**RESEARCH AND PRACTICE II**

Wayne Journell

Racial Literacies and Social Studies:
Curriculum, Instruction, and Learning
LaGarrett J. King, Ed.

Making Classroom Discussions Work:
Methods for Quality Dialogue in the Social Studies
Jane C. Lo, Ed.

Teaching Difficult Histories in Difficult Times:
Stories of Practice
Lauren McArthur Harris, Maia Sheppard,
& Sara A. Levy, Eds.

Post-Pandemic Social Studies:
How COVID-19 Has Changed the World and How We Teach
Wayne Journell, Ed.

Teaching History for Justice:
Centering Activism in Students' Study of the Past
Christopher C. Martell & Kaylene M. Stevens

# Racial Literacies and Social Studies

Curriculum, Instruction, and Learning

Edited by LaGarrett J. King

**TEACHERS COLLEGE PRESS**

**TEACHERS COLLEGE** | COLUMBIA UNIVERSITY
NEW YORK AND LONDON

Published by Teachers College Press,® 1234 Amsterdam Avenue, New York, NY 10027

Front cover design by Peter Donahue.

This book was made possible by the Spencer Foundation Conference Grant.

*Library of Congress Cataloging-in-Publication Data*

Names: King, LaGarrett J., editor.
Title: Racial literacies and social studies : curriculum, instruction, and learning / edited by LaGarrett J. King.
Description: New York, NY : Teachers College Press, [2022] | Series: Research and practice in social studies series | Includes bibliographical references and index. | Summary: "Featuring the work of historians, researchers, and classroom teachers, this volume addresses the complexities of teaching and learning about race and racism in the secondary history classroom. Readers will learn how to help young people critique the nation's legacy of racial inequality, as well as understand the historical movements to disrupt inequality"—Provided by publisher.
Identifiers: LCCN 2022020582 (print) | LCCN 2022020583 (ebook) | ISBN 9780807766569 (paperback ; alk. paper) | ISBN 9780807766576 (hardcover ; alk. paper) | ISBN 9780807780831 (ebook)
Subjects: LCSH: Racism—United States. | Race—Study and teaching (Secondary)—United States. | Social sciences—Study and teaching (Secondary)—United States.
Classification: LCC E184.A1 R325 2022 (print) | LCC E184.A1 (ebook) | DDC 305.8009730712—dc23/eng/20220826
LC record available at https://lccn.loc.gov/2022020582
LC ebook record available at https://lccn.loc.gov/2022020583

ISBN 978-0-8077-6656-9 (paper)
ISBN 978-0-8077-6657-6 (hardcover)
ISBN 978-0-8077-8083-1 (ebook)

Printed on acid-free paper
Manufactured in the United States of America

# Contents

## PART III: RACIAL LITERACY AND STUDENT LEARNING

## PART IV: RACIAL LITERACY AND TEACHER LEARNING

# Introduction

## Social Studies, All Things Race, and Racism

*LaGarrett King*

Finishing this edited volume was particularly challenging. Completing the project was made easier by excellent contributors who were gracious with their intellect and desire to transform knowledge. Yet, as a Black man who researches the teaching of Black history and race, and who is a husband, father, brother, cousin, friend, colleague, scholar, center director, and business owner, the United States's most recent racial travesties have had a negative influence on my ability to be responsive to the identities that I hold.

This book's journey began in 2020 following the murders of Breonna Taylor and George Floyd. The brutal killings caused me extreme sadness. I was not alone. The mental health of many Black people has been negatively influenced through the history of state-sanctioned violence (Bor et al., 2018; Patterson, 2018; Woodson, 2017). My unhappiness was a culmination of pain brought on by learning and teaching about the slaughter of Black people throughout history—the Middle Passage, enslavement, lynching, racial riots, and medical experiments (Cohn, 1985; Dray, 2003; Fede, 2017; Washington, 2006). My experiences as a Black person and the constant rejection of Black people's humanity also brought me sorrow. I grew tired of seeing Black death in the news.

As the discussion of institutional racism and anti-Blackness grew in the media, an unusual number of white people became allies for Black people. Corporations such as Nike, Netflix, and Ben & Jerry's created slogans in support of Black lives. Corporations such as the National Football League (NFL) and Wrangler Jeans' allyship against racism were probably more surprising, since both companies have had past racial controversies. I was bombarded with media requests and professional development opportunities for teachers to help others make sense of both the historic implications of these brutal killings and how to teach this era in critical yet nonviolent ways. I accepted most of these requests during one of the saddest moments in my career.

I received messages via text and social media from white colleagues regarding my well-being and asking if there was anything that they could do for me. I appreciated those communications even if I did not respond. Then

I became resentful. I wanted to know what was new about this experience. Why all the sudden interest in Black folks when Black folks and other non-white folks have been telling society for years about this, and few people cared enough to do anything substantive? In 2019, a year before the murders of Taylor and Floyd, many people spoke out against *The 1619 Project* for high-lighting similar concerns (Hannah-Jones, 2021; Wood 2020).

A year later, in 2021, the "racial reckoning" of 2020 became a distant memory. Historically, most societal advancements made by people of color get rolled back by legislation or white society's resentment of said gains. The year 2021 the anti–critical race theory crowd brought about verbal and phys-ical attacks on K–12 public school teachers and academics (including myself and other contributors to this book). Many have been harassed and fired for teaching about racial issues or supporting racial equity in classrooms. At the moment, at least twenty-three states (mostly with conservative elected lawmakers) have written state laws to ban any resources that provide racial knowledge within K–12 public and some private schools, in particular criti-cal race theory and/or *The 1619 Project*. There were even provisions to ban racial teaching at the higher education level as well.

Editing this book became secondary to the murders of Taylor, Floyd, and countless others, along with how the COVID-19 pandemic affected racialized communities. Yet much of my scholarly identity stems from frustration with how the United States has dealt with (or not dealt with) race and racism. So, despite these tragedies, this work had to be completed. Many people need this information, and it is our responsibility to be good stewards of knowledge to our field and the public. The academy does not stop, especially for scholars of color. Many of my colleagues needed this work to *prove* their academic worth in the eyes of their evaluators. Even while facing threats on our lives for teaching and researching about race and racism, academic work never ceases.

## SOCIAL STUDIES AND RACISM

Race should be a central component within the field's teaching, and histori-cally, that concept has been both visible and invisible (Ladson-Billings, 2003). Race and racism are highly visible within social studies because racism was the reason for the field. Social studies founders such as Samuel Armstrong and Thomas Jesse Jones, with Booker T. Washington's assistance, developed and pushed the Hampton Institute social studies curriculum to assimilate Indigenous populations and Black Americans into the American way of life in the late 19th and early 20th centuries (Dilworth, 2004; King, 2014; Lybarger, 1983; Watkins, 1996; Woyshner & Bohan, 2012). Labeled as progressive ed-ucators because they believed that both Indigenous and Black people were in-tellectually capable but morally bankrupt, Hampton's social studies ideology was to teach subservience, civic obedience, and racial evolution (Anderson,

1988; Jones, 1906; King, 2014; Woyshner & Bohan, 2012). They believed that Black people were historically oppressed, and that they were 2,000 years behind white people due to a lack of cultural evolution, making them the subordinate race (Anderson, 1988; Fallace, 2012; Watkins, 1996). Social studies was meant for Indigenous and Black people's evolution, which was code for them to passively assimilate into a society where they would accept roles as second-class citizens with limited rights.

The committee of 1916 of the National Educational Association is widely viewed as the foundations of social studies (Lybarger, 1983; Saxe, 1992). Thomas Jesse Jones, whom W. E. B. Du Bois (1919) called the "evil genius of the Negro race," was the committee's chairperson because many wanted to emulate Hampton's social studies curriculum. Again, we see racism as a motivating force to create a social studies program. Assimilation took center stage, but in addition to the Indigenous and Black populations, the newly immigrant class of Eastern Europeans and, more specifically, the Irish and the Italians, who were considered "white niggers" or "Negros turned inside out," became the target (Ignatiev, 2009; Staples, 2019). These individuals, the underclass, needed to be civilized and educated to help them assimilate. They needed to become white. Social studies, therefore, became the subject of all things race and racism, not in an effort to educate and transform society, but to sustain a racist society's belief in classifying human beings based on skin color.

Social studies is part of the racial apparatus of the United States. Social studies students have historically been taught to be racially illiterate through its curriculum, policies, and popular pedagogies. When I say racially illiterate, I am borrowing closely from Ladson-Billings's (1991) concept of multicultural illiteracy, where social studies has not taught students basic racial ideas, issues, and events that reflect people's racialized perspectives and experiences other than those of white, middle-class males. It is impossible not to have some racial knowledge and teach about it within a racial state such as the United States. Yet the concern is what racial knowledge is accepted as fact. Typically, the racial knowledge social studies curriculum and teaching does not deliver any critical concepts.

Early social studies curriculum and teaching were more directly racist, and the ideology that certain human beings were superior based on skin color was accepted as truth (Au et al., 2016; King et al., 2012). More recently, social studies racial illiteracy has been based on a societal policy of racial liberalism (Guinier, 2004). In other words, racial knowledge is based on individual transgressions, tangible and visible actions, perceived equalities in society, simple quantitative or token representations of people of color, color-blindness or color evasion, and decontextualized presentism.

Popularized after the 1960s Civil Rights Movement's perceived success, racial liberalism equates to a racial etiquette where race talk has specific parameters. In other words, white folks directed when, where, and how we talk about race and racism. Racial liberalism condemned what we perceive as individual racism and largely ignored structural aspects of racism because "people" run systems. If people are not outwardly racist, then racism cannot be a problem. Racial liberalism was a practical approach for the mainstream because race and racism became an issue for non-white people and made racial issues palatable for white folks. Racial illiteracy is about ignoring or refusing to understand BIPOC racial epistemologies, experiences, and expectations. To move past racial liberalism and illiteracy, scholars have begun to promote racial literacy to improve our understandings of race.

## RACIAL LITERACY: FOUNDATIONAL SCHOLARSHIP

Racial literacy is an international and transdisciplinary concept (Brown et al., 2021; Twine, 2004) that encompasses various definitions spanning many academic fields, including sociology, psychology, law, anthropology, and education. Generally, racial literacy is the ability to be racially conscious about the world and provide racially equitable solutions to racial issues. Racial literacy is to understand the nuances of how race operates with power and agency in society. Racially literate persons have a moderate to advanced understanding of race's histories and the various academic concepts that make up different critical racial theories. They can discern the differences and similarities of such theories and might trace the intellectual roots of critical race scholarship such as critical race theory, anti-racism, racial formation, the racial contract, anti-Blackness, and whiteness. A successfully racially literate society sees those who have racial privilege become more anti-racist, while those who have been historically excluded and racially oppressed resist themes of victimhood (Price-Dennis & Sealey-Ruiz, 2021).

As an academic concept, racial literacy comes in many different iterations. Some of its foundational scholarship can be traced to sociology, critical legal studies, and counseling psychology through such scholars as France Twine (2004), Lani Guinier (2004), and Howard Stevenson (2014). Twine (2004) defines racial literacy as "an analytical orientation and a set of practices that reflect shifts in perceptions of race, racism, and whiteness. It is a way of perceiving and responding to the racism that generates a repertoire of discursive and material practices" (Twine, 2004, p. 92). According to Twine (2004), racial literacy includes being able to understand that:

1. The definition of racism is a contemporary issue rather than strictly a historical problem.
2. Understanding racism is more than an analysis of the perception of skin color—this understanding also encompasses intersectional connections with class, gender, and sexuality.
3. Whiteness has cultural and symbolic value.
4. Race and racialization are social constructs.

5. There is a racial vocabulary and grammar that can aid in our understanding of the world around us.
6. Racialized codes and practices exist and need to be properly interpreted.

Within sociology, Twine's (2004) concept of racial literacy was theorized within the context of how multiracial families in Great Britain negotiate racial hierarchies. Her ethnographic work sought to understand white birth parents or transracial parents, their racial consciousness, and how they transmitted that knowledge to their biracial children. Twine's work diverted from previous studies where Black parents (typically Caribbean Black parents in this context) or other parents of color were studied to understand their processes on how they transferred their racial knowledge to their children, a concept similar to critical race parenting or ParentCrit (DePouw & Matias, 2016; Matias, 2016; Montoya & Sarcedo, 2018; Nishi & Montoya, 2018). Twine's research also diverged from previous whiteness studies that looked at the fragility of whiteness and the inability or resistance to fully comprehend the complexities of race. Instead, her study examined racially conscious white people and understood the potential dangers of racism. The goal of these people was to help their multiracial children manage racial hierarchies and microaggressions, and enact agency against racist encounters. To protect the racial selves of their children, they engaged in critical racial media literacy (Hawkman & Shear, 2020; King, 2017) and provided Black histories and aesthetics within the home. The study's importance centered on the racial socialization and anti-racist teaching that transracial parents exhibited within their parenting practices that helped their children confront and counter racism.

Lani Guinier's (2004) explanation of racial literacy centered on the failure of the *Brown v. Board of Education* Supreme Court case to create meaningful school integration. While *Brown* succeeded in eliminating state-sponsored segregation and overturning *Plessy v. Ferguson*, the case was an example of intersectionality and interest convergence. *Brown* ultimately privileged the white middle and/or elite class, not Black people or poor white people. The concept of interest convergence suggests that advances in society are based not on morality or the right thing to do, but on how those laws will eventually benefit and advance those of power and privilege. Additionally, the case revealed the nuances of whiteness. So, while white people access privilege from their whiteness, that privilege is conditional and fluctuates based on their socioeconomic status. The case underestimated the psychological benefits of segregation for poor white people and disregarded how Black students in integrated Northern schools still experienced intense prejudice, a case of intersectionality (Brown, 2017; Crowley & Smith, 2020).

Guinier's (2004) interpretation of *Brown* is an example of racial literacy. She defines racial literacy as "the capacity to decipher the durable racial grammar that structures racialized hierarchies and frames the narratives of our republic" (p. 100). For Guinier, racial literacy "is an interactive process in which race functions as a tool of diagnosis, feedback, and assessment, emphasizes the relationship between race and power" (p. 115), and is a living literacy that considers the "psychological, interpersonal, and structural dimensions."

Guinier's vision for racial literacy encompasses three principles:

1. Racial literacy should mainly be understood as an institutional and structural phenomenon and recognize that individual agency plays a role.
2. Racial literacy should be read as "contextual rather than Universal" (p. 114). This means that race becomes an analytical and conceptual framework for "diagnosis, feedback, and assessment" (p. 44). Becoming racially literate is about action, but the action is about learning as much as possible.
3. Racial literacy is about understanding intersectionalities between race and other social factors. A racially literate analysis puts race at the forefront but also interrogates how other social factors intersect with race, such as class, geography, gender, and other explanatory variables. (p. 115)

Her understanding of racial literacy was influenced by racial liberalism. As stated earlier, racial liberalism is the belief that racism is tangible. Racism is an individual phenomenon described by Brown and Brown (2010) as "bad men doing bad things" (p. 60). Racism is color-neutral, meaning that the proper way not to be racist is to be color-blind, or what some scholars prefer to call color-evasive (Annamma et al., 2017). In addition, this understanding of racism as neutral also eliminates the concept of power from its definitions. By excluding power benefits, white people can now situate people of color as racists, given that perceived prejudice and discrimination are enacted no matter the racial category.

Additionally, excluding power has made merely talking about race or racism a negative thing, making the accuser racist. Racial liberalism, therefore, becomes a passive, ineffective, and deficit approach to true racial equality. This understanding subjugates people of color as simply victims (or even violators) with limited agency and power. Additionally, racial liberalism does not require people to become anti-racist and challenge racial injustice actively, especially when examining their racial ideas, actions, and blind spots.

Howard Stevenson's (2014) foray into racial literacy comes through a combination of education, psychology, health, and counseling fields. Stevenson's approach to racial literacy focuses on coping with and managing racial emotions and encounters. He cites neuroscience research on Anxiety Uncertainty Management theory, which notes that there is racial anxiety or even fear of Black people's presence for many white people. He explains that racial encounters are highly stressful for many white people because of the stigma of being called racist in society; they attempt to regulate their thought processes and behaviors to cope with racial stress. This racial evasion can cause extreme fatigue because there is contention within the psyche, which understands that racism is immoral, but there are also conscious or unconscious negative attitudes toward Black people. This anxiety is based on a fear of not being politically correct or appearing racist, which can be interpreted through emotional expressions, involuntary spastic movements, or saying or doing something racially inappropriate (Stevenson, 2014).

Black people, as well as other racialized persons, also have racial anxiety through racially stressful encounters with white people and a society that favors whiteness. In the United States, the top of the racial hierarchy is defined through whiteness, which is the standard on which society is based. Blackness is on the other end of the spectrum, where anything associated with Blackness is deemed inappropriate or deficient. Therefore, Black people (and other people of color) are stereotyped and judged through a white lens. If they fail to meet standards of whiteness, their humanity is questioned, and racial power is exhibited either to make them conform to the rules of whiteness or to punish their Blackness. Black people, therefore, are in a constant state of racial trauma or what Stevenson (2014) refers to as Catch 33, the understanding that your Blackness is systemically at odds and contradictory to society for your life span no matter your socioeconomic status, educational attainment, or accomplishments. This realization of anti-Blackness (Dumas, 2016) influences Black lives through physical and mental health, educational attainment, and mortality rates (Stevenson, 2014).

Stevenson believes that racial literacy can be taught as a coping mechanism or through stress reduction strategies that can effectively lessen our emotions when confronted with racial encounters. Therefore, Stevenson defines racial literacy as the ability to read, recast, and resolve racially stressful social interactions. First, racially literate persons can read and recognize what racial encounters are and respond to them. To do this, individuals must be aware of racism and understand why racial encounters can be challenging. Second, after reading racial encounters, the ability to recast leads to the reduction of anxiety and stress. Third, the ability to resolve is about making a healthy decision about reacting to the racially stressful encounter. Racially literate persons understand and identify those emotions but do not overreact to how the moment makes them feel.

To read, recast, and resolve requires strategies such as relaxation, storytelling, journaling, debating, and role-playing. Through these processes, Stevenson (2014) believes, we can build healthy racial relationships. Both healing and deprogramming racial trauma will result from knowing and practicing the various strategies over time.

The work of Twine (2004), Guinier (2004), and Stevenson (2014) supply important constructs, as it allows us to see the broadness and complexities of racial literacy. For Twine, race is a constant in society. That racial literacy is not only an individual endeavor, but it also reifies the socialization of family dynamics associated with racial identity. The purpose of racial literacy is to help young people of color manage and survive in racial states. The teachers, in this case, are white parents who serve as a proxy of a racist society. While strategies involved building Black racial identity, the racial identity of those white parents is also being developed and constantly evolving because of its juxtaposition with the Blackness of their children.

Guinier's (2004) approach to racial literacy focuses on the institutional and structural forces that drive our racial state and racialized behaviors. Education helps us understand how oppression is legitimized along with racially aligned social, legal, media, political, and economic systems. Stevenson's racial literacy allows us to understand the psychology of race and racism. While racial literacy is seen as more individualized, the structures of a racial society heavily influence racial behaviors. Stevenson's most important work is the counseling mechanisms put in place to manage racial behaviors. While it seems that Guinier is advocating for a racial literacy that seeks to challenge and change systems, and Stevenson and Twine are not, it is important to see all these approaches as interlocking to create a racially equitable society.

## RACIAL LITERACY IN EDUCATION

The past decade has seen an increase in educational scholarship on racial literacy. I contribute this popularity to the appeal of the scholarship of Twine, Guinier, and Stevenson; increased attention to understanding racial issues in society; and the majority population of students of color in public schools. An enduring concern for educational researchers has always been teacher demographics that point to an overwhelmingly white, female, and mostly middle-class teaching field (National Center for Education Statistics, 2021). The concern has not been simply about Black, Brown, Asian, or Indigenous representation in classrooms. Studies indicate that all students are likely to learn more from a diverse teaching population (Bristol & Martin-Fernandez, 2019). Teachers of color are more likely to understand their students of color, more willing to promote racial equity and justice, and have racialized experiences themselves (Cherng & Halpin, 2016; Villegas & Irvine, 2010). While white teachers can be effective teachers for students of color (Cooper, 2003; Ladson-Billings, 2009), the research has shown that when teachers lack racial awareness and knowledge or are simply uncomfortable teaching about race and racism, problems arise, including curriculum and instructional violence, racial microaggressions, and anti-Black and restrictive school policies (Hines-Datiri & Carter Andrews, 2020; King & Woodson, 2017; Kohli & Solórzano, 2012). When teachers lack racial literacy about students' culture and society, they are underprepared to teach and see their students' full humanity.

Significant scholarship on racial literacy has been used to understand and scrutinize the complexities of racial knowledge within K–12 curriculum and pedagogical decisions (Epstein & Gist, 2015; King et al., 2018; Rogers & Mosley, 2006), educational leadership (Coleman & Stevenson, 2014; Douglass

Horsford, 2014), and teacher education and development (Allen, 2019; King, 2016; Price-Dennis & Sealey-Ruiz, 2021). Racial literacy scholarship in the education field has seen much of its work within English education, with seminal foundational research done by Rogers and Mosley (2006, 2008) and Skerrett (2011). Central to racial literacy development of English educators has been reading critical texts, assigning writing assignments, or examining films about race and racism (Ohito, 2022).

Racial literacy scholars believe that race and racism are integral parts of the educative process. Boutte (2021) notes that racial literacy can be used to disrupt five common types of racial violence that students of color experience in schools: physical, symbolic, linguistic, curricular/instructional, and systemic violence. Therefore, the process of racial literacy promotes cognitive skills that help engage the nuances of race and racism and transform schooling to become more anti-racist and equitable within curriculum development, instructional approaches, assessments, school policies, professional education, and classroom culture/management (Sealey-Ruiz, 2021).

The pedagogy surrounding racially literate teaching is conceptualized as an active and social classroom experience with racial dialogue. Scholars of racial literacy advocate for preservice teachers to discuss racial issues in an open safe space, read critical texts that explore racial issues, write or journal about race privilege or oppression from personal experiences, be held accountable for practicing racial literacy in field placements, and when given the opportunity, exert agency to fight against injustices (Mosley, 2010; Sealey-Ruiz & Greene, 2015). These moment-to-moment interactions help shape an interactive process where support for, challenges against, and multiple perspectives between preservice teachers helped them gain more racial literacy (Rogers & Mosley, 2008).

Within education, racial literacy is more than a theory; it is a praxis, a critical pedagogy that provides certain activities and pedagogical practices that will expand students' and educators' racial identity and racial knowledge. It is important to know that racial literacy as praxis is not static but fluid and an ongoing development process for teachers, students, administrators, and teacher educators (Sealey-Ruiz, 2021).

## RACIAL LITERACY AND SOCIAL STUDIES

While racial literacy as a theoretical approach and praxis is relatively new in the field, racial knowledge and how race is conceived in educative spaces have always been an enduring concern for social studies scholars (Givens, 2019; King, 2014). Social studies scholarship within racial literacy has been concerned with curriculum, teaching, teacher education, students' racial literacy, and media literacy (An, 2020; Busey, 2020; Epstein & Gist, 2015; Hawkman & Shear, 2020; Smith, 2016; Woodson, 2019). For social studies teachers, racial literacy means taking social science concepts and dissecting how race influences individuals and groups. Racially literate social studies teachers can identify racial liberal discourse and mainstream racial grammar that uncritically defines what race is, how race is examined, and why race is important.

King et al. (2018) explain racially literate social studies. First, to be racially literate, one has to understand that race and racism are not static. Still, our definitions will continuously evolve and be based on geographical (local and global) and historical/presentism contexts. Second, racially literate people understand that racism is more than "bad men doing bad things" (Brown & Brown, 2010) or individual racial transgressions. Racism can be classified as individual, but racism also has its manifestations within systems, both institutional and structural. Racial literacy teaches that racism is about power. Even when there is not "racist intent" by individuals, racism still exists through power inequalities, unequal access to opportunities, and policy outcomes. Individual agency is not ignored, but racially literate persons understand that equality is measured by eliminating institutional and environmental structures that impede racial progress. Third, racially literate persons understand intersectionality, which classifies individuals' other identities/social categories of oppression (class, geography, gender, sexualities). Intersectionality analysis explains how racial hegemony reifies itself in society through different forms.

Fourth, racial literacy possesses a sort of grammar and vocabularies associated with racial discourse, such as *white supremacy, anti-Blackness, racialization, racial identity,* and *intersectionality,* while differentiating among terms such as *ethnicity, nationality, discrimination, prejudice,* and *stereotyping.* Last, racial literacy is about understanding the appropriate pedagogies involved in racial teaching. Racially literate social studies teaches one how to "read, recast, and resolve" racially stressful situations within classroom spaces (Stevenson, 2014). Racial literacy is not only the ability to recognize a racial moment or have students leave with more racial knowledge, but it is also about doing something with this newfound knowledge. For social studies educators, this can mean understanding and recognizing how race connects to our curriculum (even when it is not explicit), implementing the appropriate pedagogies for racial topics, or developing racial literacy audits to ensure equity in learning.

For social studies educators, becoming racially literate involves sociohistorical literacy that understands content and context. This means that racially historical content knowledge is a start, but it is not enough. Racially literate social studies moves the needle from what Derrick Bell (1992) refers to as general knowledge—"knowing of" rather than "knowing about" race (cited in Brown, 2017). To *know of* refers to a simple knowledge that something had happened in the past. To *know about* recognizes the significance of that history. For example, within the social studies curriculum of most schools, teachers are expected to teach about the institution of slavery, but rarely do curriculum guides explicitly state that teachers should delve into "the nature of its practice, its relationship to the body politic and its impact on and legacy to the nation-state" (Brown, 2017, p. 87). Therefore, racial literacy within social studies education is about knowing and respecting multiple historical discourses, as sociohistorical knowledge recognizes the genealogy of race that comprehends historic racial problems but can also ascertain how these racial issues are recursive, evolve, and manifest in the present day.

## STRUCTURE OF THIS BOOK

Using the above understandings of racial literacy as a starting point, Terrie Epstein, from Hunter College, CUNY, and I were awarded a Spencer Conference grant to convene a network of social studies scholars working on racial literacy education. The Racial Literacy Spencer Conference was held during the summer of 2019 at Hunter College in New York City. Over 20 presentations and five distinct panels of papers were explored. These panels were:

- Racial Literacy and History Standards and Frameworks
- Textbooks, Racial Literacy, and Classroom Instruction and Interactions
- Racial Literacy and Student (un)Learning
- Racial Literacy and Teacher (un)Learning
- Racial Literacy and Intersectionality

The conference began with an opening keynote address by Dr. Yolanda Sealey-Ruiz, who discussed how she conceptualized her racial literacy framework. Her framework is conceptualized in her most recent book, *Advancing Racial Literacies in Teacher Education* (2021). Except for ArCasia James-Gallaway, all contributors to this book participated in the conference.

The book includes four parts with chapters that are closely aligned with the conference. The first section is titled Racial Literacy and Curriculum. The authors were asked to consider how U.S. history curricular standards, frameworks, and textbooks conceptualize race and racism. Sohyun An begins this section with her chapter, "The COVID-19 Pandemic, Racial Literacy, and Asian Americans in the History Curriculum." Her chapter posits that the lack of racial literacy in the social studies curriculum is one reason for the physical and psychological violence against Asian American students. She notes that the social studies curriculum is exclusive and reinforces white supremacy. Suggestions to enhance the presence of Asian Americans in social studies education for both classroom practice and research are included.

Maribel Santiago and Eliana Castro's chapter, "'Movin' On Up': The Growing Role of Latinx Social Studies Topics Through the Grade Levels," is next. The chapter derives from a national data set studying K–12 teachers' instructional patterns teaching Latinx social studies topics. The chapter presents a complicated narrative of why teachers throughout all grade levels chose or did not teach social studies content regarding Latinx histories. The last in this section is Christine Stanton's chapter, "'It's Gonna Be *My* History': The Need for (Re)Indigenizing Curricular Literacies." Her research delves into Indigenous representation in standards, frameworks, and textbooks. She concludes with recommendations for curriculum developers, teachers, and scholars to advance racial literacies through (re)centering Indigenous perspectives within the curriculum.

The next section is titled Racial Literacy and Social Studies Instruction. The authors were asked to answer how teachers' instructional practices inhibit and/or advance students' historical knowledge, skills, and dispositions related to racial inequalities and movements to disrupt them.

We begin with Gabriel Reich's chapter, "Between the General and the Particular: Theoretical Tensions in Historical Consciousness and Racial Literacy for the Classroom." Reich explores the tensions between historical consciousness and racial literacy using a diverse set of historical consciousness frameworks. These tensions have implications for how educators explore teaching, student learning, and curriculum design. The last chapter in the section is Noreen Rodríguez's chapter, "'We Gotta Make a Change': Developing Racial Literacy with Elementary Preservice Teachers through Angie Thomas's *The Hate U Give*." This chapter describes the role of racial literacy in an elementary social studies methods course at a Midwestern public university. Using Angie Thomas's young adult novel *The Hate U Give*, the teacher candidates emerged with a more robust understanding of race and racism in American history and more confidence dealing with race issues in elementary classrooms.

The third section is Racial Literacy and Student Learning. The section begins with Karen Burgard's chapter, "The National Curriculum of Whiteness Created by Our Public Spaces." Burgard explores the origins, implementation, and impact of the public curriculum. She posits that educators can use public spaces to deconstruct social studies topics and artifacts. In turn, they become more critical consumers of histories and social studies. Tadashi Dozono follows with his chapter, "The Refusal to Learn: Inquiry Through Marronage in the History Classroom." Using the conceptual framework of marriage and three disciplinary spaces, first as epistemology, second as geography, and third as historical case studies, Dozono challenges teachers to understand students differently and create opportunities for academic inquiry based on disciplinary work from and of the margins.

Kristen Duncan's chapter, "Racial Literacy and Historic Plantation Sites: A Tale of Two Plantations," uses racial literacy to analyze plantation tours. She visited Magnolia Plantation and Gardens in South Carolina and the Whitney Plantation in Louisiana. She notes how these two public history spaces converge and diverge as useful and sometimes useless historical spaces. Natasha Merchant's chapter follows. "Beyond Curricular Acknowledgment: Islam in the Classroom" considers Muslim high school girls' experiences to imagine a curriculum that honors complexity in Islam's lived heritage and community practices. Merchant exposes the many instances of disjuncture between the official curriculum on Islam and the students' lived experiences.

The last section is Racial Literacy and Teacher Learning. The authors were asked how teachers can prepare preservice history teachers to incorporate racially literate approaches. Tommy Ender's chapter, "Developing Racial Literacy With White Social Studies Teachers: Reflections from a Critical Teacher Educator," explores the practicability of critical reflection in helping preservice and inservice teachers develop racial literacy. Ender shares how essential reflections of teacher education, through digital spaces, in-class presentations, or final papers, can help enhance preservice teachers' racial views.

Andrea Hawkman's chapter, "'You and Your Racist Friend': Programmatic Considerations for Building Racial Literacy Through Anti-Racist Teacher Education," provides programmatic considerations for building racial literacy through an anti-racist teacher education framework by reimagining the curriculum, practices, structures, and pedagogues that prepare future teachers. The next chapter is by Chris Martell and Kaylene Stevens, "Learning to Teach History for Justice: Racial Literacies and Teacher Education." The authors argue that justice must be at the center of history teacher education, including preservice teacher preparation and inservice professional development. The chapter is a precursor to their most recent book, *Teaching History for Justice* (2020). Martell and Stevens describe the concept of teaching history for justice, which aims to foster activist thinking through the study of the past. They argue that teacher preparation and professional development programs should be built around a pedagogical framework that includes three core components: social inquiry, critical multiculturalism, and transformative democratic citizenship.

Tiffany Patterson's chapter, "Knowing Is Not Enough, Action Is Required: Toward Racial Literacy and Activism in Teacher Development," promotes racial literacy development across a continuum of teacher learning to engage teachers as activists. She notes that preservice teachers are prompted to action as they become racially literate and understand how racism is operationalized in America. This chapter is an entry point for racial justice activism to build capacity and solidarity across the teaching-learning continuum, thereby increasing the likelihood of transformative change for preservice and inservice teachers.

In the last chapter, "I Stay Mad: A Black Woman Social Studies Educator's Fight to Be Seen, Heard, and Heeded," ArCasia James-Gallaway takes a different approach to teacher learning as she examines herself and how racial literacy shaped her praxis as a social studies (teacher) educator. Examining her development as a social studies (teacher) educator, she explores her enduring rage when she feels resistance from students. She uses racial literacy to examine how the tenets of seeing, hearing, and heeding underserved Black children and communities have served as racial trauma.

These scholarly works serve as one of the beginnings of social studies scholars exploring race through racial literacy. We leave much desired as social studies continues to build and maintain a solid base of racial research. We honor scholars before us who may have seen social studies as too benign for racial justice work (Ladson-Billings, 2003). We want to say that we are trying, working hard, and theorizing in our work spaces. Most importantly, we are taking our work outside the ivory towers to influence school policy and community spaces.

It was a pleasure to work with these dynamic scholars within a challenging racial context. It is hard to work on race and experience racism simultaneously. In many ways, the work the book chapter authors and I produce is both celebrated and vilified. I am in awe of their work. Reading these chapters eased my sadness. As a Black scholar, it is easy to be pessimistic; we have centuries of racial histories that seem like progress, but race and racism persist. I am cautiously hopeful that with the continued push of racial literacy, we will get social studies to the point where we are not merely reifying racist beliefs. Still, racial literacy is an act to destroy racism so that it can never be resurrected purposely. Most importantly, social studies scholars, teachers, administrators, and policymakers need to understand that social studies is all things race and racism. We need to do our part not to transmit those ideas but to transform our society for a more equitable world.

## REFERENCES

Allen, K. M. (2019). Transformative vision: Examining the racial literacy practices of a Black male teacher with his Black male students. *Journal for Multicultural Education, 13*(1), 82–93. https://doi.org/10.1108/ JME-04-2017-0029

An, S. (2020). Learning racial literacy while navigating white social studies. *The Social Studies, 111*(4), 174–181.

Anderson, J. D. (1988). *The education of Blacks in the South, 1860–1935.* University of North Carolina Press.

Annamma, S. A., Jackson, D. D., & Morrison, D. (2017). Conceptualizing color-evasiveness: Using dis/ability critical race theory to expand a color-blind racial ideology in education and society. *Race Ethnicity and Education, 20*(2), 147–162.

Au, W., Brown, A. L., & Calderón, D. (2016). *Reclaiming the multicultural roots of US curriculum: Communities of color and official knowledge in education.* Teachers College Press.

Bell, D. (1992). Learning the three I's of America's slave heritage. *Chicago-Kent Law Review, 68,* 1037.

Bor, J., Venkataramani, A. S., Williams, D. R., & Tsai, A. C. (2018). Police killings and their spillover effects on the mental health of Black Americans: A population-based, quasi-experimental study. *The Lancet, 392*(10144), 302–310.

Boutte, G. S. (2021). Critical racial literacy in educational and familial settings. In *Oxford Research Encyclopedia of Education.*

Bristol, T. J., & Martin-Fernandez, J. (2019). The added value of Latinx and Black teachers for Latinx and Black students: Implications for policy. *Policy Insights from the Behavioral and Brain Sciences, 6*(2), 147–153.

Brown, K. D. (2017). Why we can't wait: Advancing racial literacy and a critical sociocultural knowledge of race for teaching and curriculum. *Race, Gender & Class, 24*(1–2), 81–96.

Brown, A. L., & Brown, K. D. (2010). Strange fruit indeed: Interrogating contemporary textbook representations of racial violence toward African Americans. *Teachers College Record, 112*(1), 31–67.

Brown, L., Kelada, O., & Jones, D. (2021). "While I knew I was raced, I didn't think much of it": The need for racial literacy in decolonising classrooms. *Postcolonial Studies, 24*(1), 82–103.

Busey, C. L. (2020). Diaspora literacy and Afro-Latin humanity: A critical Studyin' case study of a world history teacher's critical sociohistorical knowledge development. *Race Ethnicity and Education, 23*(6), 820–840.

Cherng, H. Y. S., & Halpin, P. F. (2016). The importance of minority teachers: Student perceptions of minority versus white teachers. *Educational Researcher, 45*(7), 407–420.

Cohn, R. L. (1985). Deaths of slaves in the Middle Passage. *The Journal of Economic History, 45*(3), 685–692.

Coleman, S., & Stevenson, H. C. (2014). Engaging the racial elephant: How leadership on racial literacy improves schools. *Independent School, 73*(4), n4.

Cooper, P. M. (2003). Effective white teachers of black children: Teaching within a community. *Journal of Teacher Education, 54*(5), 413–427.

Crowley, R. M., & Smith, W. L. (2020). A divergence of interests: Critical race theory and white privilege pedagogy. *Teachers College Record, 122*(1), 1–24.

DePouw, C., & Matias, C. (2016). Critical race parenting: Understanding scholarship/activism in parenting our children. *Educational Studies, 52*(3), 237–259.

Dilworth, P. P. (2004). Competing conceptions of citizenship education: Thomas Jesse Jones and Carter G. Woodson. *International Journal of Social Education, 18*(2), 1–10.

Douglass Horsford, S. (2014). When race enters the room: Improving leadership and learning through racial literacy. *Theory Into Practice, 53*(2), 123–130.

Dray, P. (2003). *At the hands of persons unknown: The lynching of Black America.* Random House Digital.

Du Bois, W. E. B. (1919). My mission. Opinion. *The Crisis, 18*, 7–9.

Dumas, M. J. (2016). Against the dark: Antiblackness in education policy and discourse. *Theory Into Practice, 55*(1), 11–19.

Epstein, T., & Gist, C. (2015). Teaching racial literacy in secondary humanities classrooms: Challenging adolescents' of color concepts of race and racism. *Race Ethnicity and Education, 18*(1), 40–60.

Fallace, T. (2012). Recapitulation theory and the new education: Race, culture, imperialism, and pedagogy, 1894–1916. *Curriculum Inquiry, 42*(4), 510–533.

Fede, A. (2017). *Homicide justified: The legality of killing slaves in the United States and the Atlantic world* (Vol. 2). University of Georgia Press.

Givens, J. R. (2019). "There would be no lynching if it did not start in the schoolroom": Carter G. Woodson and the occasion of Negro History Week, 1926–1950. *American Educational Research Journal, 56*(4), 1457–1494.

Guinier, L. (2004). From racial liberalism to racial literacy: *Brown v. Board of Education* and the interest-divergence dilemma. *Journal of American History, 91*(1), 92–118.

Hannah-Jones, N. (Ed.) (2021). *The 1619 project: A new origin story.* One World.

Hawkman, A. M., & Shear, S. B. (2020). "Who made these rules? We're so confused": An introduction to the special issue on critical race media literacy. *International Journal of Multicultural Education, 22*(2), 1–4.

Hines-Datiri, D., & Carter Andrews, D. J. (2020). The effects of zero tolerance policies on Black girls: Using critical race feminism and figured worlds to examine school discipline. *Urban Education, 55*(10), 1419–1440.

Ignatiev, N. (2009). *How the Irish became white.* Routledge.

Jones, T. J. (1906). *Social studies in the Hampton curriculum.* Hampton Institute Press.

King, L. J. (2014). When lions write history: Black history textbooks, African-American educators, & the alternative Black curriculum in social studies education, 1890–1940. *Multicultural Education, 22*(1), 2–11.

King, L. J. (2016). Teaching Black history as a racial literacy project. *Race Ethnicity and Education, 19*(6), 1303–1318.

King, L. J. (2017). The media and Black masculinity: Looking at the media through race[d] lenses. *Critical Education, 8*(2), 31–40.

King, L. J., Davis, C., & Brown, A. (2012). African American history, race, and textbooks: An examination of the works of Harold O. Rugg and Carter G. Woodson. *Journal of Social Studies Research, 36*(4), 359–386.

King, L. J., Vickery, A. E., & Caffrey, G. (2018). A pathway to racial literacy: Using the LETS ACT framework to teach controversial issues. *Social Education, 82*(6), 316–322.

King, L. J., & Woodson, A. N. (2017). Baskets of cotton and birthday cakes: Teaching slavery in social studies classrooms. *Social Studies Education Review, 6*(1), 1–18.

Kohli, R., & Solórzano, D. G. (2012). Teachers, please learn our names!: Racial microaggressions and the K-12 classroom. *Race Ethnicity and Education, 15*(4), 441–462.

Ladson-Billings, G. (1991). Beyond multicultural illiteracy. *The Journal of Negro Education, 60*(2), 147–157.

Ladson-Billings, G. (2003). Lies my teacher still tells: Developing a critical race perspective toward the social studies. In G. Ladson-Billings (Ed.), *Critical race theory perspectives on the social studies* (pp. 1–11). Information Age.

Ladson-Billings, G. (2009). *The dreamkeepers: Successful teachers of African American children.* John Wiley & Sons.

Lybarger, M. (1983). Origins of the modern social studies: 1900–1916. *History of Education Quarterly, 23*(4), 455–468.

Martell, C. C., & Stevens, K. M. (2020). *Teaching history for justice: Centering activism in students' study of the past.* Teachers College Press.

Matias, C. E. (2016). "Mommy, is being Brown bad?": Critical race parenting in a post-race era. *Race and Pedagogy Journal: Teaching and Learning for Justice, 1*(3), 1.

Montoya, R., & Sarcedo, G. L. (2018). Critical race parenting in the Trump era: A Sisyphean endeavor? A parable. *International Journal of Qualitative Studies in Education, 31*(1), 70–81.

Mosley, M. (2010). "That really hit me hard": Moving beyond passive anti-racism to engage with critical race literacy pedagogy. *Race Ethnicity and Education, 13*(4), 449–471.

National Center for Education Statistics. (2021). *Characteristics of public-school teachers.* U.S. Department of Health, Education, and Welfare, Education Division, National Center for Education Statistics.

Nishi, N. W., & Montoya, R. (2018). ParentCrit: Critical race parenting for our children's lives and humanity introduction. *International Journal of Qualitative Studies in Education, 31*(1), 1–2.

Ohito, E. O. (2022). "I'm very hurt":(Un) justly reading the Black female body as text in a racial literacy learning assemblage. *Reading Research Quarterly, 57*(2), 609–627.

Patterson, O. (2018). *Slavery and social death: A comparative study, with a new preface.* Harvard University Press.

*Plessy v. Ferguson,* 163 U.S. 537, 16 S. Ct. 1138 (1896)

Price-Dennis, D., & Sealy-Ruiz, Y. (2021). *Advancing racial literacies in teacher education.* Teachers College Press.

Rogers, R., & Mosley, M. (2006). Racial literacy in a second-grade classroom: Critical race theory, whiteness studies, and literacy research. *Reading Research Quarterly, 41*(4), 462–495.

Rogers, R., & Mosley, M. (2008). A critical discourse analysis of racial literacy in teacher education. *Linguistics and Education, 19*(2), 107–131.

Saxe, D. W. (1992). An introduction to the seminal social welfare and efficiency prototype: The founders of 1916 Social Studies. *Theory & Research in Social Education, 20*(2), 156–178.

Sealey-Ruiz, Y. (2021). Racial literacy: A policy research brief produced by the James R. Squire Office of the National Council of Teachers of English. *National Council for English Education.* SquireOfficePolicyBrief_RacialLiteracy_April2021.pdf (ncte.org).

Sealey-Ruiz, Y., & Greene, P. (2015). Popular visual images and the (mis)reading of Black male youth: A case for racial literacy in urban preservice teacher education. *Teaching Education, 26*(1), 55–76.

Skerrett, A. (2011). English teachers' racial literacy knowledge and practice. *Race Ethnicity and Education, 14*(3), 313–330.

Smith, W. (2016). Knowing Obama: How high school students of color learn about the 44th president. *The High School Journal, 100*(1), 26–44.

Staples, B. (2019). How Italians became "white." *The New York Times, 14.*

Stevenson, H. (2014). *Promoting racial literacy in schools: Differences that make a difference.* Teachers College Press.

Twine, F. W. (2004). A white side of black Britain: The concept of racial literacy. *Ethnic and Racial Studies, 27*(6), 878–907.

Villegas, A. M., & Irvine, J. J. (2010). Diversifying the teaching force: An examination of major arguments. *The Urban Review, 42*(3), 175–192.

Washington, H. A. (2006). *Medical apartheid: The dark history of medical experimentation on Black Americans from colonial times to the present.* Doubleday.

Watkins, W. H. (1996). Thomas Jesse Jones, social studies, and race. *International Journal of Social Education, 10*(2), 124–134.

Wood, P. W. (2020). *1620: A critical response to the 1619 Project.* Encounter Books.

Woodson, A. N. (2017). "Being Black is like being a soldier in Iraq": Metaphorical expressions of blackness in an urban community. *International Journal of Qualitative Studies in Education, 30*(2), 161–174.

Woodson, A. N. (2019). Racial code words, re-memberings and Black kids' civic imaginations: A critical race ethnography of a post–civil rights leader. *Anthropology & Education Quarterly, 50*(1), 26–47.

Woyshner, C., & Bohan, C. H. (2012). *Histories of social studies and race: 1865–2000.* Springer.

# Part I

# RACIAL LITERACY
# AND CURRICULUM

## CHAPTER 1

# The COVID-19 Pandemic, Racial Literacy, and Asian Americans in the History Curriculum

*Sohyun An*

## INTRODUCTION

A 16-year-old student in California's San Fernando Valley was sent to a hospital after he was physically attacked by peers in his high school. The bullies accused him of having the coronavirus simply because he is Asian American.

—CBS News, February 14, 2020

A 59-year-old Asian man in New York City was kicked in the back and told to go back to his country by a teen who also yelled at him "F-king Chinese coronavirus."

—*New York Post*, March 11, 2020

Two students at Bolsa Grande High School in California verbally harassed and mocked Vietnamese American classmates, yelling "coronavirus" at them during a school cultural assembly.

—*Orange County Register*, March 12, 2020

An Asian American couple in Minnesota came home and found a hateful note taped to their front door. The note said, "We're watching you f-king chinks. Take your Chinese virus back to China. We don't want you here infecting us with your diseases. From your friendly neighborhood."

—KARE 11 News, March 26, 2020

Three Asian American family members in Texas, including a 2-year-old and a 6-year-old child, were stabbed while grocery shopping. The father and the son were hurt badly in the attack with large cuts on their faces. The 19-year-old assailant said he stabbed the family because he thought the family was Chinese and infecting people with the coronavirus.

—CBS News, March 30, 2020

From the first reports of the coronavirus outbreak in China in December 2019 and the World Health Organization's declaration of COVID-19 as a pandemic on March 11, 2020, anti-Asian rhetoric has risen in the United States and globally. On January 26, 2020, a French newspaper, *Courrier picard*, featured an Asian woman wearing a mask on its front page with a headline, "Yellow Alert," as well as a similar headline, "New Yellow Peril," in its online version (Yeung, 2020). Other French newspapers referred to COVID-19 as the "Chinese virus" at the beginning of the outbreak (Yeung, 2020). On January 26, 2020, the Australian newspaper *Herald Sun* ran the headline "Chinese Virus Pandemonium," while Sydney's *The Daily Telegraph*'s headline read "China Kids Stay Home" (Kim, 2020). Consequently, there has been a significant increase in microaggressions, discrimination, and hate crimes against individuals, families, and communities of Asian heritage in France and Australia (Cho, 2020).

A similar pattern has been observed in other parts of the world, too (Giuffrida & Wills, 2020). In the United States, then-President Trump insisted on referring to COVID-19 as the "Chinese virus." Although the president's tone shifted on March 23, 2020, when he tweeted that it was "very important that we totally protect our Asian American community in the U.S., and all around the world," it was too late (Trump, 2020). One month after its official launch on March 19, 2020, the Stop AAPI Hate reporting center had received almost 1,500 reports of COVID-19–related racist incidents against Asian American communities. Asian Americans have reported being spit on, yelled at, threatened, kicked, and stabbed (Stop AAPI Hate Initiative, 2020; Wang, 2020). The incidents captured at the beginning of the chapter are just a small snapshot of the viral racism. As fear surrounding COVID-19 grew, Asian American communities in the United States faced increased hatred and violence.

This is not the first time the fear of disease has fanned anti-Asian violence and discrimination (Mohr, 2005; Shah, 2001). When the first large group of Chinese workers arrived in the mid-19th century, Chinese were racialized as uncivilized, unclean, filthy, and dangerous to white people (Lee, 2016). This racist stereotype led to discrimination against Chinese immigrants during the 1876 outbreak of smallpox in San Francisco. Chinatown was blamed as a laboratory of infection and quarantined amidst calls to halt Chinese immigration (Trauner, 1978). The 1882 Chinese Exclusion Act banned the entire ethnic group and excluded Chinese nationals from eligibility for U.S. citizenship.

Similarly, when the bubonic plague spread in San Francisco in 1900, government officials racialized the epidemic. Despite the fact that the spread of the bubonic plague was largely due to rats carrying infected fleas, health officials disregarded this information and quarantined the city's Chinatown with barbed wire and ropes. While white people were allowed to leave, 30,000 Chinese were segregated and confined (Shah, 2001). Government officials in Honolulu, Hawaii, also acted on the long-held stereotypes about the dirtiness of Chinese immigrants in their response to the bubonic plague. They sprayed the homes of Chinese residents with carbolic acid, threw out their belongings, forced Chinese residents to shower at public stations, and even burned down the homes of plague victims. The fires quickly spread out of control to surrounding areas, burning for 17 days and displacing 8,000 residents, mostly of Chinese and Japanese descent (Mohr, 2005).

My children, Asian American students, then 7 and 12 years old, were scared and worried as they watched and heard the news about people looking like themselves being assaulted and harassed in the wake of the COVID-19 pandemic throughout 2020. They worried, "Mom, is it safe to go outside and take a walk? What if people attack us?" They also worried, "Mom, are you okay to go to a grocery store? What if people do something bad to you?" For them, racism was scarier than the disease. Then, in 2021, the Atlanta mass shooting happened. A 21-year-old white man traveled to three different locations in metro Atlanta and shot eight people to death on March 16, 2021. Six of the victims were Asian immigrant women. A witness remembered that the murderer said, "I am going to kill all Asians" (Wilkinson, 2021). It was an outright hate crime against people of Asian heritage. My children and I were beyond horrified and heartbroken. Although we had seen, heard, and personally experienced anti-Asian harassment during the pandemic, the mass killing of Asian immigrant women was too difficult to fathom. It was also too close to home. We live just 15 minutes away from the mass shooting sites. The tragedy could have happened to us or our families and friends. We might have even passed the victims in a grocery store or a restaurant in metro Atlanta's Koreatown.

I write this chapter as a motherscholar (Lapayese, 2012) with hope that all children, including mine, can live in an anti-racist world where they feel safe and confident of who they are not only in a "peaceful" time but also in a time of "crisis" or "emergency." Fallout from the COVID-19 pandemic has revealed that our country is in dire need of racial literacy. We need to educate our future citizens to critically read, call out, and act against racially motivated violence and discrimination. Otherwise, we will continue to see a recurring pattern in U.S. history, particularly during public health crises, wartime, or economic downturn, of one group of people on the margins of society being scapegoated and discriminated against for society's problems.

In this chapter, I contend that U.S. history curriculum that is inclusive of all marginalized voices, including Asian Americans, is necessary for educating racially literate citizens for an anti-racist world. First, I discuss why the history curriculum matters by building on what Cridland-Hughes and King (2015) called a curriculum of violence versus a curriculum of support. Next, I review previous curriculum studies and identify continued exclusion and misrepresentation of Asian Americans in the official story of the United States. I then explicate how such an exclusive curriculum becomes a source of physical and psychological violence against Asian Americans and, further, a source of reinforcing white supremacy. Last, I discuss how Asian American history included in the official curriculum of U.S. history can contribute to building racial literacy and provide a curriculum of support for all children.

## THE POWER OF HISTORY CURRICULUM

Let me begin with explaining why school curriculum, particularly history curriculum, matters. As many scholars have noted, a school curriculum "is never simply a neutral assemblage of knowledge, somehow appearing in the texts and classrooms of a nation" (Apple, 1996, p. 22). Instead, what is included and how the included is depicted in school curricula sends an important message to students about whose knowledge counts and whose does not, thus implicitly and explicitly shaping social reality (Apple, 1996; Ladson-Billings, 2003). United States history curricula, in particular, define whose experiences and perspectives are necessary and worthy in telling its story (Brown & Brown, 2010). When the U.S. history curriculum promotes whiteness as the norm and excludes people of color or includes them in a way in which their voices are marginalized or truncated, the curriculum becomes a "curriculum of violence" (Cridland-Hughes & King, 2015).

According to Cridland-Hughes and King (2015), excluding non-white people or presenting them as insignificant, inferior, illegitimate, or dangerous in the official story of the United States reifies ideologies that non-white people are not and should not be valued, cared for, or respected. Such ideologies, when not interrupted by teachers through their teaching, tell students of color that they have no value in their country and thus kill the spirit and humanity of these students (Johnson & Bryan, 2016). The message leaves non-white youth vulnerable to violent physical attacks (Cridland-Hughes & King, 2015). For example, Black youths' physical deaths are preceded by depictions of them as thugs and criminals who are uneducable and subhuman. This racialization, according to Johnson, Jackson, Stovall, and Baszile (2017), starts in classrooms where teachers do not interrupt curricula built on dehumanizing assumptions about the history of African Americans. As such, "while violence on unarmed Black bodies occurs on the streets, the idea of violence against non-white bodies begins in the classroom" (Cridland-Hughes & King, 2015, p. 100).

Curriculum scholars have long fought difficult battles to disrupt the curriculum of violence (Banks, 1970; Ladson-Billings, 2003). Owing to their efforts, history curricula today afford more space to historically oppressed communities than in the past (Wineburg & Monte-Sano, 2008). However, there is still much work to do (Santiago, 2017; Shear et al., 2015; Stanton, 2014; Vasquez-Heilig et al., 2012). For example, studies have continued to find that history curricula limit space for African Americans to the topics of slavery and the Civil Rights Movement, focus on noncontroversial histories, present racial violence as acts detached from larger structural and institutional issues, and frame challenges to racism as the actions of a few heroic individuals rather than an organized struggle (Alridge, 2006; Brown & Brown, 2010; Busey & Walker, 2017; Vasquez Heilig et al., 2012; Vickery et al., 2015). Curriculum studies have also noted continued distortions in the curricular treatment of Indigenous people, such as limiting the place of Indigenous people to the distant past, denying their historical agency and voices, and presenting them in negative ways (Sanchez, 2007; Shear et al., 2015; Stanton, 2014). Meanwhile, studies indicate that Latin Americans are still largely absent in history curriculum, and that when they are included, they are misrepresented simply as blue-collar workers or immigrants reluctant to assimilate while making little contribution to nation- building (Cruz, 2002; Davis, 2019; Noboa, 2006).

Given the limited progress in transforming this exclusive and oppressive history curriculum, it is painful, but not surprising, to see continued symbolic and physical violence against Black and Brown youth in school and society.

## THE CURRICULAR TREATMENT OF ASIAN AMERICANS

There has been a relative lack of curriculum studies on Asian American inclusion and representation. I searched databases such as EBSCO Host and ERIC using search terms such as "Asian American," "Asian immigrant," "curriculum," "textbook," "standards," "history education," "social studies," and "content analysis" in various combinations. The searches resulted in 15 studies that were conducted over the last 60 years with a focus on the curricular treatment of Asian Americans in U.S. history. By no means is this a complete, exhaustive list of all studies ever conducted on Asian American inclusion or representation in the history/social studies curriculum. Yet the search results suggest that Asian Americans and their experiences have received relatively little attention in and of themselves in curriculum studies.

In the meantime, the existing studies reach a similar conclusion. That is, Asian Americans are virtually absent from the U.S. history curriculum, and when they are visible, they are generally depicted as foreigners or a model minority. For example, the earliest study I found was Zuercher's (1969) analysis of U.S. history textbooks. Featured in the *Indiana Social Studies Quarterly* in 1969, this article reported and criticized the omission and misrepresentation of Asian Americans in U.S. history textbooks published in the 1960s. This problem seems to have continued into the 1980s and 1990s, as Chin's (1984) and Harada's (2000) studies found omissions and misrepresentations of Asian Americans in textbooks used in California and Hawaii, respectively. Specifically, Chin (1984) found that, despite the fact that California has a long history of Asian Americans and the largest Asian population in the United States, 4th-grade California state history textbooks have failed to reflect the past or present realities of the Asian American experience. Harada (2000) found that the U.S. history textbooks used in Hawaii's high schools contained little about the history of Asian Americans and that conventional attention was paid to the Chinese and Japanese while other Asian American groups were seldom addressed.

Today's history curriculum does not seem much different from that of the past. Chan (2007) analyzed two U.S. history textbooks widely used in 2005 and found inadequate and incomplete coverage of Asian American experiences. When included, Asian Americans were excluded from the main text, instead being presented in supplemental insertions. Further, attention was paid to Chinese and Japanese Americans, while other Asian groups were given limited attention or left out entirely. More recently, Suh, An, and Forest's (2015) analysis of U.S. history textbooks used in Virginia secondary schools found a similar pattern. In the reviewed textbooks, Asian Americans were largely absent, and when included, they appeared as victims of nativist racism. Additionally, the diversity among Asian American groups and the complexities of their experiences were oversimplified. Hartlep and Scott (2016) found a similar trend in today's K–12 social studies textbooks and teacher manuals used across the country. A common message across the reviewed texts was:

> Asian Americans are immigrants who come to America for a better life. These immigrants are able to succeed due to the construction of American society. While they may be temporarily impeded by little obstacles such as racism and bigotry, these impediments are easily surpassed through hard work. (p. 82)

According to Hartlep and Scott, this message is problematic because it not only distorts the Asian American experience but also perpetuates a false story about the American dream, equal opportunity for all, and meritocracy.

Along with textbooks, curriculum standards also tend to ignore Asian Americans in scripting official knowledge of U.S. history. In an analysis of U.S. history curriculum standards from 10 states, An (2016) found that Asian Americans and their experiences were virtually invisible. Except for the Chinese Exclusion Act of 1882 and the incarceration of Japanese Americans during World War II, no other Asian American figures or events were commonly included in the state-level standards. When included, Asian Americans were largely depicted as dangerous foreigners, such as Chinese immigrants who were inassimilable foreign workers taking jobs away from white people or Japanese immigrants who were incarcerated during World War II because of their questionable loyalty. An's (2022) recent analysis of 50 states' U.S. history curriculum standards found similar patterns.

Meanwhile, three curriculum studies that I found paid specific attention to the curricular treatment of Japanese incarceration. Romanowski (1995), for example, analyzed how Japanese incarceration was presented in U.S. history textbooks published between 1988 and 1992. His analysis revealed that most of the textbooks did not address the loss of personal property, a variety of possible motives for the incarceration, and the government's role in ordering and carrying out the incarceration, thus failing to provide students with complete, accurate information on the topic. Ogawa (2004) found a similar pattern in his analysis of textbooks adopted in Idaho schools in 2002. For example, the textbooks attributed the causes of the incarceration simply to fear and defense of national security without discussing other underlying issues such as racial discrimination. Hawkins and Buckendorf (2010) noted some improvement in textbooks published between 2005 and 2008. Recent textbooks provide more details on the loss of individuals' personal property and the government's motives for incarceration. However, there are still some limitations, such as the failure to explain why there were no incarceration camps in Hawaii or omitting anti-Japanese violence at the end of World War II.

Some curriculum studies have included Asian Americans in multiethnic group analyses. Kane (1970), for example, analyzed 45 secondary social studies textbooks published in the 1960s in terms of their treatment of minorities. Regarding Asian Americans, he found "there has been virtually no improvement of Americans of Orient descent. The achievements, varied characteristics, and current status of Chinese Americans and Japanese Americans are still a neglected subject" (p. 136). Wolf (1992) examined the depiction of minorities in secondary U.S. history textbooks published between 1945 and 1985. He found that over the four decades, there was an increase in the accounts of people of color in textbooks, with the greatest improvement given to the history of Black and Indigenous people. Hispanic and Asian people, however, tended to be neglected, and this neglect continued over 40 years. Sleeter and Grant (1991) analyzed 47 elementary textbooks published between 1980 and 1988 in the field of social studies as well as language arts, science, and mathematics. They found that white people continued to receive the most attention in the textbooks, dominating story lines and lists of accomplishments. They also found that the textbooks depicted Asian Americans as isolated figures with virtually no history or contemporary ethnic experience.

Again, curriculum standards seem not so much different from textbooks in scripting official knowledge of U.S. history. In an analysis of history standards from California, Sleeter (2002) found that among 96 Americans who were selected for study in the standards, there were no Asian Americans, while there were 77% white people, 18% African Americans, 4% Native Americans, and 1% Latinx. Vasquez-Heilig and co-researchers (2012) found a similar pattern in their analysis of history standards from Texas. That is, the Texas standards highlighted events and figures involving white people while paying limited attention to groups of color in the U.S. historical narrative. In particular, Asian Americans, along with Latin Americans, were virtually absent from the reviewed history standards.

## EXPLICATING THE CURRICULAR EXCLUSION OF ASIAN AMERICANS

How can we explain this continued underrepresentation and misrepresentation of Asian Americans in U.S. history curricula? Furthermore, how can we explain the lack of scholarly interest when it comes to Asian Americans? AsianCrit provides a conceptual lens to explicate the limited scholarly and curricular attention paid to Asian Americans. As a branch of critical race theory, AsianCrit emerged in the early 1990s among Asian American scholars in the field of law in order to recognize and foreground the racialized history of Asian immigrants and its subsequent impact on Asian American experiences in U.S. society

(Chang, 1993; Iftikar & Museus, 2018). From an AsianCrit perspective, the two most apparent forms of racism against Asian Americans are racialization of Asian Americans as foreigners and as a model minority (Ancheta, 2000; Chang, 1993; Wu, 2002). This anti-Asian racism is pervasive in U.S. society, including the school curriculum (An, 2016; Hartlep & Scott, 2016).

First, no matter how long Asian Americans have been in the United States or how assimilated into mainstream society they have become, Asian Americans are regarded as foreigners (Kim, 1999; E. Lee, 2016). Discussions about race in the United States continue to be conducted based on a white-Black dichotomy in which "'American' means 'white' and 'minority' means 'black'" (Wu, 2002, p. 20). In this racial framework, Asian Americans have been civically ostracized as "perpetual foreigners" (Wu, 2002, p. 81) who can never be American and whose presence poses economic, social, military, and moral threats—the yellow peril—to the United States as the country of the white race (E. Lee, 2016). This sense of dangerous foreignness is what distinguishes anti-Asian racism from racism against many other groups (Iftikar & Museus, 2018). Furthermore, this racialization has been a common underlying cause of much historical and contemporary anti-Asian discrimination and violence, as we saw during the bubonic plague in 1900 as well as in the COVID-19 pandemic in 2020.

While civically ostracized as foreigners (Kim, 1999), Asian Americans are often valorized relative to other people of color for being a model minority, that is, the right kind of racial minority, are quiet, diligent, and uncomplaining about the status quo (Iftikar & Museus, 2018). Despite seeming flattering, this racialization functions as a hegemonic device to oppress non-white people and maintain white supremacy. For example, the model minority discourse pits Asian Americans against other minority groups as an exemplar case of hard work and a model of nonpolitical upward mobility. In doing so, the discourse negates charges of racial injustice, blames communities of color for their struggle, and upholds the myth of the American dream, colorblindness, and meritocracy (Hartlep, 2013). Far from being neutral, the model minority discourse serves those in power by proclaiming that U.S. legal, economic, and educational systems operate objectively and reward individual merit when, in fact, these systems are based on white norms and only serve the interests of the dominant white race (Chubbuck, 2004).

From an AsianCrit perspective, racialization of Asian Americans as dangerous foreigners and a model minority is pervasive in U.S. society to the extent that it is reflected in curricular exclusion or misrepresentation of Asian Americans (Iftikar & Museus, 2018). In other words, the dominant society racializes Asian Americans as perpetual foreigners who can never become a part of U.S. society or as a model minority who do well in school and society and thus need little help (Chang, 1993; Iftikar & Museus, 2018). This racialization can create an audience that is unsympathetic to the needs and problems of Asian Americans, and further makes a call for more research or more inclusive curricula for Asian Americans seem unwarranted and inappropriate

(S. Lee, 2005). Besides, when included, the curriculum would mirror the dominant societal racialization of Asian Americans, presenting them as a foreign threat or model minority (An, 2016; Hartlep & Scott, 2016).

## THE DANGER OF CURRICULAR EXCLUSION OF ASIAN AMERICANS

History curriculum that excludes and misrepresents Asian Americans in the official story of the United States is a source of psychological and physical violence to Asian American students. Studies show that invisibility and misrepresentation of Asian Americans in school curriculum confuses and alienates Asian American students, which may lead to their civic disempowerment (An, 2009, 2020; S. Lee, 2005; Ngo, 2015; Park, 2011). For example, a study by the Center for Information and Research on Civic Learning and Engagement (2011) found that Asian American youths were one of the most civically alienated groups. According to the study findings, Asian American youths were less likely to vote, discuss politics, or engage in political activities compared with white people and other youth groups of color. From an AsianCrit perspective, this civic and political alienation can be partly explained by the racialization, starting in school, of Asians as foreigners and a model minority. That is, curricular exclusion and misrepresentation of Asian Americans send an official message to Asian American students that they are foreigners or a compliant, quiet minority. This message may lead Asian American youth to think they do not fully belong to mainstream society or to feel pressured to be the right kind of minority that is quietly successful without challenging the status quo.

Beyond civic alienation, the exclusionary curriculum can lead to physical violence toward Asian American students. As COVID-19 has spread, Asian American students have increasingly become the target of suspicion, discrimination, and harassment. They have been called "coronavirus" and told to "go back to China!" They have been shunned, taunted, threatened, and physically assaulted (Hong, 2020; Stop AAPI Hate Initiative, 2020). This can be partly explained by the exclusionary curriculum that produces and reproduces the dominant racialization of Asian Americans as dangerous foreigners who can be expelled and mistreated when they are perceived as an existential threat to "Americans."

Meanwhile, anti-Asian violence and bullying do not occur only during a time of "crisis" or "emergency." A study conducted a few years ago by the Asian American Legal Defense and Education Fund (2013) found that about 50% of Asian American youth in New York City public schools experienced racist harassment at school. Another study conducted by the U.S. Departments of Justice and Education revealed that 54% of Asian American teenagers were bullied in school, which was sharply above the percentages for other ethnic groups (DeVoe & Murphy, 2011).

Unfortunately, this violence toward Asian American youth is part of a long history of anti-Asian violence in the United States. Ever since the first Asians arrived on U.S. soil, Asian Americans have been subjected to harassment and hostility as "yellow peril" (E. Lee, 2016). As early as 1885, a mob of white miners in Rock Springs, Wyoming, massacred 28 Chinese laborers, as they felt threatened because Chinese laborers accepted lower wages and poorer working conditions (E. Lee, 2019). The white miners opened fire at a crowd of unarmed Chinese, burned their huts to the ground, and threw the bodies of the dead, as well as the wounded Chinese who were still alive, into the flames. A grand jury did not indict a single person. One hundred years later, in 1982, two unemployed white auto workers in Detroit, Michigan, beat Vincent Chin, a Chinese American man, to death with a baseball bat because they assumed Chin was Japanese and blamed him for their layoff and the U.S. auto industry's meltdown. The men were never sent to jail (Chang, 1993).

In the post-9/11 and Trump eras, with their heightened anti-Muslim and anti-immigrant sentiments, there has been a dramatic increase in hate crimes against South Asian, Muslim, Sikh, and Hindu communities as well as Asian immigrant communities (South Asian Americans Leading Together, 2018). Yet the criminal justice system and mass media remained inattentive to anti-Asian violence, producing and reproducing the myth that Asian Americans do not experience racism (Chen, 2000). Then, on March 16, 2021, a 21-year-old white man traveled to three different locations in metro Atlanta and killed six Asian immigrant women. A white police spokesperson tried to justify the hate crime by stating that the murderer simply had a "bad day" (Shapiro, 2021).

At the heart of anti-Asian violence and hate crimes is the racial ideology that Asian Americans are dangerous foreigners. This racial ideology is being produced and reproduced in the classroom and, when uninterrupted by teachers through their enacted curriculum, can allow, ignore, or justify anti-Asian violence in school and society.

Furthermore, the insidious effects extend to other students because such curriculum contributes to reinforce the dominant ideology that "America is a white nation" (Wu, 2002, p. 88). As history has taught us, this ideology of the white national identity has been an underlying cause of countless unjust acts of violence against communities of color, ranging from the extermination of Indigenous people and the enslavement of African Americans to a multitude of present-day racial violence, including mass incarceration and police brutality against Black and Brown communities. Therefore, omission and distortion of Asian American experience in the official curriculum of U.S. history is not a trivial matter. Such a curriculum would ultimately allow, ignore, and justify symbolic and physical violence against all non-white students.

## INCLUSIVE HISTORY CURRICULUM FOR RACIAL LITERACY BUILDING

A call for a more inclusive and accurate presentation of Asian American history in the U.S. history curriculum can be further justified in terms of racial literacy development. As a "skill and practice in which individuals are able to discuss the social construction of race, probe the existence of racism and examine the harmful effects of racial stereotyping" (Sealey-Ruiz & Greene, 2015, p. 60), racial literacy is vital for students to critically read and challenge the racism that has plagued the United States since its founding. Racially literate citizens would understand that race is socially constructed; that racism is normal, pervasive, and permanent; and that racism is more than individual prejudice, instead involving the institutional, systemic, and cultural processes that perpetuate racial hierarchies (King, 2016; King & Chandler, 2016). Like other racialized, ethnic histories, Asian American history can be a vehicle for racial literacy learning (King, 2016).

The story of Asian immigration and settlement, in particular, vividly shows that the preservation of whiteness as the national identity was not something conceived through a natural process, but a conscious, deliberate process constructed through government policy (Chang, 1993; E. Lee, 2016, 2019). At its formation, the United States defined citizenship as the province of white male property owners and limited naturalization only to free white persons (E. Lee, 2019). Against whiteness as the norm of citizenship, Asians were positioned as unassimilable others or dangerous foreigners who would never become a part of U.S. society (E. Lee, 2016). This racialization justified the exclusion of Asians entering the United States through a series of anti-Asian immigration laws such as the Chinese Exclusion Act of 1882, the Asiatic Barred Zone Act of 1917, and the Asian Exclusion Act of 1924. This foreigner racialization justified the exclusion of Asian immigrants from becoming naturalized citizens once in the United States and allowed a wide range of anti-Asian legislation in housing, schooling, employment, marriage, and political participation (E. Lee, 2016; Wu, 2002). It was not until 1952 that all Asian immigrants were finally eligible for naturalization, and it was not until 1965 that Congress finally abolished the discriminatory national quotas for Asian immigration (E. Lee, 2019).

Of course, many other immigrant groups have faced antagonism and prejudice upon arrival in the United States. However, it was only Asian people whose arrival created opposition sufficient enough to initiate a series of exclusionary, discriminatory laws regarding immigration, naturalization, and civic participation (Okihiro, 1994). This long history of excluding and discriminating against Asians entering the U.S. and becoming American citizens has served to maintain whiteness as the national identity and strengthen white supremacy, "a racialized social system that upholds, reifies, and reinforces the superiority of whites" (Leonardo, 2005, p. 127).

When included in the study of U.S. history, these stories of Asian Americans can help students develop critical race knowledge. For example, an inquiry into a series of anti-Asian immigration and naturalization laws can engage students in exploring how the government and the dominant group have answered the following questions: Who are we as a nation? What does it mean to be an American? Who may live among us and become an American, and who should not? Through these inquiries, students would realize that white supremacy has been a major feature of U.S. citizenship and that racism is not just what Brown and Brown (2010) called "bad men doing bad things" (p. 60), but a systematic tool for maintaining white supremacy (Delgado & Stefancic, 2012). The inquiry can also assist students in moving beyond the white-Black binary of race by uncovering that white dominance has depended on racializing all non-white groups, including Asians, in different and related ways (E. Lee, 2019). Through the inquiry, students will be able to further disrupt the dominant racialization of Asian Americans as foreigners or a quiet compliant minority by learning that Asian Americans have long been a part of this country and have fought hard against white supremacy in the court, street, and workplace (Aguirre & Lio, 2008).

I contend that these racial understandings are vital for both Asian and non-Asian students. Such critical race knowledge will, first, guide the students to more fully understand how racism and white supremacy shape the social realities of all people and, second, to envision and create a new social reality.

## WHERE DO WE GO FROM HERE?

Cridland-Hughes and King (2015) maintained that if we want to provide a curriculum of support, not violence, we must push for an inclusive curriculum that includes marginalized voices. More curricular and scholarly efforts should be made to make the U.S. history curriculum inclusive and accurate for all marginalized groups, including Asian Americans. Such a curriculum will become a source of support for all students for racial literacy learning and civic empowerment. Without this inclusive curriculum, we will reproduce a population that has problematic perspectives on the issues of race, racism, and citizenship. Further, we will continue to see surges in symbolic and physical violence against students of color. The rise of hate crimes and violence against Asian communities in the wake of the COVID-19 pandemic is a poignant reminder of this danger.

## REFERENCES

Aguirre, A., & Lio, S. (2008). Spaces of mobilization: The Asian American/Pacific Islander struggle for social justice. *Social Justice, 35*(2), 1–17.

Alridge, D. (2006). The limits of master narratives in history textbooks: An analysis of representations of Martin Luther King, Jr. *Teachers College Record, 108*(4), 662–686.

An, S. (2009). Learning U.S. history in an age of transnational migration. *Journal of Curriculum Studies, 41*(6), 763–787.

An, S. (2016). Asian Americans in American history: An AsianCrit perspective on Asian American representation in US history curriculum standards. *Theory and Research in Social Education, 44*(2), 244–276.

An, S. (2020). Racial literacy learning while navigating white social studies. *The Social Studies, 111*(4), 174–181.

An, S. (2022). Re/presentation of Asian Americans in 50 states U.S. history standards. *The Social Studies.* https://doi.org/10.1080/00377996.2021.2023083

Ancheta, A. (2000). *Race, rights and the Asian American experience.* Rutgers University Press.

Apple, M. W. (1996). *Cultural politics and education.* Open University Press.

Asian American Legal Defense and Education Fund. (2013). *One step forward, half a step back: A status report on bias-based bullying of Asian American students in New York city schools.* aaldef.org/2013_NYC_bullying_report.pdf

Banks, J. (1970). *Teaching the Black experience: Methods and materials.* Fearson.

Brown, A. L., & Brown, K. D. (2010). Strange fruit indeed: Integrating contemporary textbook representations of racial violence toward African Americans. *Teachers College Record, 112*(1), 31–67.

Busey, C., & Walker, I. (2017). A dream and a bus: Black critical patriotism in elementary social studies standards. *Theory & Research in Social Education, 45*(4), 456–488.

CBS News. (2020, February 14). Bullies attack Asian American teen at school, accusing him of having coronavirus. https://www.cbsnews.com/news/coronavirus-bullies-attack-asian-teen-los-angeles-accusing-him-of-having-coronavirus/

CBS News. (2020, March 30). FBI calling stabbing at Midland Sam's a hate crime. https://www.cbs7.com/content/news/FBI-calling-stabbing-at-Midland-Sams-a-hate-crime-569233691.html

Center for Information and Research on Civic Learning and Engagement. (2011). *Understanding a diverse generation: Youth civic engagement in the U.S.* http://www.civicyouth.org/wp-content/uploads/2011/11/CIRCLE_cluster_report2010.pdf

Chan, C. (2007). Breadth versus depth: The treatment of Asian Americans in US history textbooks. In C. Park, R. Endo, S. Lee & X. Long (Eds.), *Asian American education, acculturation, literacy development, and learning* (pp. 131–154). Information Age Publishing.

Chang, R. S. (1993). Toward an Asian American legal scholarship: Critical race theory, poststructuralism, and narrative space. *California Law Review, 19*, 1243–1323.

Chen, T. (2000). Hate violence as border patrol: An Asian American theory of hate violence. *Asian American Law Journal, 7* (3), 69–101.

Chin, C. (1984). Asian Americans and California state textbooks. *Social Studies Review, 23* (3), 46–48.

Cho, D. (2020, March 17). Racist attacks against Asians continue to rise as the coronavirus threat grows. *People.* https://people.com/health/coronavirus-racist-attacks-against-asians/

Chubbuck, S. (2004). Whiteness enacted, whiteness disrupted: The complexity of personal congruence. *American Educational Research Journal, 41*(2), 301–333.

Cridland-Hughes, S., & King, L. (2015). Killing me softly: How violence comes from the curriculum we teach. In K. Fasching-Varner & N. Hartlep (Eds.), *The assault on communities of color: Exploring the realities of race-based violence* (pp. 99–102). Rowman & Littlefield.

Cruz, B. C. (2002). Don Juan and rebels under palm trees: Depictions of Latin Americans in US history textbooks. *Critique of Anthropology, 22*(3), 323–342.

Davis, E. (2019). (Mis)representation of Latinxs in Florida social studies standards. *Social Studies Research and Practice, 14*(1), 1–13.

Delgado, R., & Stefancic, J. (2012). *Critical race theory: An introduction.* New York University Press.

DeVoe, J., & Murphy, C. (2011). *Student reports of bullying and cyber-bullying: Results from the 2009 School Crime Supplement to the National Crime Victimization Survey.* http://nces.ed.gov/pubs2011/2011336.pdf

Giuffrida, A., & Wills, K. (2020, January 31). Outbreaks of xenophobia in the west as coronavirus spreads. *The Guardian.* https://www.theguardian.com/world/2020/jan/31/spate-of-anti-chinese-incidents-in-italy-amid-coronavirus-panic

Harada, V. H. (2000). *The treatment of Asian Americans in U.S. history textbooks published 1994–1996.* ERIC Clearinghouse for Social Studies/Social Science Education, Document No. ED448072

Hartlep, D. (2013). *The model minority stereotype: Demystifying Asian American success.* Information Age.

Hartlep, N. D., & Scott, D. P. (2016). *Asian/American curricular epistemicide: From being excluded to becoming a model minority.* Sense Publishers.

Hawkins, J. M., & Buckendorf, M. (2010). A current analysis of the treatment of Japanese Americans and internment in U.S. history textbooks. *Journal of International Social Studies, 1*(1), 34–42.

Hong, A. (2020, March 12). Amid the coronavirus outbreak, Asian-American students like my son face racist taunting. Let's change that. *Chalkbeat.* https://chalkbeat.org/posts/us/2020/03/12/amid-coronavirus-outbreak-asian-american-students-like-my-son-face-racist-taunting-lets-change-that/

Iftikar, J., & Museus, S. (2018). On the utility of Asian critical (AsianCrit) theory in the field of education. *International Journal of Qualitative Studies in Education, 31*(10), 935–949.

Johnson, L., & Bryan, N. (2016). Using our voices, losing our bodies: Michael Brown, Trayvon Martin, and the spirit murders of Black male professors in the academy. *Race Ethnicity and Education*, 20 (2), 163–177.

Johnson, L., Jackson, J., Stovall, D., & Baszile, D. (2017). "Loving Blackness to death": (Re)imagining ELA classrooms in a time of racial chaos. *English Journal, 106* (4), 60–66.

Kane, M. (1970). *Minorities in textbooks: A study of their treatment in social studies texts.* Quadrangle Books.

KARE 11 News. (2020, March 26). We can control the spread of hate during the coronavirus pandemic. https://www.kare11.com/article/news/local/breaking-the-news/we-can-control-the-spread-of-hate-during-the-coronavirus-pandemic/89-b3d40 6e0-9e14-4794-9e5e-727b48d0d275

Kim, C. (1999). The racial triangulation of Asian Americans. *Politics and Society, 27*(1), 105–38.

Kim, H-J. (2020, February 2). Fears of new virus trigger anti-China sentiment worldwide. AP News. https://apnews.com/04f18aafe1074a1c06b4203edcbd c661

King, L. (2016). Teaching black history as a racial literacy project. *Race Ethnicity and Education, 19*(6), 1303–1318.

King, L., & Chandler, P. (2016). From non-racism to anti-racism in social studies teacher education: Social studies and racial pedagogical content knowledge. In A. Crowe & A. Cuenca (Eds.), *Rethinking social studies teacher education in the twenty-first century* (pp. 3–21). Springer International Publishing.

Ladson-Billings, G. (2003). Lies my teacher still tells: Developing a critical perspective toward social studies. In G. Ladson-Billings (Ed.), *Critical race theory perspectives on social studies* (pp. 1–11). Information Age.

Lapayese, Y. V. (2012). Mother-scholar: (Re)imagining K–12 education. *Transgressions: Cultural Studies and Education, 85,* 1–10.

Lee, E. (2016). *Making of Asian America.* Basic Books.

Lee, E. (2019). *America for Americans. A history of xenophobia in the U.S.* Basic Books.

Lee, S. (2005). *Up against whiteness.* Teachers College, Columbia University.

Leonardo, Z. (2005). *Race, whiteness, and education.* Routledge.

Mohr, J. (2005). *Plague and fire: Battling Black Death and the 1900 burning of Honolulu's Chinatown.* Oxford University Press.

*New York Post.* (2020, March 11). Asian man is victim in latest coronavirus-fueled hate crime. https://nypost.com/2020/03/11/asian-man-is-victim-in-latest-coronavirus-fueled-hate-crime/?fbclid=IwAR0RGrFQfZTlbj2oAKntgKbYg3CMshM0s3MyOStQG4XX5NbUEjHktWMwKN4

*New York Post.* (2020, March 14). Victim of possible coronavirus hate crime in Queens speaks out. https://nypost.com/2020/03/14/victim-of-possible-coronavirus-hate-crime-in-queens-speaks-out/

Ngo, B. (2015). Hmong culture club as a place of belonging: The cultivation of Hmong students' cultural and political identities. *Journal of Southeast Asian American Education and Advancement, 10*(2), 1–16.

Noboa, J. (2006). *Leaving Latinos out of history: Teaching U.S. history in Texas.* Routledge.

Ogawa, M. (2004). Treatment of Japanese-American internment during World War II in U.S. history textbooks. *International Journal of Social Education, 19*(1), 35–47.

Okihiro, G. Y. (1994). *Margins and mainstreams: Asians in American history and culture.* University of Washington Press.

*Orange County Register.* (2020, March 12). Garden Grove students scream "coronavirus," mock Asian teens. https://www.ocregister.com/2020/03/12/video-garden-grove-students-scream-coronavirus-mocks-asian-teens/

Park, G. (2011). Are we real Americans? Cultural production of forever foreigners at a diversity event. *Education and Urban Society, 43*(4), 451–467.

Romanowski, M. (1995). Impressions of the democratic ideals of justice and equality in U.S. history textbooks: The treatment of Japanese Americans during World War II. *Journal of Social Studies Research, 19* (1), 31–49.

Sanchez, T. R. (2007). The depiction of Native Americans in recent (1991–2004) secondary American history textbooks: How far have we come? *Equity & Excellence in Education, 40,* 311–320.

Santiago, M. (2017). Erasing differences for the sake of inclusion: How Mexican/Mexican American students construct historical narratives. *Theory and Research in Social Education, 45*(1), 43–74.

Sealey-Ruiz, Y., & Greene, P. (2015). Popular visual images and the (mis) reading of Black male youth: A case for racial literacy in urban preservice teacher education. *Teaching Education, 26*(1), 1–22.

Shah, N. (2001). *Contagious divides: Epidemics and race in San Francisco's Chinatown.* University of California Press.

Shapiro, E. (2021, March 19). Georgia sheriff's department under fire after official says spa shooting suspect had 'really bad day.' *ABC News.* https://abcnews.go.com/US

/georgia-sheriffs-department-fire-official-spa-shootings-suspect/story?id
=76533598

Shear, S. B., Knowles, R. T., Soden, G. J., & Castro, A. J. (2015). Manifesting destiny: Re/presentations of indigenous peoples in K–12 U.S. history standards. *Theory & Research in Social Education, 43*(1), 68–101.

Sleeter, C. E. (2002). State curriculum standards and student consciousness. *Social Justice, 29*(4), 8–25.

Sleeter, C. E., & Grant, C. A. (1991). Race, class, gender, and disability in current textbooks. In M. W. Apple & L. K. Christian-Smith (Eds.), *The politics of the textbook* (pp. 78–110). Routledge.

South Asian Americans Leading Together. (2018). *Communities on fire: Confronting hate violence and xenophobic political rhetoric.* http://saalt.org/report-communities-on-fire-confronting-hate-violence-and-xenophobic-political-rhetoric/

Stanton, C. R. (2014). The curricular Indian agent: Discursive colonization and Indigenous (dys)agency in U.S. history textbooks. *Curriculum Inquiry, 44*(5), 649–676.

Stop AAPI Hate Initiative. (2020). STOP AAPI HATE receives over 1,100 incident reports of verbal harassment, shunning and physical assault in two weeks. http://www.asianpacificpolicyandplanningcouncil.org/stop-aapi-hate/

Suh, Y., An, S., & Forest, D. (2015). Immigration, imagined communities, and collective memories of Asian American experiences: A content analysis of Asian American experiences in Virginia U.S. history textbooks. *Journal of Social Studies Research, 39*(1), 39–51.

Trauner, J. (1978). Chinese as medical scapegoats, 1870–1905. *California History, 57*(1), 70–87.

Vasquez-Heilig, J. V., Brown, K., & Brown, A. (2012). The illusion of inclusion: A critical race theory textual analysis of race and standards. *Harvard Educational Review, 82* (3), 403–424.

Vickery, A. E., Holmes, K., & Brown, A. L. (2015). Excavating critical racial knowledge in economics and world geography. In P. T. Chandler (Ed.), *Doing race in social studies: Critical perspectives* (pp. 253–282). Information Age Publishing.

Wang, J. (2020, March 18). Vandals tag downtown Asian restaurants with racist messages. KOB4 News. https://www.kob.com/coronavirus/vandals-tag-downtown-asian-restaurant-with-racist-message/5677160/

Wilkinson, J. (2021, March 17). Hear it: 911 calls from 2 Atlanta spa shootings released. https://www.nydailynews.com/news/national/ny-atlanta-spa-shootings-911-calls-20210318-555ybojhhzdt5mbwphoz5tbzfa-story.html

Wineburg, S., & Monte-Sano, C. (2008). Famous Americans: The changing pantheon of American heroes. *Journal of American History, 94*(4), 1186–1202.

Wolf, A. (1992). Minorities in U.S. history textbooks, 1945–1985. *The Clearing House, 65*(5), 291–297.

Wu, F. (2002). *Yellow: Race in America beyond black and white.* Basic Books.

Yeung, J. (2020, January 31). As the coronavirus spreads, fear is fueling racism and xenophobia. CNN. https://www.cnn.com/2020/01/31/asia/wuhan-coronavirus-racism-fear-intl-hnk/index.html

Zuercher, R. (1969). The treatment of Asian minorities in American history textbooks. *Indiana Social Studies Quarterly, 22* (Autumn), 19–27.

## CHAPTER 2

# "Movin' On Up"

## The Growing Role of Latinx Social Studies Topics Through the Grade Levels[1]

*Maribel Santiago and Eliana Castro*

Educators are expected to teach in increasingly diverse classrooms. Latinx[2] students comprise a quarter of the children in the United States, making them the largest ethnic group in K–12 schools (Ceasar, 2011). School districts have responded with efforts to create a more culturally relevant curriculum to be more inclusive of their Latinx students. The Los Angeles Unified School District (LAUSD), the second-largest school district in the country, made ethnic studies a high school graduation requirement (Ceasar, 2014). Chicago Public Schools adopted a Latino and Latin American Studies curriculum (Chicago Public Schools, 2015). Even Indiana—a state people do not usually associate with Latinx populations—offers ethnic studies courses in all high schools (Lindsay, 2018). This is happening as states like Texas and California try to make social studies standards more inclusive of Latinx perspectives (Fogo, 2015; Swaby, 2018). These advances serve as evidence of a nationwide trend calling for educators to teach about Latinx communities.

While commendable, these shifts give teachers little guidance on *how* to teach Latinx topics. Empirical research on teaching and learning about Latinx topics in social studies classrooms is a small but burgeoning field (e.g., Busey & Russell, 2016; Salinas et al., 2016; Santiago, 2017). These studies have usually focused on individual classrooms. Broader understanding of which topics are covered and how Latinx contributions are represented across the country is essential.

This chapter addresses a critical need: preparing educators to teach the contributions of Latinx communities in K–12 social studies courses. This requires an understanding of both the content taught in the classroom and the factors that encourage or discourage educators from teaching Latinx topics in their social studies classrooms. One such factor may be the need for teachers to not only learn about Latinx communities and experiences, but also to develop the racial literacy (Guinier, 2003, 2004) necessary to teach Latinx social studies topics with nuance.

## LITERATURE REVIEW

Research on K–12 social studies instruction and the representation of communities of color in curriculum is essential to understanding what content social studies educators currently teach about Latinx communities and what factors influence their uptake (or lack thereof). Literature on K–12 instruction and communities of color in the curriculum offer insight into the marginalization of social studies content and Latinx contributions.

### Grade-Level Differences

Social studies instruction varies remarkably by grade level, with elementary curriculum marginalizing this content area the most. Scholarship points to several reasons for this trend. The pressure of standardized testing is one major culprit (Au, 2009, 2011; Grant & Salinas, 2010; Pace, 2008, 2011). Since social studies is typically not subject to standardized, high-stakes tests at the state or national levels, teachers favor other tested subjects, particularly literacy and mathematics (Abernathy-Dyer et al., 2013; Berson & Camicia, 2013; Heafner & Fitchett, 2012; Pace, 2008, 2011). The diminished time allotted to social studies instruction restricts elementary teachers' potential content coverage (Bisland, 2011; Fitchett, Heafner, & Lambert, 2014; Fitchett, Heafner, & VanFossen, 2014).

However, the prevalence of testing may not be the only factor at fault. Elementary social studies instruction tends to be marginalized in teacher education as well. Specifically, preservice teachers' field experiences may have an equal or greater impact on their classroom practice than programs of study and methods instruction (Bolick et al., 2010; Hawkman et al., 2015; Starr, 2012). When mentor teachers dedicate less instructional time to social studies, teacher candidates receive less exposure to models for designing and implementing quality social studies learning opportunities (Hawkman et al., 2015).

Other challenges surface with the perceived relevance of social studies content across grade levels, shaped by states' course requirements. Secondary social studies instruction research tends to focus on *how*, not *whether*, social studies topics are taught (Jaffee, 2016; Russell, 2010; Salinas et al., 2008). More social studies content is presumed to be taught as students get older. This assumption makes sense, since secondary courses in world history, U.S. history, government, and economics are required in many states (e.g., California State Board of Education, 2016; Florida Department of Education, 2019; Illinois State Board of Education, 2016; New York State Education Department, 2019). Although the secondary social studies scholarship is necessary, it often overlooks which topics teachers prioritize over others and why.

One exception is the Survey on the Status of the Social Studies (S4, led by a research team from 35 states across the country), which found that teachers emphasize less history instruction when they prioritize civics instruction, and vice versa (Fitchett & VanFossen, 2013). Drawing from S4 data, Bigler and colleagues (2013) investigated the frequency with which elementary, middle, and high school teachers addressed race and class in their classrooms. Teachers reported addressing race and class more frequently as grade level increased. Less than one-fourth of elementary teachers reported highlighting these themes frequently or almost daily. In contrast, one-half of middle school teachers and two-thirds of high school teachers reported emphasizing race or class frequently or almost daily. Bigler and colleagues (2013) suggest that the greater emphasis in middle and high school may be related to elementary teachers' concerns that issues of race and class are developmentally inappropriate for their students (e.g., Demoiny, 2017) and to the greater disciplinary focus of social studies courses in the middle and high school grades (e.g., Reisman, 2012).

## Representation in Social Studies Content

Social studies content also routinely excludes or minimizes the histories, agency, and perspectives of communities of color. Scholars who have examined state social studies content standards and textbooks have found the representation of Black, Indigenous, Asian American, and Latinx communities to be lacking. World history standards reflect Eurocentrism (Marino & Bolgatz, 2010), minimizing and distorting the role of Latin America and other parts of the Global South (Noboa, 2012). In U.S. history, racial violence against African Americans is minimized or distorted in K–12 textbooks, and when depicted, incidents tend to be divorced from structural and institutional forces (A. L. Brown & K. D. Brown, 2010; K. D. Brown & A. L. Brown, 2010). Standards from all 50 states and Washington, D.C., present Indigenous peoples in a pre-1900 context and relegate their importance and presence to the distant past (Shear et al., 2015). Further, An's (2016) AsianCrit analysis of U.S. history standards in 10 states revealed that even in New York, the state with the most Asian-related events in its standards, there were no events of Asian American movements for justice and organized activism listed in the standards.

This study seeks to complicate this literature by illuminating the treatment of Latinidad and its treatment across K–12 social studies. We use the term Latinidad even though we are aware that, although meant to bring together the Latinx diasporas, it can also erase the distinct racial, linguistic, national, and migrant experiences of the same diverse communities it attempts to include (Salazar, 2019). Our chapter highlights these nuances specifically in relationship to how educators represent Latinx communities in K–12 social studies classrooms. Understanding and addressing this complexity requires a degree of racial literacy, or "the ability to read race in conjunction with institutional and democratic structures" (Guinier, 2003, p. 120). Racial literacy is contextual. It illuminates the operation of psychological, interpersonal, and structural processes and interrogates intersectional dynamics like race, geography, and other variables (Guinier, 2004). In developing this study, we considered this complexity, specifically how discrete Latinx groups and their distinct experiences might be taught differently. We discuss this further in the "Methods and Analysis" section below.

### Latinidad in Social Studies Education

While some scholars have documented how Latinx communities are under-represented in textbooks and state standards (Noboa, 2013), other scholars have turned their attention to *how* they are represented (Busey & Cruz, 2017; Díaz & Deroo, 2020). This scholarship includes how Mexican American histories must conform to the Black/white racial binary (Santiago, 2017, 2019) and how Afro-Latinxs are excluded altogether (Busey, 2018; Busey & Cruz, 2017).

Given these limited representations, scholars have developed research-based classroom interventions to challenge such narratives (Bondy & Pennington, 2016; Chiodo, 2013). However, these interventions tend to target the upper grades. For example, in suggesting ways to develop historical thinking among Latinx immigrant students across place and time, Fránquiz and Salinas (2011) focused on high school students' examinations of the Chicanx movement in the 1960s and 1970s, and current Mexican immigration. Whether and how these techniques for interrogating Latinx representations might be adapted for elementary students has yet to be explored.

## METHODS AND ANALYSIS

To understand which Latinx topics teachers are including, we considered the following research questions: Which Latinx-related topics are elementary, middle, and high school educators including in their social studies lessons? What differences occur between grade levels? What accounts for why grade-level teachers include certain topics over others?

### Data Collection

We designed a survey for K–12 educators in four cities to share whether and how they teach Latinx topics. Specifically, we selected four sites with significant Latinx student populations: Los Angeles, New York City, Chicago, and Orange County, Florida.

These areas are populated by the three largest Latinx-origin groups in the U.S.—people of Mexican, Puerto Rican, and Cuban origin (United States Census, 2010)—and Latinx communities unique to each city. In Los Angeles, 74% of the public school student population was Latinx in 2018–2019 (Education Data Partnership, 2020), most of whom were of Mexican (40%) and Central American (11%) origin (U.S. Census, 2010). New York City was

28.6% Latinx, primarily of Puerto Rican (8.9%) and Dominican (7.1%) origin (U.S. Census, 2010). Although Florida is known for its Cuban-origin community, Orange County is only 2% Cuban-origin, with 13% of Puerto Rican origin (U.S. Census, 2010). Chicago, home to the fifth-largest concentration of Latinxs in the United States (Ready & Brown-Gort, 2005), was 28.9% Latinx, mostly of Mexican and Puerto Rican origin (U.S. Census, 2010).

### Survey Instrument

To design the survey, we cross-referenced sample scales and pre-existing instruments in the field (Fitchett & VanFossen, 2013; Passe & Fitchett, 2013). We also pulled social studies topics from content standards in participating states. These topics reflect benchmarks surrounding Latinx history and/or culture, broadly defined as any topic referring to Mexico, Central America, South America, Cuba, Puerto Rico, or the Dominican Republic. This list includes content not typically considered "Latinx" but with significance for Latinx people in the United States. For instance, Manifest Destiny is often presented as the westward movement of white European Americans based on governmental and religious support for their settlement. However, educators may use this topic to also expose the systematic displacement of Indigenous and Mexican communities from their land and the attempted erasure of their languages and ways of life. The latter framing allows this topic to be perceived as one in which Latinx history *is* U.S. history.

Our instrument had 28 items, with three categories of open- and close-ended questions. Demographic questions focused on the school, students, and teacher. Instructional items asked about their overall approach to teaching Latinx topics and their frequency. Rationale questions addressed factors that would help teachers incorporate more Latinx topics into their instruction. This chapter focuses solely on analyses of the close-ended responses. Specifically, we consider two types of frequency questions: how often educators taught a specific topic and how often they integrated Latinx topics in their overall teaching. For this chapter we compared what educators taught and how often by grade level.

### Sample

We disseminated the online survey via our professional networks to a voluntary convenience sample of K–12 social studies teachers in all four districts. We collected responses for 14 months through the Qualtrics® data management system. One hundred and thirty K–12 teachers took the survey: 60 Los Angeles teachers, 31 New York City teachers, 25 Chicago teachers, and 14 Orange County teachers. The participating teachers identified as white (48.84%), Latinx (25.58%), two or more races (11.63%), East Asian/Asian American (5.43%), Black/African American (3.88%), South Asian/Asian

American (3.10%), Middle Eastern/Asian American (0.77%), and American Indian or Alaska Native (0.77%).

Teachers self-reported their grade level by selecting as many of the following categories as applied to them: early childhood (pre-K–3); elementary (K–5); elementary (K–6); middle (6–8); junior high (7–9); secondary (9–12); and senior high (10–12). We subsequently regrouped responses as elementary (pre-K–3, K–5, and K–6), middle (6–8 and 7–9), and high school (9–12 and 10–12). There were 44 elementary, 19 middle, and 64 high school teacher participants. Three teachers were not included in the three-level analysis because they indicated that they taught multiple grades across more than one category. One teacher whose responses belonged to both the lower and upper categories was not included in the two-level grade comparison.

## Data Analysis

To compare what content educators taught in different grades, we first grouped teachers by grade levels. The variables of teachers' grade levels were constructed using both two grade-level and three grade-level categories. In the two-level analysis, teachers were grouped as lower (elementary) or upper grades (middle and high school). The three-level analysis categorized teachers as elementary, middle, or high school.

Teachers' coverage of Latinx topics across the school year was assessed using the following four categories: (1) no coverage, (2) slight coverage (one class/lesson or less), (3) moderate coverage (two to five classes/lessons), and (4) sustained coverage (more than five classes/lessons). In addition to how often they taught specific Latinx topics, teachers were asked how they integrated Latinidad throughout their curriculum. Teachers' answers were grouped into three categories: low coverage (do not teach; rarely teach; or teach Latinx topics when there is time left over); middle coverage (taught during a particular portion of the school year); and high coverage (taught during a portion of school day, or integrated throughout the curriculum).

We then conducted the chi-square test of independence and Fisher's exact test to examine the relationship between teachers' grade levels and their coverage of Latinx topics in social studies. The analysis methods were selected given that levels of measurement for both teachers' coverage of Latinx topics and teachers' grade levels are categorical. A null hypothesis in both tests is that there is no association between teachers' grade levels and their coverage of Latinx topics, whereas the alternative hypothesis is that there is a relationship. Chi-square tests provide $z$-statistics and a corresponding $p$-value to determine whether the null hypothesis is rejected, while Fisher's exact tests directly provide $p$-values for hypothesis testing. We utilized the chi-square test for a case where every cell has an observed frequency larger than 5 and the Fisher's exact test for the cases in which one or more of the observed frequencies is 5 or less (e.g., 4 levels of topic coverage).

## FINDINGS

In this section, we examine the trends that emerged across participants' coverage of Latinx topics according to the grade level and content they teach. Four findings became evident: (1) the higher the students' grade level, the more likely teachers were to report covering Latinx topics on a regular basis; (2) the topics with the highest coverage among middle school teachers *directly aligned* with content standards, but the topics with the highest coverage among high school teachers *related less explicitly* to the standards; (3) elementary teachers also reported teaching Latinx content that we later found were related to standards; and (4) one topic was an outlier—not aligned with standards but one that middle and high school educators reported teaching consistently.

### The Higher the Grade Level, the More Coverage

One finding was abundantly clear across all participants and topics listed on the survey: Middle and high school educators were more likely to report covering Latinx topics on a consistent basis. When comparing two grade-level bands (pre-K–6 and 6–12), the difference in classroom coverage of Latinx topics was statistically significant and considerably higher for teachers who work with upper grades.

Table 2.1 below represents how teachers in upper and lower levels describe their approach to teaching Latinx social studies topics. These results indicate that there is an association between the grade levels that educators teach and their frequency of covering Latinx topics (Fisher's exact = .04, $p < .05$).[3] To be specific, teachers in the lower grades showed relatively low levels of Latinx topic coverage (56.10%), while teachers who taught upper grades were more likely to exhibit middle levels of Latinx topic coverage (60.00%).

**Table 2.1. Fisher's Exact Test of the Relationship Between Grade Levels and Teachers' Approach to Covering Latinx Topics**

| Level | Lower Grades (pre-K–6) | Upper Grades (6–12) | Total |
|---|---|---|---|
| Low Latinx topic teaching coverage | 23 (56.10%) | 27 (33.75%) | 50 (41.32%) |
| Middle Latinx topic teaching coverage | 15 (36.59%) | 48 (60.00%) | 63 (52.07%) |
| High Latinx topic teaching coverage | 3 (7.32%) | 5 (6.25%) | 8 (6.61%) |
| Total | 41 (100%) | 80 (100%) | 121 (100%) |

*Note:* Fisher's exact test = .04.

As further proof of the upward trend in Latinx topic coverage by grade levels, when we ran three-level comparisons for individual topics, we found no Latinx topics that had the highest reported coverage among teachers in the elementary grades. There were, however, topics with the highest coverage in upper grades (for two-level comparisons), and in middle and high school grades (in three-level comparisons).

### Standards-Aligned in Middle Grades, Standards-Related in High School

While no elementary teachers reported sustained coverage for any topic, middle school teachers reported both moderate and sustained coverage for four topics: Spanish exploration and colonization, Mexican rule in what is now U.S. territory, the U.S.-Mexico War, and the Brown Berets (a Chicanx youth power movement). With the exception of the Brown Berets, these Latinx topics directly aligned with their respective social studies content standards.

There was a statistically significant association between teachers' grade levels and topic coverage of Spanish exploration, Mexican rule in the U.S., and the U.S.-Mexico War. Middle school teachers reported moderate and sustained coverage more often than their high school and elementary colleagues. For example, high school teachers reported moderate coverage (37.50%) of Spanish exploration and colonization, but middle school teachers' coverage rates were almost the same (31.58%). More importantly, middle school teachers reported a higher percentage of sustained coverage (36.84%) than their high school colleagues (see Table 2.2).

Two topics not directly aligned with content standards demonstrated the highest reported coverage among high school teachers. These topics were the effects of assimilationist policies, and Latinx people as a rising voting bloc in the U.S. Although not explicitly listed in content standards, these topics are

**Table 2.2. Chi-Square Test of the Relationship Between Three Grade Levels and Topic Coverage of Spanish Exploration and Colonization in What Is Now U.S. Territory**

| Topic Coverage | Elementary | Middle | High | Total |
|---|---|---|---|---|
| None, Not Covered | 18 (40.91%) | 4 (21.05%) | 15 (23.44%) | 37 (29.13%) |
| Slight Coverage (One class/lesson or less) | 13 (29.55%) | 2 (10.53%) | 13 (20.31%) | 28 (22.05%) |
| Moderate Coverage (Two to five classes/lessons) | 7 (15.91%) | 6 (31.58%) | 24 (37.50%) | 37 (29.13%) |
| Sustained Coverage (More than five classes/lessons) | 6 (13.64%) | 7 (36.84%) | 12 (18.75%) | 25 (19.69%) |
| Total | 44 (100%) | 19 (100%) | 64 (100%) | 127 (100%) |

*Note:* Fisher's exact = .04.

related to other civics and U.S. government standards. Each state has some high school content standard(s) relating to analysis of voting, including voter turnout trends (Florida Department of Education, 2014), limitations and opportunities with voting (Illinois State Board of Education, 2017), historical development with civil rights (California State Board of Education, 2016), and critical analysis of political arguments when participating as a voter (New York State Education Department, 1996).

We found that high school teachers were more likely to teach the effects of assimilationist policies in comparison to their middle school colleagues. For example, 6.25% of high school teachers reported sustained coverage on the effects of assimilationist policies, while their middle school counterparts reported sustained coverage 5.26% of the time. The differences are more striking for moderate coverage: 26.56% of high school teachers reported moderate coverage, compared to only 10.53% of middle school teachers (see Table 2.3). These results indicate coverage being proportional to students' grade levels.

Unlike the middle and high school teachers, the majority of elementary teachers reported not teaching the effects of assimilationist policies (59.09%). Yet those who did teach this content reported moderate coverage in greater numbers (20.45%) than their middle school counterparts (10.53%). This pattern may exist because elementary social studies content often includes assimilation-based activities (e.g., learning state and national symbols, roles of citizens, following rules and laws), which encourage patriotism and ideas regarding who is a "good" citizen.

Data on Latinx people as a rising voting bloc also support the finding that high school teachers are more likely to teach content not directly connected to the standards. Specifically, 70% of high school teachers reported teaching at least one lesson on Latinxs as a rising voting bloc, whereas almost 56% of middle school teachers reported the same (see Table 2.4). This is in sharp

**Table 2.3. Chi-Square Test on the Relationship Between Three Grade Levels and Topic Coverage of the Effect of Assimilationist Policies**

| Topic Coverage | Elementary | Middle | High | Total |
|---|---|---|---|---|
| None, Not Covered | 26 (59.09%) | 7 (36.84%) | 18 (28.13%) | 51 (40.16%) |
| Slight Coverage (One class/lesson or less) | 7 (15.91%) | 9 (47.37%) | 25 (39.06%) | 41 (32.28%) |
| Moderate Coverage (Two to five classes/lessons) | 9 (20.45%) | 2 (10.53%) | 17 (26.56%) | 28 (22.05%) |
| Sustained Coverage (More than five classes/lessons) | 2 (4.55%) | 1 (5.26%) | 4 (6.25%) | 7 (5.51%) |
| Total | 44 (100%) | 19 (100%) | 64 (100%) | 127 (100%) |

*Note:* Fisher's exact = .02.

**Table 2.4. Chi-Square Test on the Relationship Between Three Grade Levels and Topic Coverage on Latinxs as a Rising Voting Bloc in U.S. Elections**

| Level | Elementary | Middle | High | Total |
|---|---|---|---|---|
| None, Not Covered | 31 (70.45%) | 8 (42.11%) | 19 (26.69%) | 58 (45.67%) |
| Slight Coverage (One class/lesson or less) | 11 (25.00%) | 7 (36.84%) | 31 (48.44%) | 49 (38.58%) |
| Moderate Coverage (Two to five classes/lessons) | 0 (0.00%) | 4 (21.05%) | 9 (14.06%) | 13 (10.24%) |
| Sustained Coverage (More than five classes/lessons) | 2 (4.55%) | 0 (0.00%) | 5 (7.81%) | 7 (5.51%) |
| Total | 44 (100%) | 19 (100%) | 64 (100%) | 127 (100%) |

*Note:* Fisher's exact < .01.

contrast to elementary teachers, 70% of whom reported not covering this topic at all. Latinxs as a rising voting bloc are not listed in any state standards for any grade level. However, voting rights and laws in general are included at the high school level, but not the middle or elementary level. This disparity gives us some insight into why high school teachers might include standards-related content.

**The Outlier: The Lives of Undocumented Workers**

Secondary teachers are more likely to report sustained coverage (more than five lessons) of the lives of undocumented workers, a topic not listed in any state standards. Specifically, 31.82% of lower-grade-level teachers reported never covering this topic, and only 12.94% of upper-grade-level teachers gave the same response. Also, 4.55% of lower-grade-level teachers reported sustained coverage of this topic, while 21.18% of upper-grade-level teachers did the same (see Table 2.5). In sum, upper-grade-level teachers cover this topic more consistently than lower-grade-level teachers.

This topic was statistically significant at the two-level comparison but not the three-level comparison. Thus, upper-grade teachers were more likely to teach about undocumented workers than their elementary colleagues, while middle and high school teachers were equally likely to teach about the lives of undocumented workers.

The lives of undocumented workers topic was an outlier in yet another way. It was the only topic that did not appear in or relate closely to content standards of participating districts. When combined with the finding that teaching about undocumented workers was statistically significant at the secondary level, it seems that secondary teachers might be more likely to include topics not explicitly stated in their state's social studies content standards.

Table 2.5. Chi-Square Test of the Relationship Between Two Grade Levels and Topic
Coverage of the Lives of Undocumented Workers

| Topic Coverage | Lower Grade | Upper Grade | Total |
|---|---|---|---|
| None, Not Covered | 14 (31.82%) | 11 (12.94%) | 25 (19.38%) |
| Slight Coverage (One class/lesson or less) | 13 (29.55%) | 25 (29.41%) | 38 (29.46%) |
| Moderate Coverage (Two to five classes/lessons) | 15 (34.09%) | 31 (36.47%) | 46 (35.66%) |
| Sustained Coverage (More than five classes/lessons) | 2 (4.55%) | 18 (21.18%) | 20 (15.50%) |
| Total | 44 (100%) | 85 (100%) | 129 (100%) |

*Note:* Fisher's exact = .01.

## DISCUSSION

Select findings from our national survey data reveal several patterns in how K–12 educators in four districts teach Latinx social studies topics, but these data call for further contextualization. Rather than demonstrating that teachers of the elementary grades are outright *choosing* not to teach Latinx topics, our study extends the literature by showing how grade-level structures may contribute to disproportionate patterns of coverage. Pressure to teach content determined by grade-level standards appeared to drive teachers' curricular decision-making with Latinx topics in different ways at each grade level. We also acknowledge that despite the pressures of standards and standardized testing, teachers possess autonomy in how they implement instructional guidelines in their respective classrooms.

These findings show that the power of standards and testing manifests differently at the secondary level. Middle school teachers lean on the standards to teach some Latinx topics, while high school teachers deviate from the standards. Last, while the survey data are informative, they do not tell the full story of how each teacher envisions the various degrees of topic coverage in practice. In this regard, we do not assume that more coverage ensures an adequate representation of the complexity of Latinidad, nor that participants share definitions of terms like "integration" of Latinx topics. Both topics raise questions to guide future directions of this project. For instance, future stages of this study can interrogate the racial literacy tools educators use to teach a Latinidad that is contextual, multidimensional, and intersectional (Guinier, 2004).

Elementary educators are teaching Latinx topics the least. This was true for both teachers' self-reported approach to teaching Latinx topics and the coverage of specific Latinx topics. As other scholars have noted, elementary teachers offer little social studies instruction (Abernathy-Dyer et al., 2013;

Berson & Camicia, 2013; Heafner & Fitchett, 2012), consistent with its de-emphasis during their preparation (Bolick et al., 2010; Hawkman et al., 2015; Starr, 2012). Given how little elementary educators teach social studies to begin with (Bisland, 2011; Fitchett, Heafner, & Lambert, 2014; Fitchett, Heafner, & VanFossen, 2014), it follows that they reported teaching fewer Latinx topics. Thus, the marginalization of social studies in the elementary grades contributes to the marginalization of Latinx topics. Elementary schooling structures (such as the prioritizing of math and literacy due to standardized testing) limit teachers' ability to include Latinx topics, rather than a lack of teacher interest.

The fact that secondary teachers are more likely to include Latinx topics supports our claim that the upward trend in coverage results from the lack of emphasis on social studies at the elementary level. At first glance, this might seem contradictory because prior research indicates the exclusion of Black, Latinx, Asian American, and Indigenous groups from social studies standards, textbooks, and curricula across grades (An, 2016; A. L. Brown & K. D. Brown, 2010; Shear et al., 2015). However, most states require three years of social studies instruction in both middle and high schools (e.g., California Department of Education, 2020; Florida Department of Education, 2019; Illinois State Board of Education, 2016; New York State Education Department, 2019). Just as Bigler et al. (2013) found that issues of race and class were broached most often in high school classrooms, the specific experiences of Latinxs are more likely to appear in middle and especially high school. Although Latinx topics might not be consistently present in the curriculum, we agree with Bigler and colleagues (2013) that having discrete social studies courses at the secondary level gives teachers more latitude regarding racial/ethnic group content—in this case, to explore Latinx topics in their classes. The data suggest that grade-level structures are important. This gives middle school educators flexibility to teach Latinx topics that directly connect to standards and high school educators' opportunities to include Latinx topics related to standards, even if not explicitly connected. This approach differs from the elementary grades, where social studies standards exist, but the content is either pushed aside in favor of math and literacy (Lane, Parke, & Stone, 2002; Pace, 2011), or subsumed into other content-area instruction (Fitchett, Heafner, & VanFossen, 2014).

Although upper-level teachers might have more flexibility to include Latinx topics, doing so remains challenging. Our findings also highlight the difficulties of integrating Latinx topics throughout the curriculum. The majority of upper-level teachers (60%) reported teaching Latinx topics only during a portion of the school year. Only 6.25% of secondary teachers reported integrating Latinx topics throughout their curriculum or during a particular portion of each school day. This outcome reveals that high coverage in any grade level is challenging. We argue that this is because allowing such coverage requires teachers to rewrite the social studies narrative in a way that centers Latinx communities, instead of simply adding them into existing curriculum. As Banks (1993) has pointed out, taking either an additive or contributions-focused approach to teaching multicultural content—rather than transforming the structure or narrative of curriculum—is the most common strategy. Latinx topics are no exception. The content standards and textbooks that exclude Latinx topics (e.g., Noboa, 2012) still limit teachers' curricular decision-making.

Other data from this study indicate that teachers would be more likely to include Latinx topics if they were part of the required curriculum or content standards. Consistent with the findings analyzed above, elementary teachers might teach more Latinx topics if they could teach more social studies in general. Middle school teachers demonstrated that they are more likely to include Latinx topics when they are explicitly stated in the standards, whereas their high school counterparts include those that are tangentially related to the standards. Combined, these findings strongly suggest that curricula and content standards greatly influence which Latinx social studies topics educators teach and how often. This discovery may come as a surprise, given the connection often made in the literature between standardized testing and the content of instruction. Since social studies is not a "tested" subject, one might reasonably expect a wider scope in coverage.

Yet educators are not without agency. Overall, the Latinx topic most often taught is the lives of undocumented workers, a topic not listed in any of the state content standards for California, New York, Illinois, or Florida. The fact that so many teachers taught it highlights that the content standards are not the sole guiding force in which Latinx topics educators teach.

This complicates what we know about the teaching and learning of Latinidad. The survey indicated that teachers are attempting to include topics that are relevant to current events, despite the minimized or distorted representations of Black (K. D. Brown & A. L. Brown, 2010; Busey & Cruz, 2015), Indigenous (Calderón, 2014; Conrad, 2019; Stanton, 2012), and other people of color (Suh, An, & Forest, 2015) in curricular materials. Educators may be choosing which Latinx topics to include based on their students and communities, even if it means teaching topics not aligned with the state content standards. The standards are not completely restrictive, even if they offer educators little guidance on which Latinx topics to teach. However, the association of Latinx people with undocumented status raises questions about the narrative unfolding around this topic and about the aspects of Latinidad that teachers choose to highlight when exercising their pedagogical discretion in their classrooms. Advancing racial literacy could provide educators with a framework to disrupt harmful racial stereotypes about Latinx people in curriculum and instruction.

One of the promising findings of the survey was that more than half of the participants reported teaching Latinx topics during some portion of the school year or integrated throughout their curriculum. However, gauging what teachers consider "integrating" is impossible because the term can be subjective. For example, elementary educators might teach Latinx topics during Latinx Heritage Month in September and October, host a Cinco de Mayo "fiesta," and participate in a "multicultural" fair. Each of these might be considered integrating Latinx social studies topics because they are interspersed throughout various times of the year. However, they are more in line with what Banks (1993) describes as a "contributions approach"—educators focusing on holidays without having to change the curriculum. Through a contributions approach, educators can sprinkle Latinidad throughout their curriculum while still upholding stereotypes, misinformation, or reductive ideas about Latinx people (Díaz & Deroo, 2020; Santiago, 2017). Educators might include Latinx topics while still aligning the content with existing curricular materials and narratives. This may be especially true of middle school teachers, whose high coverage of content was directly aligned with standards.

We are also cognizant that "integrating" might imply increased inclusion, but not necessarily "better" coverage. Including Latinx topics throughout the school year without depth does not necessarily represent the experiences of Latinidad accurately or meaningfully. For example, although middle school teachers reported high coverage of the U.S.-Mexico War, we do not know exactly what they are teaching about it. Topics related to the war can range from battles and historical figures to the impact of postwar policies. Teaching this content can emphasize U.S. citizens' actions and perspectives without considering the actions and perspectives of Mexican citizens brought into the United States as a result of the Treaty of Guadalupe Hidalgo. Even if they consider U.S. and Mexican citizens, educators might exclude Indigenous communities colonized by both Mexico and the United States. Although some educators teach about the U.S.-Mexico War, they can do so without discussing the structures and institutions that created the circumstances and perpetuate inequities (K. D. Brown & A. L. Brown, 2010). The goal of a more diverse curriculum is to depict the experiences of Latinx communities, complete with their complexities and contradictions (Lee, 2003; Novoa, 2007; Parker, 2003). Doing so requires a degree of racial literacy that not all teachers have had the opportunity to develop.

## IMPLICATIONS

This study has implications for pedagogy, teacher education, school and district leadership, and state-level education policy. Based on the low self-reported coverage of Latinx topics, elementary teachers require more support in teaching Latinx social studies topics. These supports could range from changes in teacher education courses to fieldwork, professional development, and curricular resources. However, these are band-aid solutions until social studies content can be given more instructional time at the elementary level. As this study's findings show, the largest influence on teachers' curricular decision-making with Latinx content are grade-level standards. Changing these standards requires structural policy reforms with substantial teacher input in order to understand their needs.

Since the middle school teachers in our sample responded to standards by incorporating Latinx topics in class instruction when they were directly mentioned, future versions of these standards could encourage deeper and more comprehensive coverage. Three of the four topics taught consistently by middle school educators focus on exploration, colonization, and warfare. Those topics can center the role of official authority, perhaps to the detriment of delving into the everyday lives of ordinary people. They may thus undermine the power of collective action and the untold stories of unofficial actors. Alongside increased social studies instructional time and greater presence of Latinx topics in the standards, states must consider what narratives we teach students.

The study raises questions about the narratives being constructed and the aspects of Latinidad being foregrounded in classrooms. More coverage does not guarantee "better" representation. If teachers opt to integrate issues like immigration into their instruction, they benefit from access to materials that strengthen their content and pedagogical content knowledge. These tools include historical documents, immigration statistics, and narratives told from the perspective of immigrants and their children. They can enhance teachers' and students' understanding of the reasons why people migrate, the hardships they experience, and the impact of policies on human beings. The histories of individuals and communities across Latinx ethnicities (including nationality, Afro descent, and Indigeneity) can more accurately depict the kaleidoscope that is Latinidad. In the absence of supports for advancing teachers' racial literacy, this expectation will continue unmet.

Last, the overwhelming response to the lives of undocumented workers—a topic not referenced in the content standards of any state in our sample—bears reiterating. This finding offers hope about the agency that teachers possess and how they can wield it to address a contemporary issue at the center of political debate, one that affects millions of lives. When educators align their pedagogy to their students' needs and present Latinidad in its human complexity, they serve as models for others.

## REFERENCES

Abernathy-Dyer, J., Ortlieb, E., & Cheek, E. H. (2013). An analysis of teacher efficacy and perspectives about elementary literacy instruction. *Current Issues in Education*, 16(3).

An, S. (2016). Asian Americans in American history: An AsianCrit perspective on Asian American inclusion in state US history curriculum standards. *Theory & Research in Social Education*, 44(2), 244–276. https://doi.org/10.1080/00933104.2016.1170646

Au, W. (2009). Social studies, social justice: W(h)ither the social studies in high-stakes testing? *Teacher Education Quarterly*, 36(1), 43–58.

Au, W. (2011). Teaching under the new Taylorism: High-stakes testing and the standardization of the 21st century curriculum. *Journal of Curriculum Studies*, 43(1), 25–45. https://doi.org/10.1080/00220272.2010.521261

Banks, J. A. (1993). Approaches to multicultural curriculum reform. In J. A. Banks & C. A. M. Banks (Eds.), *Multicultural education: Issues and perspectives.* John Wiley & Sons.

Berson, I. R., & Camicia, S. P. (2013). Early childhood social studies: A national study of challenges and promising practices. In J. Passe & P. G. Fitchett (Eds.), *The status of social studies: Views from the field* (pp. 65–76). Information Age Publishing.

Bigler, E., Shiller, J. T., & Willox, L. (2013). The teaching of race and class in American social studies classrooms. In J. Passe & P. G. Fitchett (Eds.), *The status of social studies: Views from the field* (pp. 153–168). Information Age Publishing.

Bisland, B. M. (2011). The marginalization of social studies in the elementary grades. In W. E. Russell III (Ed.), *Contemporary social studies: An essential reader* (pp. 173–191). Information Age Press.

Bolick, C. M., Adams, R., & Willox, L. (2010). The marginalization of elementary social studies in teacher education. *Social Studies Research & Practice, 5*(2), 1–14.

Bondy, J. M., & Pennington, L. K. (2016). Illegal aliens, criminals, and hypersexual spitfires: Latin@ youth and pedagogies of citizenship in media texts. *The Social Studies, 107*(3), 102–114. https://doi.org/10.1080/00377996.2016.1149045

Brown, A. L., & Brown, K. D. (2010). Strange fruit indeed: Interrogating contemporary textbook representations of racial violence toward African Americans. *Teachers College Record, 112*(1), 31–67.

Brown, K. D., & Brown, A. L. (2010). Silenced memories: An examination of the sociocultural knowledge on race and racial violence in official school curriculum. *Equity & Excellence in Education, 43*(2), 139–154.

Busey, C. L. (2018). Diaspora literacy and Afro-Latin humanity: A Critical Studyin' case study of a world history teacher's critical sociohistorical knowledge development. *Race Ethnicity and Education, 21*(3), 1–21. https://doi.org/10.1080/13613324.2018.1511531

Busey, C. L., & Cruz, B. C. (2015). "A shared heritage: Afro-Latin@s and Black history." *The Social Studies, 106*(6), 293–300. https://doi:10.1080/00377996.2015.1085824.

Busey, C. L., & Cruz, B. C. (2017). Who is Afro-Latin@? Examining the social construction of race and négritude in Latin America and the Caribbean. *Social Education, 81*(1), 37–42.

Busey, C. L., & Russell III, W. B. (2016). "We want to learn": Middle school Latino/a students discuss social studies curriculum and pedagogy. *Research in Middle Level Education—RMLE Online, 39*(4), 1–20. https://doi.org/10.1080/19404476.2016.1155921

Calderón, D. (2014). Speaking back to manifest destinies: A land education-based approach to critical curriculum inquiry. *Environmental Education Research, 20*(1), 24–36.

California Department of Education. (2020). *High school graduation requirements.* https://www.cde.ca.gov/ci/gs/hs/cefhsgradreq.asp

California State Board of Education. (2016, July). *History-social science framework for California schools.* California Department of Education. https://www.cde.ca.gov/ci/hs/cf/documents/hssappendixc.pdf

Ceasar, S. (2011, March 24). Hispanic population tops 50 million in U.S. *Los Angeles Times.* http://www.latimes.com/la-na-census-hispanic-20110325,0,3497296.story

Ceasar, S. (2014, December 4). L.A. Unified to require ethnic studies for high school graduation. *Los Angeles Times*. https://www.latimes.com/local/education/la-me -ethnic-studies-20141209-story.html

Chicago Public Schools. (2015, March 12). *Celebrating Latino history and culture: CPS introduces new Interdisciplinary Latino & Latin American Studies curriculum*. https://cps.edu/spotlight/pages/spotlight642.aspx

Chiodo, J. J. (2013). The zoot suit riots: Exploring social issues in American history. *The Social Studies, 104*(1), 1–14. https://doi.org/0.1080/00377996.2011.642421

Conrad, J. (2019). The Big History Project and colonizing knowledges in world history curriculum. *Journal of Curriculum Studies, 51*(1), 1–20.

Demoiny, S. B. (2017). Are you ready? Elementary pre-service teachers' perceptions about discussing race in social studies. *Multicultural Education, 24*(2), 25–33.

Díaz, E., & Deroo, M. R. (2020). Latinxs in contention: A systemic functional linguistic analysis of 11th grade US history textbooks. *Theory & Research in Social Education*, 1–28. https://doi.org/10.1080/00933104.2020.1731637

Education Data Partnership. (2020). *Los Angeles Unified*. California Department of Education, EdSource, and the Fiscal Crisis and Management Assistance Team/California School Information Services. http://www.ed-data.org/district/Los-Angeles /Los-Angeles-Unified

Fitchett, P. G., Heafner, T. L., & Lambert, R. G. (2014). Examining elementary social studies marginalization: A multilevel model. *Educational Policy, 28*(1), 40–68. https://doi.org/10.1177/0895904812453998

Fitchett, P. G., Heafner, T. L., & VanFossen, P. (2014). An analysis of time prioritization for social studies in elementary school classrooms. *Journal of Curriculum and Instruction, 8*(2), 7–35.

Fitchett, P. G., & VanFossen, P. J. (2013). Survey on the Status of Social Studies: Development and analysis. *Social Studies Research & Practice, 8*(1), 1–23.

Florida Department of Education. (2014, June). *Next generation Sunshine State standards—Social studies*. http://www.fldoe.org/academics/standards/subject-areas /social-studies.stml

Florida Department of Education. (2019). *Standard diploma requirements*. http://www .fldoe.org/core/fileparse.php/7764/urlt/StandardDiplomaRequirements.pdf

Fogo, B. (2015). The making of California's history-social science standards: Enduring decisions and unresolved issues. *The History Teacher, 48*(4), 737–775.

Fránquiz, M. E., & Salinas, C. S. (2011). Newcomers to the U.S.: Developing historical thinking among Latino immigrant students in a central Texas high school. *Bilingual Research Journal, 34*(1), 58–75. https://doi.org/10.1080/15235882.2011 .568831

Grant, S. G., & Salinas, C. (2010). Assessment and accountability in the social studies. In L. S. Levstik & C. A. Tyson (Eds.), *Handbook of research in social studies education* (pp. 219–236). Routledge.

Guinier, L. (2003). Admissions rituals as political acts: Guardians at the gates of our democratic ideals. *Harvard Law Review, 117*, 113.

Guinier, L. (2004). From racial liberalism to racial literacy: *Brown v. Board of Education* and the interest-divergence dilemma. *Journal of American History, 91*(1), 92–118.

Hawkman, A. M., Castro, A. J., Bennett, L. B., & Barrow, L. H. (2015). Where is the content?: Elementary social studies in preservice field experiences. *The Journal of*

Social Studies Research, 39(4), 197–206. https://doi.org/10.1016/j.jssr.2015
.06.001

Heafner, T. L., & Fitchett, P. G. (2012). National trends in elementary instruction: Exploring the role of social studies curricula. The Social Studies, 103(2), 67–72. https://doi.org/10.1080/00377996.2011.592165

Illinois State Board of Education. (2016). State graduation requirements. https://www
.isbe.net/Documents/grad_require.pdf

Illinois State Board of Education. (2017, June.) Illinois social science standards. https://
www.isbe.net/Documents/K-12-SS-Standards.pdf

Jaffee, A. T. (2016). Social studies pedagogy for Latino/a newcomer youth: Toward a theory of culturally and linguistically relevant citizenship education. Theory & Research in Social Education, 44(2), 147–183. https://doi.org/10.1080/00933104
.2016.1171184

Lane, S., Parke, C. S., & Stone, C. A. (2002). The impact of a state performance-based assessment and accountability program on mathematics instruction and student learning: Evidence from survey data and school performance. Educational Assessment, 8(4), 279–315. https://doi.org/10.1207/S15326977EA0804_1

Lee, C. D. (2003). Why we need to re-think race and ethnicity in educational research. Educational Researcher, 32(5), 3–5.

Lindsay, J. (2018, July 16). Indiana high schools to offer new ethnic studies elective. Indiana Public Media. https://indianapublicmedia.org/news/indiana-high-schools
-offer-ethnic-studies-elective-151984.php

Marino, M., & Bolgatz, J. (2010). Weaving a fabric of world history? An analysis of US state high school world history standards. Theory & Research in Social Education, 38(3), 366–394. https://doi.org/10.1080/00933104.2010.10473431

New York State Education Department. (1996). Learning standards for social studies. http://www.nysed.gov/common/nysed/files/sslearn.pdf

New York State Education Department. (2019). General education and diploma requirements. http://www.nysed.gov/curriculum-instruction/general-education-and
-diploma-requirements.

Noboa, J. (2012). Missing pages from the human story: World history according to Texas standards. Journal of Latinos and Education, 11(1), 47–62.

Noboa, J. (2013). Teaching history on the border: Teachers voice their views. International Journal of Qualitative Studies in Education, 26(3), 324–345. https://doi.org
/10.1080/15348431.2012.631441

Novoa, A. (2007). Teaching modern Latin America in the social science curriculum: An interdisciplinary approach. Social Education, 71(4), 187–190.

Pace, J. L. (2008). Inequalities in history-social science teaching under high stakes accountability: Interviews with fifth-grade teachers in California. Social Studies Research and Practice, 3(1), 24–40.

Pace, J. L. (2011). The complex and unequal impact of high stakes accountability on untested social studies. Theory & Research in Social Education, 39(1), 32–60. https://doi.org/10.1080/00933104.2011.10473446

Parker, W. C. (2003). Teaching democracy: Unity and diversity in public life. Teachers College Press.

Passe, J., & Fitchett, P. G. (Eds.). (2013). The status of social studies: Views from the field. Information Age Publishing.

Ready, T., & Brown-Gort, A. (2005). The state of Latino Chicago: This is home now. Institute for Latino Studies, University of Notre Dame.

Reisman, A. (2012). The "document-based lesson": Bringing disciplinary inquiry into high school history classrooms with adolescent struggling readers. *Journal of Curriculum Studies*, *44*(2), 233–264. https://doi.org/10.1080/00220272.2011.591436

Russell III, W. B. (2010). Teaching social studies in the 21st century: A research study of secondary social studies teachers' instructional methods and practices. *Action in Teacher Education*, *32*(1), 65–72. https://doi.org/10.1080/01626620.2010 .10463543

Salazar, M. (2019, September 16). The problem with Latinidad. *The Nation*. https:// www.thenation.com/article/archive/hispanic-heritage-month-latinidad/

Salinas, C., Fránquiz, M. E., & Reidel, M. (2008). Teaching world geography to late-arrival immigrant students: Highlighting practice and content. *The Social Studies*, *99*(2), 71–76. https://doi.org/10.3200/TSSS.99.2.71-76

Salinas, C. S., Fránquiz, M. E., & Rodríguez, N. N. (2016). Writing Latina/o historical narratives: Narratives at the intersection of critical historical inquiry and LatCrit. *The Urban Review*, *48*(2), 264–284. https://doi.org/10.1007/s11256-016 -0355-z

Santiago, M. (2017). Erasing differences for the sake of inclusion: How Mexican/Mexican American students construct historical narratives. *Theory & Research in Social Education*, *45*(1), 43–74. https://doi.org/10.1080/00933104.2016.1211971

Santiago, M. (2019). Historical inquiry to challenge the narrative of racial progress. *Cognition and Instruction*, *37*(1), 93–117. https://doi.org/10.1080/07370008.20 18.1539734

Shear, S. B., Knowles, R. T., Soden, G. J., & Castro, A. J. (2015). Manifesting destiny: Re/presentations of Indigenous peoples in K–12 US history standards. *Theory & Research in Social Education*, *43*(1), 68–101. https://doi.org/10.1080/00933104 .2014.999849

Stanton, C. R. (2012). Hearing the story: Critical Indigenous curriculum inquiry and primary source representation in social studies education. *Theory & Research in Social Education*, *40*(4), 339–370.

Starr, J. D. (2012). A lack of depth: One preservice teacher's experiences in a post-NCLB world. *The Social Studies*, *103*(6), 241–246. https://doi.org/10.1080/003 77996.2011.630698

Suh, Y., An, S., & Forest, D. (2015). Immigration, imagined communities, and collective memories of Asian American experiences: A content analysis of Asian American experiences in Virginia U.S. history textbooks. *Journal of Social Studies Research*, *39*(1), 39–51.

Swaby, A. (2018, April 11). Texas education board approves course formerly known as Mexican-American studies. *Texas Tribune*. https://www.texastribune.org/2018 /04/11/texas-education-board-mexican-american-studies-course/

United States Census. (2010). Hispanic or Latino by type. https://data.census.gov/cedsci /all?q=hispanic%20or%20latino%20by%20type&hidePreview=false&tid =ACSDP1Y2018.DP05&t=Hispanic%20or%20Latino

## CHAPTER 3

# "It's Gonna Be *My* History"

## The Need for (Re)Indigenizing Curricular Literacies

*Christine Stanton*

Several years ago, I interviewed Sara[1], a young Indigenous[2] woman, about her experiences in the history classroom. She asked, "Why should I even go? It ain't gonna be *my* history." As a teacher and instructional coach at Sara's school, and as someone who had known her for three years, I was not surprised to hear her assessment of the history curriculum. I was already familiar with the deficiencies of the textbooks, and I understood that our predominantly white faculty—myself included—had limited knowledge about the histories and experiences of Indigenous peoples. However, after visiting with Sara, I became disheartened by the realization that our students *knew* about these problems, and—worse yet—that they perceived we did not care enough to confront the limitations of our own curriculum and preparation.

In addition to discouraging Indigenous students from engaging with the subject matter, the absence of Indigenous histories[3] in curriculum limits content accuracy and depth for all students, conflicts with democratic principles supporting public education, and obstructs efforts to advance sovereignty (Carjuzaa et al., 2010; Kincheloe, 2006; Loewen, 1995, 2010).

Through a synthesis of knowledge shared by both Indigenous and non-Indigenous scholars, this chapter overviews ways curriculum (mis)represents Indigenous experiences and describes the potential to advance racial literacies and (re)Indigenize history education through curricular change. Since over 80% of teachers are white (National Center for Education Statistics (NCES), 2020), developing racial literacies requires learning not only by students, but also by teachers. Given my positionality as a white woman and settler, I strive to learn from Indigenous scholars, mentors, and students—like Sara—while simultaneously acknowledging that it is not the responsibility of Indigenous peoples to educate me or other white people (Sabzalian, 2019a; Stanton, 2019). Too often, we white people occupy space that should belong to scholars and educators of color and/or demonstrate "chronic apathy" toward anti-colonial education (Kovach, 2013, p. 117). Unfortunately, history education has not been particularly welcoming to scholars and educators of color, and to date the vast majority of publications focusing on representations of Indigenous peoples within the field have not been authored by Indigenous scholars. The good news is that by expanding conversations about racial literacies, taking responsibility for our own learning, and committing to increased visibility of and leadership by Indigenous historians, scholars, and educators, we can begin to re-Indigenize experiences within history education and research.

## HISTORY CURRICULUM AND RACIAL LITERACIES

In its broadest sense, *curriculum* can be defined as the aims, policies, and practices that guide educational decision-making (Flinders & Thornton, 2004; Short, 1991). Within most contemporary K–12 public schools, curriculum is typically operationalized through tangible resources, including standards, frameworks, and textbooks. Curriculum is influential across all aspects of education (Apple & Christian-Smith, 1991), both in explicit ways and through the "hidden curriculum"—what is excluded and/or implied through educational practices (Freire, 1972/2000). Therefore, this chapter investigates what is said *and* unsaid about Indigenous knowledges and ways of knowing within the curriculum, while operating under the assumption that curriculum forms the foundation for teacher practice.

In particular, history instruction is greatly shaped by curriculum. History teacher education programs focus heavily on content, and practicing teachers often rely on textbooks and other externally developed resources to inform their instructional decision-making (Brophy & Alleman, 2008; Levstik, 2008; Whitney, Golez, Nagel, & Nieto, 2012). To investigate the interrelatedness of content and pedagogy, this chapter focuses on the intersections between critical questions (i.e., those surrounding social norms, equity, etc.) and evaluative questions (i.e., those exploring the practical implementation of curriculum) (Short, 1991).

*Racial literacy* can be defined as both "content knowledge about the operation of racism and an interpretive framework that recognizes racism as varied in expression" (Brown, 2017, p. 84). Racial literacy extends beyond culturally relevant curriculum and pedagogy—and certainly beyond mainstream curriculum and pedagogy—because it demands complicated conceptualizations of race through deep, critical understanding of historical and political influences on identity, access, and (in)equity (Epstein & Gist, 2015). Guinier (2004) identifies three key expectations for developing racial literacy: (1) confronting racism as systemic, institutional, and structural; (2) balancing "knowing" about race with learning and action; and (3) recognizing the dynamic intersections between race and other social constructs. Interwoven within the understanding of racial literacy is an attention to the role of language in reinforcing racism (Guinier, 2004; Smith, 2016). Given this focus, this chapter purposefully uses the plural form of the term (i.e., racial literacies) to acknowledge the diversity between, within, and beyond Indigenous groups. In other words, there is not, and cannot be, a single "racial literacy," "Indigenous experience," or "Indigenous racial literacy."

Unfortunately, while schools can support racial literacies, they often struggle to do so for a variety of reasons, including limited teacher knowledge about racism, inadequate educator preparation and professional development, fear of offending students or of being accused of political agendas, and deficient or restrictive curricula (Brown, 2017; King, 2016; King et al., 2018; Sealey-Ruiz & Greene, 2015; Stanton, 2014, 2015). Brown (2017) argues that since schools often perpetuate racism, either explicitly or through inaction, "we can no longer wait until the 'just right time' emerges for us to address race and racism" (p. 93). Students (and teachers) who demonstrate racial literacies "need to learn how to see a racial moment, do something about it, and leave with a greater understanding of its complexity" (King et al., 2018).

To consider how curriculum develops—or fails to develop—Indigenous racial literacies, this chapter begins with an overview of how fragmentation of Indigenous worldviews within education serves as a structural instrument to encourage racialized "othering." To provide specific examples of racial literacies in curricular practice, I overview ways that standards, frameworks, and textbooks (mis)represent Indigenous experiences and limit application of Guinier's (2004) elements of racial literacy. To (re)Indigenize curriculum and advance racial literacies, teachers and students must move beyond a basic appreciation for and/or inclusion of Indigenous knowledges in order to gain a critical awareness of complex topics such as settler colonialism, cultural genocide, and contemporary issues that perpetuate racism. Furthermore, as Indigenous scholars McCarty and Lee (2014) argue, (re)Indigenizing education demands that teachers demonstrate active commitments to social justice, language revitalization, and community-centered pedagogy. Given these goals, this chapter concludes with a section exploring recommendations to (re)Indigenize racial literacies within history curriculum.

## INDIGENOUS EDUCATION, HISTORIES, AND WORLDVIEWS

Before the invasion of settlers, thousands of unique cultures and language groups inhabited the Americas (Hixon, 2013). There remain over 500 distinct, federally recognized Indigenous Nations in the United States, as well as many other nonrecognized tribes and peoples who identify with multiple groups (Castagno & Brayboy, 2008). Given the "survivance"—or integrated view of survival and resistance (Vizenor, 2008)—of these diverse Indigenous communities and individuals, this chapter recognizes the importance of looking to ways education can be *re*-claimed, by and with Indigenous peoples, for the purpose of sustaining and revitalizing distinct and community-specific knowledges.

Traditionally, many Indigenous peoples engaged in learning about their histories using integrated, place-conscious, and experiential practices grounded in cultural knowledges, sovereignty, and resilience (Eage Shield et al., 2020; Kimmerer, 2013; Sabzalian, 2019a; Stanton et al., 2019). Community experts used Indigenous languages, which served as vehicles for carrying unique knowledges, to share contextualized oral histories. Such an approach valued the interactive roles of teacher and students through highly relevant curriculum. In setting after setting around the world, Indigenous peoples faced—and continue to face—efforts of colonists to oppress and/or exterminate knowledges and modes of knowledge transmission.

In the United States, settler colonialism sought to control the Indigenous population and remove Indigenous peoples from land desired by settlers (Hixon, 2013). As part of these efforts, settlers endeavored to disrupt the transmission of cultural knowledges by forcibly removing children from families and sending them to boarding schools, where they were punished for practicing their traditional ways and speaking their languages (Lomawaima, 2004; McCoy, 2017). As a result, the U.S. government, religious institutions, educational systems, and other formal and informal settler colonial structures were/are directly responsible for many of the complex racialized issues that affected—and continue to affect—Indigenous peoples and communities.

While forced assimilative education is no longer officially mandated, many Indigenous communities continue to feel its reverberation through intergenerational trauma and the ongoing influence of externally developed curricular resources and policies. In fact, a 2014 report declared the education of Indigenous youth to be "in a state of emergency" (Executive Office of the President, 2014, p. 19). Indigenous youth graduate at the lowest rates among public school students and are disproportionately represented in special education and school discipline (Executive Office of the President, 2014; Quijada Cerecer, 2014; Whitford, 2017). In response to this emergency, today's Indigenous communities have increased their call to (re)Indigenize education. As a result of these efforts, Lomawaima (2000) argues that Indigenous communities are now re-entering the "battle for power" and educational sovereignty (p. 1).

To restore educational self-determination, many scholars look to TribalCrit (Brayboy, 2005) and Culturally Sustaining and Revitalizing Pedagogy (CSRP) (McCarty & Lee, 2014). *TribalCrit* centers Indigenous communities' "desire to obtain and forge . . . self-determination" through recognition of their cultural histories and identities as independent from and influenced by settler colonialism (Brayboy, 2005, p. 429). Similarly, CSRP emphasizes the importance of sustaining *and* revitalizing the unique and essential Indigenous knowledges that have become endangered due to settler colonialism (McCarty & Lee, 2014). Both TribalCrit and CSRP rely upon (1) recognition of the unique and independent histories and experiences of Indigenous peoples, (2) confrontation of the effort of settler colonialism to disrupt the transmission of Indigenous knowledges, and (3) active engagement with efforts to elevate, sustain, and reinvigorate Indigenous knowledge systems.

## STANDARDS: EXPECTATIONS FOR RACIAL LITERACIES, OR FOR ASSIMILATION?

Standards—or sets of specific target learning outcomes—form the curricular foundation of most U.S. schools. Standards may include content details, skills, and/or dispositions and are designed to provide grade-level and subject-specific benchmarks regarding learner progress. Today's teachers are often expected to apply multiple sets of standards (e.g., district, state, and national). While it is unclear how faithfully teachers adhere to standards, pressure stemming from accountability discourse has expanded the role of state and national standards in shaping curricular and pedagogical choices of teachers (Shear et al., 2015). Notably, research demonstrates the potential for standards to shape *what* teachers teach and *how* they teach it (Barton & Levstik, 2004; Journell, 2009).

Both advocates for and opponents of standards note their usefulness in shaping a consistent, or "standardized," version of the subject matter. Such consistency can make it easier to develop resources (e.g., textbooks), prepare teachers for a wide variety of contexts, and measure progress for both teachers and students. However, consistency also means greater potential for minoritized voices, perspectives, and ways of knowing to be excluded, while the views and narratives of the dominant group are normalized (Journell, 2009). In particular, the basic goal to standardize curriculum runs counter to the complexity and diversity of Indigenous ideologies and experiences.

Although few studies have looked specifically at how standards represent Indigenous peoples, the results consistently highlight three main areas of deficiency. First, history standards rarely include explicit discussions of Indigenous experiences, and the few that exist focus on pre-1890 history (i.e., events that occurred before the Massacre at Wounded Knee, often described as the end of the "Indian Wars"). Journell's (2009) study noted that standards focus primarily on early U.S. history, and that such representations are typically "demeaning" to Indigenous peoples (p. 24). Similarly, a mixed-methods analysis by Shear and colleagues (2015) found that within national and state history standards, "Indigenous Peoples were largely confined within a pre-1900 context devoid of any significant voice" (p. 89), with over 86% of the standards focusing on that distant history. This focus encourages both teachers and students to falsely believe that Indigenous peoples no longer exist in the United States, that Indigenous traditions and worldviews are irrelevant to recent history, and/or that Indigenous peoples who resisted U.S. policy were eliminated or subdued.

Second, standards tend to situate Indigenous experiences exclusively within the context of a broader Eurocentric, settler colonial narrative, without allowing critical examination of the interaction and intersections between contexts. Typically, such positioning suggests that Indigenous peoples are somehow "other" within the story of America, while portraying settlers in an overwhelmingly positive light. For example, very few states include standards that focus on the purposeful introduction of disease in order to remove tribes from traditional lands (Journell, 2009). Furthermore, instead of using benchmarks relevant to Indigenous history, most state standards rely upon Eurocentric definitions of important moments in history, such as the arrival of the Pilgrims and the "discovery"[4] of gold in California. Shear et al. (2015) also note that Indigenous interactions with settlers, government officials, and other European Americans are typically described as either cooperating to advance *or* conflicting with the narrative of American progress. For example, "cultural exchanges" and references to Thanksgiving promote beliefs about cooperation, while standards that call attention to the French and Indian War, the Battle of Little Big Horn, and other conflicts reinforce views of Indigenous peoples as savages and incompatible with American progress.

Finally, the language used in history standards often suggests inevitability in terms of the oppression of Indigenous peoples. As Shear et al. (2015) note, almost all state standards position the United States as an institution "pushing at the edge of the Mississippi River," eager to follow Lewis and Clark "into the heart of a wild and empty landscape" (p. 86). By framing learning targets around the "Corps of Discovery," the Homestead Act, and "westward expansion," standards reinforce the doctrine of Manifest Destiny, arguing that European Americans were superior to Indigenous peoples and therefore destined to settle the "wild and empty landscape." Furthermore, specific language choices normalize "territorial expansion" and federal policymaking, while minimizing or ignoring treaty rights, tribal sovereignty, and the role of individual actors. Such normalization encourages students to view history as objective and static, instead of understanding its interpretive and dynamic nature (Stanton, 2014; Wineburg, 2001). Along these lines, standards rarely use language that encourages critical thinking and dialogue about the complicated nature of history, particularly if such language encourages critique of settler colonial actions. For example, standards in only one state—Washington—use the word "genocide" to describe the systematic efforts by policymakers, settlers, and military leaders to exterminate Indigenous cultures and peoples (Shear et al., 2015, p. 87).

While the standards typically encourage students to view Indigenous peoples as doomed relics of the distant past who are important only in terms of interactions/cooperation/conflict with settlers or colonists, the research highlights several exceptions. More specifically, four states (Arizona, Kansas, Oklahoma, and Washington) directly call for students to learn about the influence of assimilative boarding schools on sovereignty and identity (Shear et al., 2015). Such efforts demonstrate the potential for standards to support teachers in guiding critical thinking and action about settler colonialism and self-determination, thereby advancing racial literacies, TribalCrit, and CSRP.

## FRAMEWORKS: GUIDELINES FOR RACIAL LITERACIES
## OR SUPERFICIAL TEACHING?

While similar in many ways to standards, curricular frameworks claim to be more flexible. Standards typically focus on discrete content elements and/or specific skills, while frameworks strive to develop more complex concepts and advanced skills, such as "critical thinking and historical inquiry" (Shear et al., 2015, p. 73). Therefore, in theory, frameworks offer more potential to support racial literacies, in particular Guinier's (2004) second tenet, which emphasizes the importance of balancing thinking with action. Frameworks appear at both state and national levels and across grades and content areas. Examples include Montana's *Essential Understandings Regarding Montana's Indians* (Montana Office of Public Instruction (MOPI), 1999/2019), which provides a framework for teaching across all subject areas; the *Advanced Placement U.S. History* (APUSH) *Framework* (College Board, 2019), which encourages teaching of specific content and skills within AP classrooms; and the national *College, Career, and Civic Life* (C3) *Framework* (National Council for the Social Studies (NCSS), 2013), which guides teaching and learning across grade levels and social studies disciplines.

The influence of frameworks on curriculum and pedagogy is unknown at this point. For instance, while Thacker and colleagues (2016) found that a majority of surveyed teachers claim to use instructional strategies that may support ideas within the *C3 Framework*, they acknowledged uncertainty with more critically oriented concepts and inquiry-based learning. While standards are often criticized for being too prescriptive, frameworks may be too vague, especially in terms of racial literacies and Indigenous perspectives. Given that the research is extremely limited (or nonexistent in terms of Indigenous experiences), this chapter includes insights based on an abbreviated critical discourse analysis of the *C3 Framework* to highlight potential areas of challenge and opportunity.

While the *C3 Framework* consists of 108 pages, 4 dimensions, 23 suggested pathways, and 75 indicators articulated across four grade levels, or over 300 opportunities, only two of its elements directly reference Indigenous experiences. Both of these occur as 12th-grade "indicators" for a single "suggested pathway" and focus on contemporary civic and political institutions (p. 32). These examples encourage the study of tribal governments, which *could* enhance student understanding of sovereignty and self-determination. One additional reference to "indigenous populations around the world" occurs in the glossary under "perspective" (p. 103). No references to complex concepts central to development of racial literacies (e.g., racism, discrimination, genocide, settler colonialism) exist, aside from in appendices focusing on psychology and anthropology. Overall, while the national framework vaguely encourages critical thinking and historical inquiry, it perpetuates the same challenges encountered by standards. Like state standards, the *C3 Framework* ignores and excludes direct references to Indigenous histories, and it situates Indigenous histories within (or as an appendix to) the broader mainstream narrative.

History is highlighted as one of the "core disciplines" within Dimension 2 of the *C3 Framework*, and teachers are encouraged to support conceptual understanding of "perspective," the interpretive nature of the discipline, and the "multiplicity of points of view in the past" (p. 47). Although the suggested pathways and indicators do not explicitly reference Indigenous perspectives, teachers may *choose* to adhere to expectations within the "perspective" category by recognizing Indigenous views (but they may also choose not to include those perspectives). Within this dimension, teachers and learners are also encouraged to seek out a variety of historical sources and evidence, including "oral accounts" and "artistic works" that, theoretically, might encourage inclusion of Indigenous perspectives. Overall, while frameworks do not specifically *exclude* teaching about Indigenous perspectives or critical thinking about race, they do not directly *support* development of racial literacies.

Montana's Indian Education for All, (*Essential Understandings Framework* MOPI, 1999/2019) is different from other frameworks in several ways. First, it provides explicit attention to histories, experiences, and worldviews of Indigenous peoples across subject areas and grade levels. Second, since it was developed as the result of a state-level constitutional mandate, it is more influential than many frameworks. While the framework does not dictate specific content, it does outline basic "essential understandings" expected of all students (see Table 3.1). Additional resources offer specific guidance for implementation of these essential understandings (e.g., Elser, 2010).

Research suggests that Montana's approach has helped teachers develop confidence in terms of teaching about Indigenous perspectives and supporting critical thinking about race and settler colonialism (Bachtler, 2015; Hopkins, 2020; Stanton et al., 2019; Stanton & Morrison, 2018). In 2015, an evaluation of the *Essential Understandings Framework* showed that it supported development of extensive supplemental resources, including instructional guides, lesson plans, and professional development materials (Bachtler, 2015). Furthermore, teachers who use these resources demonstrate greater willingness to apply the *Essential Understandings Framework* within their own classrooms (Bachtler, 2015).

While the *Essential Understandings Framework* has positively informed basic racial literacy efforts, most implementation remains fairly superficial (Stanton et al., 2019). Bachtler's 2015 report determined that the quality of implementation varies greatly from school to school, that 15–20% of teachers were not aware of the available curricular resources, and that another 15–30% of teachers claimed to "never" use those resources, even though they know they exist (Bachtler, 2015, p. 13). Additionally, non-Indigenous teachers remain reluctant to establish relationships with Indigenous community members or reach beyond resources developed by MOPI (Bachtler, 2015; Stanton et al., 2019; Stanton & Morrison, 2018). Some hesitation comes from a fear of "offending" Indigenous students and their families (Stanton et al., 2019). Others claim concern about seemingly "forced" connections between the *Essential Understandings* and specific content standards, skills, and

**Table 3.1. Indian Education for All, *Essential Understandings* (MOPI, 1999/2019)**

| | Description |
|---|---|
| 1 | There is great diversity among the twelve tribal nations of Montana in their languages, cultures, histories, and governments. Each tribe has a distinct and unique cultural heritage that contributes to modern Montana. |
| 2 | Just as there is great diversity among tribal nations, there is great diversity among individual American Indians as identity is developed, defined and redefined by entities, organizations, and people. There is no generic American Indian. |
| 3 | The ideologies of Native traditional beliefs and spirituality persist into modern day life as tribal cultures, traditions, and languages are still practiced by many American Indian people and are incorporated into how tribes govern and manage their affairs. Additionally, each tribe has its own oral histories, which are as valid as written histories. These histories pre-date the "discovery" of North America. |
| 4 | Though there have been tribal peoples living successfully on the North American lands for millennia, reservations are lands that have been reserved by or for tribes for their exclusive use as permanent homelands. Some were created through treaties while others were created by statutes and executive orders. The principle that land should be acquired from tribes only through their consent with treaties involved three assumptions: I. Both parties to treaties were sovereign powers; II. Indian tribes had some form of transferable title to the land; III. Acquisition of Indian lands was solely a government matter not to be left to individual colonists or states. |
| 5 | There were many federal policies put into place throughout American history that have affected Indian people in the past and continue to shape who they are today. Many of these policies conflicted with one another. Much of Indian history can be related through several major federal policy periods: Colonization/Colonial Period (1492–1800s), Treaty-Making and Removal Period (1778–1871), Reservation Period—Allotment and Assimilation (1887–1934), Tribal Reorganization Period (1934–1953), Termination and Relocation Period (1953–1968), Self-Determination Period (1975–Present). |
| 6 | History is a story most often related through the subjective experience of the teller. With the inclusion of more and varied voices, histories are being rediscovered and revised. History told from American Indian perspectives frequently conflicts with the stories mainstream historians tell. |
| 7 | American Indian tribal nations are inherent sovereign nations and they possess sovereign powers, separate and independent from the federal and state governments. However, under the American legal system, the extent and breadth of self-governing powers are not the same for each tribe. |

so forth. For example, Bachtler (2015) quoted a math teacher who craved added rigor: "It would be nice to move beyond using teepees for geometry and buffalo for counting. Some of that just seems to reinforce stereotypes" (p. 21). As implementation of the *Essential Understandings* demonstrates, having a critically oriented curricular framework—even one developed in partnership with Indigenous communities—does not independently ensure advancement of racial literacies.

In terms of both national and state-level curricular frameworks, the results are similar. Frameworks still fail to effectively support racial literacies. To move beyond superficial connections, comprehensive relationships must be developed and sustained among Indigenous communities, schools, teachers, and curriculum designers (e.g., standards revision teams). To enhance meaningful implementation of the *Essential Understandings Framework* in Montana, more Indigenous community members must be actively involved in the development of quality resources, preparation of teachers, and accountability efforts, and financial resources need to be allocated to support and sustain ongoing partnerships among MOPI personnel, practicing and preservice teachers, and Indigenous community members (Bachtler, 2015; Stanton et al., 2019). Overall, while frameworks offer the potential to advance racial literacies, they cannot take the place of meaningful relationships.

## TEXTBOOKS: TOOLS FOR RACIAL LITERACIES OR SILENCING?

Within history education, textbooks remain influential and popular curricular resources. There are only a handful of major history textbook publishers. As for-profit publishers, they strive to appeal to the largest audiences possible. In other words, school districts and states with large populations (e.g., California, Texas) typically have a greater influence on textbook content and design than those with small populations (e.g., Alaska, Wyoming). Therefore, textbook publishers, authors, and editors have little incentive to expand awareness of Indigenous experiences, given the overall small population of Indigenous peoples in the United States (only 1–2% of the total population) and the minimal influence of states with large(r) Indigenous populations. Thus, the process for textbook development is one that further impedes the potential for development of racial literacies. While some progress has been made in terms of integrating historical content related to Latinx and African Americans, very little progress has been made in terms of including more Indigenous histories (Padgett, 2015). Even when Indigenous historians participate in the textbook review process, their ideas are rarely incorporated (Fixico, personal communication, December 11, 2009).

History textbooks have been studied extensively in terms of their (mis)representations of Indigenous experiences and worldviews (Loewen, 1995, 2010; Padgett, 2015; Sanchez, 2007; Stanton, 2014). Textbook authors and editors often depict Indigenous peoples as violent, lawless, and confined to the distant pre-1890 past. While most 11th-grade history textbooks exceed 1,000 pages, they typically include discussions of Indigenous experiences on fewer than 10 pages. In these brief appearances, Indigenous peoples are often portrayed as doomed (e.g., "the Sioux were beaten"), dependent (e.g., "they had no way to sustain their way of life"), and deserving of disdain (e.g., "bands of Native Americans began raiding wagon trains and stealing cattle and horses") (Stanton, 2014). Such discourse reinforces stereotypes, neglects the complexity of the events, and minimizes or excuses the actions of the settlers and colonists. This positioning of Indigenous peoples also reduces power and agency for/with Indigenous peoples, further reinforcing racialized structures within schooling and society (Stanton, 2014). Given that most students view textbook representations as factual and unquestionable (Wineburg, 2001), and that teachers and students are rarely invited by authors and editors to critically consider the (mis)representations of Indigenous experiences, textbooks may be the greatest obstacles to advancing racial literacies within history education.

In addition to overt (mis)representations common in textbooks, textbook authors and editors also inhibit development of Indigenous racial literacies epistemologically and ontologically. For example, most U.S. history textbooks prioritize the "American Progress" narrative, suggesting that obstacles to the expansion of capitalism are anti-American (Apple & Christian-Smith, 1991; Loewen, 2010; Scott, 2008; Stanton, 2014). Such positioning discounts the intersectionality of racialized histories in the United States and privileges individuality over collectivism. In terms of Indigenous communities, histories are especially complex in this regard, given the sophisticated collective agricultural and economic networks that existed prior to invasion by Europeans, the intentional severance of nations from these highly functional food and trade systems, the lack of economic opportunities in reservation communities due to discrimination and geographic isolation, and the continued role of historical trauma in perpetuating poverty (Mann, 2006). In these examples, teachers and students deserve opportunities for deep investigations of the intersections among settler colonialism, race, class, and policy, among other aspects of social experience.

Unlike other curricular resources described in this chapter, textbooks have long shaped teacher pedagogy in very direct ways. Many teachers continue to rely heavily on teachers' editions that often accompany a textbook series (Brenner & Hiebert, 2010; Stanton, 2015; Whitney et al., 2012). While there is limited research on the pedagogical effectiveness of these resources (Lavere, 2008; Levstik, 2008), it is clear that they fall short in supporting teachers who are working to develop racial literacies. In a study investigating the five most popular U.S. history textbooks used at the 11th-grade level, pedagogical recommendations in teachers' editions reflected the deficiencies common to student textbooks and other curricular resources (see Table 3.2) (Stanton, 2015).

Teachers' editions often include "wraparound" features, which include guidance for lectures, discussions, activities, and quizzes in the margins surrounding a view of the student text. These features most frequently support basic understandings of Indigenous experiences, if they encourage such awareness at all (Stanton, 2015). One book encourages teachers to ask the question, "How did Native American resistance to white settlement end?"

Table 3.2. *Common Themes and Examples from Teachers' Editions* (Stanton, 2015)

| Themes | Examples from Textbooks |
| --- | --- |
| Exclude or minimize Indigenous experiences—especially after 1890 | 144 wraparound features reference Indigenous peoples or histories (across five textbooks, each 1,000+ pages in length). |
| Employ stereotypical and conflict-oriented language | Use "battle" to refer to massacres at Wounded Knee and "cult" to refer to the Ghost Dance. |
| Privilege Eurocentric, capitalist, and settler ideologies | "Tell students that in this chapter they will learn how the American West was transformed from unsettled territories to ranches, farms, and towns." |
| Emphasize the myth that Indigenous ways of life were doomed | "Have students think about those aspects of their culture that might keep the Native Americans and white settlers from living together peacefully." |
| Excuse actions of white settlers and/or suggest such actions benefited Indigenous peoples | "Using the computer or pencil and paper, have students make a two-column chart of positive changes and negative changes for Native Americans." |
| Encourage "compromise" and negotiation | "Tell students that they are going to try to negotiate an agreement between the Native American tribes and the United States government. . . . Have both groups consider the causes and effects of actions taken by Native Americans to expand economic opportunities and political rights in the United States. When the two groups come together, they should try to find a way to work out their differences." |

with the suggested responses noting that Indigenous peoples "were moved to reservations, captured, or defeated" (cited in Stanton, 2015, p. 183). Like many throughout the teachers' editions, this example reinforces the beliefs that Indigenous peoples were relevant only within distant historical contexts, destined to be defeated, and passive in their responses. As a result, such an example illustrates the tendency of textbooks to limit racial literacies in terms of all three of Guinier's (2004) tenets: It does not ask teachers and students to "read" racism as structural (e.g., by explaining the intent of the reservation system), balance critical thinking and action (e.g., by having students investigate continued resistance), or recognize how race intersects with other social constructs (e.g., by interrogating the origins and impacts of poverty on reservations).

While the majority of recommendations included in wraparound features in teachers' editions fail to support racial literacies, there are a few exceptions. One textbook, *America: Pathways to the Present* (Cayton et al., 2007), includes a single activity encouraging teachers to:

Tell students to research the Sioux. Have them investigate how the Sioux lived in the nineteenth century and how their culture has survived in the twenty-first century. How has their way of life changed over the years? (cited in Stanton, 2015, p. 186)

Although this example remains problematic (e.g., the authors do not explain their use of "Sioux," a contested and geopolitically complex term), it does engage students in learning about the contemporary experiences of Indigenous peoples, and it does recognize the "Sioux" as a group with unique culture and experiences. Many other textbooks group all Indigenous nations together, or into regional groups (e.g., "Plains Indians").

Of the 144 wraparound features referencing Indigenous experiences, only three (from three different teachers' editions) demonstrate a potential for teaching racial literacies (Stanton, 2015). These examples show three patterns: oral histories are recognized as valid knowledge sources (thereby confronting the popular argument that Indigenous perspectives are excluded from history because they were often not written); settler colonial perspectives are critically examined (thereby analyzing the role of structures in perpetuating racial injustice); and the actions of named white leaders are critiqued (thereby elevating attention to actions of individuals and systems, instead of "fate"). However, these few examples are exceptions to the rule that both students' and teachers' textbooks enact problematic language that not only discourages racial literacies, but actually *reinforces* racism.

## (RE)INDIGENIZING THE CURRICULUM: RECOMMENDATIONS

This chapter's synthesis of research demonstrates several common findings. First, standards, frameworks, and textbooks largely exclude Indigenous experiences. If and when described, these experiences are frequently presented in temporally distant and stereotypical ways. Second, Indigenous histories are situated almost exclusively within the narrative of settler colonialism, with descriptions confined primarily to encounters and conflicts with white people. Third, the curricular resources do not effectively equip teachers to advance racial literacies. In other words, experiences, perspectives, and histories are shared in trivial and basic ways that do little to encourage students to "read" racism as a structural force, balance critical thinking with action for justice, or learn about the intersections between race and other social constructs.

Teachers cannot assume curriculum will support teaching for racial literacies, particularly in terms of Indigenous experiences. To create change, action must occur at both the curricular design and classroom instruction levels. Standards, frameworks, and textbooks all have the potential to advance racial literacies, but to this point, these resources have neglected (or evaded) such a charge. Although this chapter focuses on history education, the recommendations below are applicable to various content areas. Such broad inclusion confronts the normalization of marginalization and encourages connectivity, contextualization, and complexity.

At the design level, several key approaches could advance racial literacies. Most importantly, a broader commitment to change is necessary. Such a commitment demands political and personal will, which also requires recognition of the existing deficiencies. Advocates for racial literacies can generate support for improved curriculum by sharing the research highlighted in this chapter, serving on state and local standards revision teams, and providing review of frameworks and textbooks. However, simply drawing attention to the problems that exist within the curriculum is only a first step. To enact change, Indigenous scholars, historians, educators, and leaders must be comprehensively and authentically engaged in the revision and development process to ensure "desire-centered" research, policymaking, and curriculum development (Tuck, 2009). Such work requires identification of the needs and interests—or desires—specific to minoritized communities, as defined by those communities, and as communicated from those communities through meaningful collaborations with the scholars, historians, educators, and leaders who shape curriculum and practice. This collaboration must extend beyond the token involvement popular within today's textbook review processes by including attention to specific discursive choices as well as broader concepts, content, and skills, given the complex influence of both the overt and hidden curriculum.

As illustrated throughout this chapter, language choices—while not directly or intentionally racist—inhibit racial literacies and reinforce racist structures. In particular, curricular discourse that describes Indigenous peoples must shift from one of conflict and doom to one of relationship, productivity, and persistence. Finally, pedagogical change can be encouraged through improving wraparound features of teachers' editions and expanding professional development for practitioners. Such professional development can help by sharing examples from curricular resources such as those described in this chapter, encouraging teachers to discuss problems with the examples, and providing planning time for teachers to work with one another and with Indigenous leaders to enhance activities.

In addition to systemic changes, classroom teachers can commit to using curriculum—including the existing curriculum—to advance racial literacies. There are extensive possibilities for this. One teacher regularly asks her students to critique the mainstream textbook by asking, "Whose story is this?," "Whose story is missing?," and "How can we learn about the missing story?" (Stanton, 2012). Through this questioning, the teacher models critique of the textbook and encourages students to delve into reading history as a dynamic and socially constructed narrative. This teacher also engaged students in community-centered, authentic oral history inquiry to learn about the missing narratives.

To frame teaching about civics, Sabzalian (2019b) offers six orientations (i.e., place, presence, political nationhood, perspectives, power, and partnerships) that can also be used to guide teaching and learning about Indigenous experiences. Purposeful attention to land, settler colonialism, and sovereignty can increase accuracy, criticality, and engagement, even for very young students (Turtle Island Social Studies Collective (TISSC), 2019). A related strategy is to integrate land acknowledgments throughout one's teaching. On day one, the teacher can ask students to identify the Indigenous peoples with historical and contemporary connections to the land where the class is meeting. Then, for each curricular topic, the teacher can encourage students to learn about Indigenous experiences, settler colonialism, and ongoing sovereignty as connected to the place(s) where events occurred. As is true with all efforts to integrate cultural knowledges, it is important for teachers who include land acknowledgments to make such inclusion purposeful and valuable (Tuck, 2019).

If teachers have the flexibility to incorporate resources outside of their school's curriculum, they can look to schools, states, and other organizations that lead the way in advancing racial literacies. The states of Montana and Washington, the National Museum of the American Indian, and many tribal nations have quality resources available online. Similarly, Rethinking Schools, Learning for Justice, Oyate, *and* American Indians in Children's Literature offer extensive online materials that can support racial literacies specific to Indigenous history. Like standards, frameworks, and textbooks, many supplemental resources fall short in terms of advancing racial literacies, so it is important to review all options critically and carefully (Stanton, 2012).

As TribalCrit scholars emphasize, Indigenous peoples have their own unique, powerful, and robust counternarratives that can inform teaching (Brayboy, 2005). To this end, teachers can include works of historical nonfiction (e.g., *Custer Died for Your Sins*) and historical fiction (e.g., *Fools Crow*) to inspire critical thinking about divergent or conflicting perspectives (Daniels, 2011). Oral histories and artifacts can offer another format for counternarratives. However, teachers must work with Indigenous peoples to ensure appropriate classroom use of such inclusion of oral histories, artifacts, and other culturally sensitive materials.

Given the shortcomings of many curricular resources and potential for misuse of culturally sensitive materials, teachers and students must collaborate in comprehensive and sustained ways with cultural mentors and leaders. Such collaboration can serve the following functions: support efforts to identify and evaluate existing or externally developed materials; provide guidance for development of standards, frameworks, textbooks, and other materials; contribute to professional development and pedagogical assistance; and offer insights for guest instructors and place-based learning. As Smith and Crowley (2018) note, determining the content of history curricula is a divisive issue, with "lines being drawn between history curricula that is cohesive, patriotic, and universal on the one hand, and multicultural, open-ended, and self-critical on the other" (p. 449). In other words, it is difficult and uncomfortable for many teachers and curriculum developers to center diverse narratives, especially if those narratives conflict with the mainstream mythology. Working with Indigenous leaders and community members can provide opportunities to access, learn about, and (re)center the experiences of Indigenous peoples. Drawing upon TribalCrit and CSRP can offer further guidance for teachers working to develop racial literacies.

## CONCLUSION

Broadly, the scholarship demonstrates that Indigenous representations within curriculum are limited and exclusionary, situated within settler colonial narratives, and devoid of opportunities that encourage critical thinking and antiracism (Chandler, 2010; Shear et al., 2015; Stanton, 2012, 2014). In fact, curriculum itself serves to reinforce the very systems, structures, and institutions (e.g., settler colonialism) that perpetuate racism. Specifically, history curriculum in the United States serves to *systematically* confine the experiences of Indigenous peoples to pre-1900 history (Shear et al., 2015), embolden educational institutions to limit the sovereignty and agency of Indigenous peoples (Stanton, 2014), and contribute to the structure of settler colonialism through emphasis on economic views of progress as tied to control of land and resources (Stanton, 2014, 2015).

This analysis suggests that Manifest Destiny remains alive and well in contemporary curriculum, both in terms of the exclusion of Indigenous perspectives and in the privileging of settler colonial ideologies. To "Indigenize" (or *re*-Indigenize) curricula, we need to recognize and include (in *meaningful* ways) the experiences of sovereign Indigenous nations, confront the historical and continued role of settler colonialism in education, and actively participate in curricular transformation through revitalization of Indigenous knowledge systems. Such efforts are vital for creating spaces where students like Sara can recognize themselves in the curriculum, feel empowered to challenge settler colonial views, and create change to improve education for all learners.

## REFERENCES

Apple, M. W., & Christian-Smith, L. K. (Eds.). (1991). *The politics of the textbook.* Routledge.

Bachtler, S. (2015). *Montana* Indian Education for All *evaluation.* Montana Office of Public Instruction.

Barton, K. C., & Levstik, L. S. (2004). *Teaching history for the common good.* Erlbaum.

Brayboy, B. (2005). Toward a tribal critical race theory in education. *The Urban Review, 37*(5), 425–446.

Brenner, D. & Hiebert, E. H. (2010). If I follow the teachers' editions, isn't that enough? Analyzing reading volume in six core reading programs. *The Elementary School Journal, 110*(3), 347–363.

Brophy, J., & Alleman, J. (2008). Early elementary social studies. In L. S. Levstik & C. A. Tyson (Eds.), *Handbook of research in social studies education* (pp. 33–49). Routledge.

Brown, K. (2017). Why we can't wait: Advancing racial literacy and a critical sociocultural knowledge of race for teaching and curriculum. *Race, Gender, & Class, 24*(1), 81–96.

Carjuzza, J., Jetty, M., Munson, M., & Veltkamp, T. (2010). Montana's Indian Education for All: Applying multicultural education theory. *Multicultural Perspectives, 12*(4), 192–198.

Castagno, A. E. & Brayboy, B. (2008). Culturally responsive schooling for Indigenous youth: A review of the literature. *Review of Educational Research, 78*(4), 941– 949.

Cayton, A., Perry, E. I., Reed, L., & Winkler, A. M. (2007). *America: Pathways to the present*. Prentice Hall.

Chandler, P. T. (2010). Critical race theory and social studies: Centering the Native American experience. *The Journal of Social Studies Research, 34*(1), 29–58.

The College Board. (2019). *AP U.S. history course and exam description*. https://apcentral.collegeboard.org/pdf/ap-us-history-course-and-exam-description.pdf

Daniels, E. A. (2011). Racial silences: Exploring and incorporating critical frameworks in the social studies. *The Social Studies, 102*(5), 211–220.

Deloria, V. (1988). *Custer died for your sins: An Indian manifesto*. University of Oklahoma Press.

Eagle Shield, A., Paris, D., Paris, R., & San Pedro, T. (2020). *Education in movement spaces: Standing Rock to Chicago Freedom Square*. Routledge.

Elser, T. (2010). *The framework: A practical guide for Montana teachers and administrators implementing Indian Education for All*. Montana Office of Public Instruction.

Epstein, T., & Gist, C. (2015). Teaching racial literacy in secondary humanities classrooms: Challenging adolescents' of color concepts of race and racism. *Race Ethnicity & Education, 18*(1), 40–60.

Executive Office of the President. (2014, December). *Native youth report*. https://obamawhitehouse.archives.gov/sites/default/files/docs/20141129nativeyouthreport_final.pdf

Flinders, D. J., & Thornton, S. J. (2004). Looking back: A prologue to curriculum studies. In D. J. Flinders & S. J. Thornton (Eds.), *The curriculum studies reader* (2nd ed., pp. 1–8). RoutledgeFalmer.

Freire, P. (1972/2000). *Pedagogy of the oppressed*. Continuum.

Guinier, L. (2004). From racial liberalism to racial literacy: *Brown v. Board of Education* and the interest-divergence dilemma. *The Journal of American History, 91*(1), 92–118.

Hixon, W. (2013). *American settler colonialism: A history*. Palgrave McMillan.

Hopkins, J. (2020). *Indian education for all: Decolonizing Indigenous education in public schools*. Teachers College Press.

Journell, W. (2009). An incomplete history: Representation of American Indians in state social studies standards. *Journal of American Indian Education, 48*(2), 18–32.

Kimmerer, R. W. (2013). *Braiding sweetgrass: Indigenous wisdom, scientific knowledge, and the teachings of plants*. Milkweed Editions.

Kincheloe, J. (2006). Critical ontology and Indigenous ways of being: Forging a postcolonial curriculum. In Y. Kanu (Ed.), *Curriculum as cultural practice: Postcolonial imaginations* (pp. 181–202). University of Toronto Press.

King, L. (2016). Teaching Black history as a racial literacy project. *Race Ethnicity & Education, 19*(6), 1301–1318.

King, L., Vickery, A., & Caffrey, G. (2018). A pathway to racial literacy: Using the LETS ACT framework to teach controversial issues. *Social Education, 82*(6), 316–322.

Kovach, M. (2013). Treaties, truths, and transgressive pedagogies: Re-imagining Indigenous presence in the classroom. *Socialist Studies, 9*(1), 109–127.

Lavere, D. B. (2008). The quality of pedagogical exercises in U.S. history textbooks. *The Social Studies, 99*(1), 3–7.

Levstik, L. S. (2008). What happens in social studies classroom? Research on K-12 social studies practice. In L. S. Levstik & C. A. Tyson (Eds.), *Handbook of research in social studies education* (pp. 50–62). Routledge.

Loewen, J. W. (1995). *Lies my teacher told me: Everything your American history textbook got wrong.* Simon & Schuster.

Loewen, J. W. (2010). *Teaching what* really *happened: How to avoid the tyranny of textbooks and get students* excited *about doing history.* Teachers College Press.

Lomawaima, K. T. (2000). Tribal sovereigns: Reframing research in American Indian education. *Harvard Educational Review, 70*(1), 1–21.

Lomawaima, K. T. (2004). Educating Native Americans. In J. A. Banks & C. A. McGee Banks (Eds.), *The handbook of research on multicultural education* (2nd ed., pp. 441–461). Jossey-Bass.

Mann, C. C. (2006). *1491: New revelations of the Americas before Columbus.* Vintage.

McCarty, T., & Lee, T. (2014). Critical culturally sustaining/revitalizing pedagogy and Indigenous education sovereignty. *Harvard Educational Review, 84*(1), 101–124.

McCoy, M. (2017). Preparing preservice educators to teach American Indian boarding school histories. In S. Shear, C. M. Tschida, E. Bellows, L. B. Buchanan, & E. E. Saylor (Eds.), *Making controversial issues relevant for elementary social studies: A critical reader* (pp. 255–277). Information Age Press.

Montana Office of Public Instruction (MOPI). (1999/2019). *Essential understandings regarding Montana Indians.* https://opi.mt.gov/Portals/182/Page%20Files/Indian%20Education/Indian%20Education%20101/essentialunderstandings.pdf?ver=2019-03-08-090932-123\

Montana Office of Public Instruction (MOPI). (2018). *Montana American Indian data report.* https://leg.mt.gov/content/Committees/Interim/2017-2018/Education/Meetings/Sept-2018/AI%20Student%20Data%20Report%20Fall%202018.pdf#:~:text=%EF%83%98%20Nine%20and%20two-tenths%20percent%20of%20Montana%E2%80%99s%20total,Native%20as%20at%20least%20one%20of%20their%20races

National Center for Education Statistics (NCES). (2020). Fast facts: Teacher characteristics and trends. https://nces.ed.gov/fastfacts/display.asp?id=28

National Council for the Social Studies (NCSS). (2013). *The college, career, and civic life (C3) framework for social studies state standards: Guidance for enhancing the rigor of K-12 civics, economics, geography, and history.* NCSS.

Padgett, G. (2015). A critical case study of selected U.S. history textbooks from a Tribal Critical Race Theory perspective. *The Qualitative Report, 20*(3), 153–171.

Quijada Cerecer, P. (2014). The policing of Native bodies and minds: Perspectives on schooling from American Indian youth. *American Journal of Education, 119*(4), 591–616.

Sabzalian, L. (2019a). *Indigenous children's survivance in public schools.* Routledge.

Sabzalian, L. (2019b). The tensions between Indigenous sovereignty and multicultural citizenship education: Toward an anticolonial approach to civic education. *Theory & Research in Social Education, 43*(3), 311–346.

Sanchez, T. R. (2007). The depiction of Native Americans in recent (1991–2004) secondary American history textbooks: How far have we come? *Equity & Excellence in Education, 40*(4), 311–320.

Scott, D. (2008). *Critical essays on major curriculum theorists*. Routledge.

Sealey-Ruiz, Y., & Greene, P. (2015). Popular visual images and the (mis)reading of Black male youth: A case for racial literacy in urban preservice teacher education. *Teaching Education, 26*(1), 55–76.

Shear, S. B., Knowles, R. T., Soden, G. J., & Castro, A. J. (2015). Manifesting destiny: Re/presentations of Indigenous peoples in K-12 U.S. history standards. *Theory & Research in Social Education, 43*(1), 68–101.

Short, E. C. (1991). Introduction: Understanding curriculum inquiry. In E. C. Short (Ed.), *Forms of curriculum inquiry* (pp. 1–25). State University of New York Press.

Smith, W. (2016). Knowing Obama: How high school students of color learn about the 44th president. *The High School Journal, 100*(1), 26–44.

Smith, W. L., & Crowley, R. M. (2018). Barack Obama, racial literacy, and lessons from "A More Perfect Union." *The History Teacher, 51*(3), 445–476.

Stanton, C. R. (2012). Context and community: Resisting curricular colonization in American history courses. In H. Hickman & B. J. Porfilio (Eds.), *The new politics of the textbook: Problematizing the portrayal of marginalized groups in textbooks* (pp. 173–194). Sense Publishers.

Stanton, C. R. (2014). The curricular Indian agent: Discursive colonization & Indigenous (dys)agency in U.S. history textbooks. *Curriculum Inquiry, 44*(5), 649–676.

Stanton, C. R. (2015). Beyond the margins: Evaluating the support for multicultural education within teachers' editions of U.S. history textbooks. *Multicultural Perspectives, 17*(4), 180–189.

Stanton, C. R. (2019). "Now you can't just do *nothing*": Unsettling the settler self within social studies education. *Social Education, 83*(5), 282–289.

Stanton, C. R., Carjuzaa, C., & Hall, B. (2019). The promises, purposes, and possibilities of Montana's *Indian Education for All. Journal of American Indian Education, 58*(3), 78–104.

Stanton, C. R., & Morrison, D. (2018). Investigating curricular policy as a tool to dismantle the master's house: *Indian Education for All* and social studies teacher education. *Policy Futures in Education*, 16(6), 729–748.

Thacker, E. S., Lee, J. K., & Friedman, A. M. (2016). Teaching with the C3 Framework: Surveying teachers' beliefs and practices. *The Journal of Social Studies Research, 41*, 89–100.

Tuck, E. (2009). Suspending damage: A letter to communities. *Harvard Educational Review* 79(3), 409–427.

Tuck, E. (2019). *Statement regarding the 2019 Meeting of the American Educational Research Association in Toronto: Indigenous Education Network*. https://www.oise.utoronto.ca/ien/UserFiles/File/AERA2019_in_Tkaronto_Indigenous_Education_Network-1.pdf

Turtle Island Social Studies Collective (TISSC). (2019). Beyond Pocahontas: Learning from Indigenous women changemakers. *Social Studies and the Young Learner, 31*(3), 7–13.

Vizenor, G. (2008). Aesthetics of survivance: Literary theory and practice. In G. Vizenor (Ed.), *Survivance: Narratives of Native presence* (pp. 1–24). University of Nebraska Press.

Welch, J. (1986). *Fools crow*. Viking.

Whitford, D. K. (2017). School discipline disproportionality: American Indian students in special education. *Urban Review, 49*, 693–706.

Whitney, L., Golez, F., Nagel, G., & Nieto, C. (2012). Listening to voices of practicing teachers to examine the effectiveness of a teacher education program. *Action in Teacher Education, 23*(4), 69–76.

Wineburg, S. (2001). *Historical thinking and other unnatural acts: Charting the future of teaching the past*. Temple University Press.

# Part II

# RACIAL LITERACY AND SOCIAL STUDIES INSTRUCTION

## CHAPTER 4

# Between the General and the Particular

## Theoretical Tensions in Historical Consciousness and Racial Literacy for the Classroom

*Gabriel A. Reich*

As teacher educators, we often confront the difficulty of bridging theory and practice. This tension is perpetually vexing because one is not reducible to the other. A general theory may not account for an individual case, and an individual case provides weak substantive evidence for a general theory. In this chapter, I explore the tension that exists between the general and the particular, the theory and the case. I will argue that tension is central to theories of racial literacy, and that understanding that tension has significant implications for teaching, learning, and curriculum design. To illustrate that tension, I will explore Guinier's (2004) theory of racial literacy. Then I will juxtapose it with King's (2019) theory of Black historical consciousness and Rüsen's (2005) universal theory of historical consciousness. Guinier (2004) describes racial literacy as a praxis of learning that emerges from cycles of analysis, reflection, and action. In that spirit, I will apply that praxis to a historical inquiry I developed with a student on Confederate monuments (Gibson & Reich, 2017).

Theories of historical consciousness emerge primarily from philosophy and attempt to describe how historians connect interpretations, claims, and evidence to construct a narrative that explains change over time (Clark & Grever, 2018; cf. Gadamer, 2004). A separate branch has emerged to describe how ordinary citizens make sense of the present and imagine possible futures with reference to what they know about the past (Clark & Grever, 2018; Seixas, 2017). In this chapter, I will focus on the theory of historical consciousness developed by Jörn Rüsen (2005), a German philosopher of history. His theory makes strong claims to universalism and attempts to synthesize historical consciousness with history education. Rüsen's project emerges from the profound rupture to modernism's promise of progress represented by the Third Reich and the Holocaust. His goal is to influence history curricula so that they promote nuance and wrestle with the inherent human capacity for good and evil, to temper nationalism and guard against another catastrophe.

Racial literacy emerges from legal scholarship, specifically a critique of the landmark *Brown v. Board of Education* (1954) case, the legal and political strategies that led up to that decision, and the integration policies that followed it (Guinier, 2004). Racial literacy outlines an analytical method for social change in which knowledge of the structural arrangements that maintain social, economic, and legal hierarchies based on race are interrogated at various geographical scales to inform direct—and preferably local—action (Guinier, 2004). Theories of historical consciousness and racial literacy recognize the problem of the general (theory) and the particular (case) and attempt to account for the tension between them. Although neither do so satisfactorily, exploring why helps to clarify the challenge of expanding students' racial literacy through the study of history, and suggests that we should consider how we engage students in dialectical thinking, particularly regarding issues of scale.

## RÜSEN'S HISTORICAL CONSCIOUSNESS

Rüsen (2004, 2005) argued that history courses are an opportunity for students to build what he calls *narrative competence*. Rüsen (2004) defined narrative competence as "the ability of human consciousness to carry out procedures that make sense of the past, effecting a temporal orientation in present practical life by means of the recollection of past actuality" (p. 69). He argued (2005) that historical consciousness is informed by historical knowledge, collective memory, historical thinking/literacy, self-awareness, identity, and ethics and that consciousness is evoked when people make decisions in the present based on their knowledge of history, their identity commitment(s), their ethics, and their self-awareness as historical beings. Rüsen believes that historical consciousness is universal, that all people make decisions in this way, but that there is great variation that depends largely on the level of sophistication and nuance of their historical knowledge and narrative competence.

Seixas (2017) described the narrative competence of professional historians and identified a central challenge they face called "the conundrum of causation" (p. 67). He wrote:

> The historian's narrative achievement is to set human decision-making in context in a way that communicates choice and intention, while accounting for historical context and conditions. Moreover, one of the pedagogical benefits of historical narratives that successfully negotiate the problem of agency is that, by analogy, they position *us* as historical agents with responsibilities toward the future. (p. 67, emphasis added)

The complexity of thought that goes into such an achievement is staggering. A challenge learners face on the path toward narrative competence is toggling between larger structures (social, geographical, technological, cultural, etc.) and more variable factors, such as human agency and contingency (i.e., luck) to understand how change occurs over time. The conundrum of causation is that at different scales, the relevant facts concerning the general (e.g., structural) and the specific (e.g., agency and contingency) sometimes support each other and at other times contradict each other.

## BLACK HISTORICAL CONSCIOUSNESS AND RACIAL LITERACY

Black historical consciousness is an emergent concept in history education that critiques the universality of theories like Rüsen's and seeks to reframe consciousness in ways that resonate with the specificity of the Black experience and the intellectual traditions that emerged from that experience (King, 2019). Black historical consciousness is, in part, a response to the need to reframe Black people as complex human subjects, to center the historical concept of race and racism in narratives of the post-1492 world, and to sustain a wide variety of cultural activities that provide a healthy orientation to the past, present, and future. As an emerging framework, it is not yet clear the extent to which Black historical consciousness will handle the tensions between the general and the particular. Specifically, that tension is manifest in the structural, cultural, and ideological frameworks of race and racism on the one hand, and the humanized Black subject on the other. Racial literacy (Guinier, 2004), however, can be conceived as a specific example of Black historical consciousness in praxis and will serve as a more concrete example for the purposes of this essay.

The term racial literacy—at least as it is employed in education research (Epstein & Gist, 2015; King, 2016; Smith & Crowley, 2018; Simmons et al., 2019)—was coined by legal scholar Lani Guinier (2004) in a work of history. In that account, Guinier (2004) uses critical race theory (Bell, 1980) to analyze the failure of the U.S. Supreme Court decision in the case of *Brown vs. Board of Education*. Guinier's account draws a causal link from the shortcomings of racial liberalism to the failure of *Brown* to alter racial hierarchies. Racial liberalism was a social theory that diagnosed the problem of *de jure* segregation as "the corrosive effect of individual prejudice . . . on black personality development" (Guinier, 2004, p. 95). That strategy garnered sympathy from many middle-class white people and led to a hard-won victory. However, the victory had the unintended consequence of deepening *de facto* segregation and re-entrenching race as a marker of social capital further dividing working-class African Americans and white people. According to Guinier's (2004) account, the failure of *Brown* was due, in part, to a failure of historical consciousness on the part of the legal team. Racial literacy emerged as a framework for reorienting historical consciousness around "the dynamic

interplay among race, class, and geography" over time, as well as the particular way that race has been used as "an instrument of social, geographic, and
economic control of both whites and blacks" (Guinier, 2004, p. 104).

Guinier's (2004) framework for racial literacy suggests that to work toward
a more equal and just future, activists and jurists should engage a praxis for
reading the dynamics of race in a variety of situations they encounter. Much
of that work involves toggling between factors related to the general and the
particular, and on an honest critical reflection regarding one's analysis and
actions. The first tenet states that "racial literacy is contextual rather than universal" (Guinier, 2004, p. 105):

> [It] depends upon the engagement between action and thought, between experi-
> mentation and feedback, between bottom-up and top-down initiatives. It is about
> learning rather than knowing. Racial literacy is an interactive process in which
> race functions as a tool of diagnosis, feedback, and assessment. (pp. 105–106)

That framing of race is a little confusing. As an ideology, racism is totalizing.
It imposes universal hierarchies on all people based on phenotypical characteristics. However, Guinier (2004) argued that race operates differently in different
places and times, and moreover that it is a versatile set of beliefs that impact
social, legal, and economic life in drastically different contexts. She develops this
line of thought further in the second tenet, which "emphasizes the relationship
between race and power" (p. 105). That relationship engages entities that are
intimate and distant, concrete and abstract. As she described it,

> Racial literacy reads race in its psychological, interpersonal, and structural dimen-
> sions. It acknowledges the importance of individual agency but refuses to lose
> sight of institutional and environmental forces that both shape and reflect that
> agency. (p. 105)

In the third tenet, intersectionality, the framework for analysis is made
more complex still, as the multiple factors that make up the particular over-
whelm the ability of the universal to offer useful explanations. Guinier (2004)
refers to the praxis of racial literacy in terms that refer to both analysis and
action, both political and legal. For example, that praxis

> constantly interrogates the dynamic relationship among race, class, geography,
> gender, and other explanatory variables. It sees the danger of basing a strategy
> for monumental social change on assumptions about individual prejudice and in-
> dividual victims. It considers the way psychological interests can mask political
> and economic interests for poor and working-class whites. It analyzes the psycho-
> logical economy of white racial solidarity for poor and working-class whites and
> blacks, independent of manipulations by "the industrialists and the lawyers and
> politicians who served them." Racial literacy suggests that racialized hierarchies
> mirror the distribution of power and resources in the society more generally. In

other words, problems that converge around blacks are often visible signs of broader societal dysfunction. (p. 105)

## TOWARD (W)RECKONING THE UNIVERSAL
## AND THE PARTICULAR

Rüsen's theory of historical consciousness is primarily interested in how people use what they know about the past to accomplish several tasks: (1) to orient themselves in time and space, (2) to express a sense of a belonging to a community, and (3) to inform ethical judgments about what to do in the present. Rüsen attempted to describe how *all* people use knowledge of history in a praxis of everyday life, particularly in regard to making ethical choices. He also argued that through learning content and thinking through historical problems, one's consciousness of history can become more nuanced and comfortable with complexity and cognitive dissonance. Racial literacy assumes that race is salient as a transhistorical and geographic identity, and that it is key to how people orient themselves in the United States. It eschews simplicity for complexity and nuance, in particular arguing that what it means to be raced varies significantly over time and space. Racial literacy also assumes an affective and ethical commitment to care for, with, and about Black people as a collective. Thus, reading race is a praxis that engages the knowledge of history—the study of how humans in different times and places engaged with the world and made choices based on the limitations imposed by social structures, cultures, and the needs of material life.

There are significant differences between Rüsen's (2005) approach and that of Guinier (2004). The most significant is Guinier's deep commitment to altering power relations and hierarchies based primarily on race that are oppressive to Black people. Guinier's (2004) commitment emerged from a consciousness of history that engenders a skepticism of universal claims that veil meaningful differences. That skepticism was informed by multiple cases of the physical, intellectual, and emotional struggles that people of African descent have engaged in since their arrival in the Americas. In King's (2019) words, "Black people's historical experiences are just different" (p. 171). However, there are also some useful parallels between these theories that suggest some cognitive challenges for learners that can serve as a useful starting point for considering classroom pedagogy.

In Guinier's (2004) historical account, and in more recent education research that employs her framework (Epstein & Gist, 2015; King, 2016; Simmons et al., 2019; Smith & Crowley, 2018), the cognitive achievement described as racial literacy consistently values nuance and complexity over overarching theories and narratives. In its insistence on the significance of the particular, nuance is the counterpoint to universalism. It affirms, challenges, and complicates theory. Guinier's historical argument is that when nuance is eschewed for the universal, as it was in the *Brown v. Board of Education* legal strategy, solutions focus on isolated factors, such as *de jure* segregation, over-estimating their significance, rather than on a more detailed analysis that might suggest a variety of institutional arrangements that maintain race- and class-based hierarchies.

Regarding King's work on black historical consciousness (2018, 2019; Simmons et al., 2019) and racial literacy (2016), the expanse of significant historical content that will provide nuance is broad. It ranges from Africa through time to the entirety of the Black diaspora in the Americas and Europe. Even in such a broad expanse, the aim is depth. Perhaps most significantly, King places greater emphasis on detailed historical knowledge as an important shaper of historical consciousness than Rüsen does. That concern is manifested, for example, in the insistence on "a holistic representation of Black people's history" (Simmons et al., 2019, p. 53), as well as "nuance and complexity" (p. 54) when dealing with historical events, actors, and key concepts, such as race. Without deep content knowledge, the result is a "disjointed understanding" (p. 53) based on misleading historical tropes and sentimentality. However, the call for nuance and complexity on the one hand, and on the other a coherent understanding, suggests that to be racially literate is to be comfortable with cognitive dissonance and ambiguity, in particular, dissonance between theory and contextualized cases (see also Milner, 2017). It is unclear to what extent such comfort is an intellectual achievement or an affective disposition, but clearly identifying it as a pedagogical goal is an important step toward designing curricula and pedagogies that support it.

Regarding K–12 history education, these works point to some useful dialectics that can help frame design. I use dialectics here not to propose that binaries are somehow a superior framework to describe the world, but rather because the authors under discussion use them, and because they are useful particularly for framing a curricular design that encourages reflexivity, self-awareness, and a social justice ethic. Framing curricular goals dialectically points to the centrality of dialectical thinking as an intellectual activity that all these scholars value. In other words, all these authors present learning aims involving the ability to hold two or more ideas as true in one's head simultaneously, including ideas that may both be true and contradictory. The most significant dialectic is between the general and the particular. That is a dialectic of scale, pointing to the phenomenon that fact-based historical representations will vary depending on the grain size of the analysis (among other factors).

A second and related dialectic concerns the relationship between the historical agent and the structural forces and arrangements of power that serve to limit agency in significant ways. The literature on curricula (King et al., 2018; Simmons et al., 2019; Smith & Crowley, 2018) and classroom praxis (Epstein & Gist, 2015) suggests that it is important for students to learn how to toggle between scales, between specific context and larger structure, between individuals and institutions, and between individuals and larger collectives. To understand the significance of Maggie Walker, America's first Black millionaire, one must consider her success *and* the deeply racist and patriarchal historical context of her times. Failure to toggle between her story and the social dynamics in which she lived distorts the narrative. Focus on her success alone and one will have a hard time understanding why it was so unique or why others were not successful. Focus primarily on the social and legal structure of her time, and one will miss how she was able to exercise her limited agency to great effect. Thus, if we follow the logic of Guinier (2004), King (2016, 2019), and others, we must be clear that we are asking teachers to design curricula that engage students in dialectical thinking. To make this idea more concrete, I will give some historical background to the construction of Confederate monuments in the U.S. South, and then I will analyze a historical inquiry on those monuments informed by the praxis of racial literacy.

## UNDERSTANDING CONFEDERATE MONUMENTS

The first wave of Confederate monument installation occurred between 1890 and 1920. In that era, the states of the former Confederacy had largely recovered economically from the Civil War. It was also the point when the remaining vestiges of postwar experiments in racial equality had been politically and socially defeated, and white supremacy had been restored. Confederate statues were "monuments to public affect" (Doss, 2010, p. 13), designed to teach future generations of white Southern children to feel proud of the Confederacy, to connect their identities to the heroes of the rebellion, and to believe in the Lost Cause narrative of the Civil War. They were also designed to remind African Americans of their place at the bottom rung of society.

There is evidence that the affect the monuments were designed to engender continues to exist among a number of white people, particularly in the South (Pew Research Center, 2011). In New Orleans, Louisiana, Mayor Mitch Landrieu decided to remove the statue of Confederate General Robert E. Lee from Lee Square late at night, under armed guard, and with the faces of the workers covered. In Richmond, Virginia, former capital of the Confederacy and home to Monument Avenue's five Confederate monuments, a mayoral commission on the future of those monuments garnered significant support for the position that nothing be done to change or alter its current configuration. While this position may not represent the majority of Richmond's residents, it appears to be the majority position of those who feel strongly enough to get politically involved in the issue (Coleman et al., 2018; Levin, n.d.). It was not until the summer 2020 protests against police brutality and white supremacy, which included the removal of some monuments by protesters themselves, that Richmond mayor Levar Stoney was politically able to remove the Confederate monuments under his jurisdiction.

## A CURRICULAR FRAMEWORK FOR THE STUDY OF
## CONFEDERATE MONUMENTS

Controversy over Confederate monuments occurs mostly in Southern cities, many of which are majority African American. The controversy presents an opportunity for students to engage in the dialectics discussed above. At a more general level is the issue of the use-of-history to create collective memories that privilege or challenge hegemonic narratives (King, 2019). Nordgren's (2016) definition of use-of-history is "the communicative process in which aspects of the historical culture are applied to communicate meaning and action-oriented messages" (p. 481). In this case, the people who commissioned monuments to the Confederacy were attempting to communicate a reverence for its leaders, the rightness of their cause, and that white supremacy is a praxis subsequent generations should take up. As Guinier, King, and others have argued, racism and white supremacy are a, if not *the*, key element of historical culture in the United States. Ignorance of that structural truth renders reading what Confederate monuments communicate more difficult. At a finer scale are the specific histories of the various localities where the statues exist, the political arguments put forth by different people in those localities, the specific actions taken at different times to support and challenge power arrangements there, and the diversity of public reactions. For the purposes of this chapter, I will focus on Richmond, Virginia, the city where I live and work.

Several years ago, I published a historical inquiry with a student in *Social Education* (Gibson & Reich, 2017). It was designed to help students understand continuity and change in controversies over Confederate monuments in Richmond as a case that illuminates similar struggles in other cities. That lesson was framed by a compelling question: "What criteria should be considered when deciding the future of controversial public monuments?" (Gibson & Reich, 2017, p. 361). That question was introduced in a warm-up exercise in which students analyzed images of Confederate monuments in Richmond and then responded to the following questions: "What story do Confederate monuments tell about the Civil War? Why would some people want to tell *that* story?" (p. 361, emphasis in the original).

Three separate controversies regarding Richmond's monuments were presented—1890, 1995, and 2015—each with its own framing question, contextual information, and primary document sets. 1890 was when the monument to Lee was unveiled; 1995 was when the monument of African American tennis champion and Richmond native Arthur Ashe was added; and 2015 was when a public controversy about the continued presence of Confederate monuments emerged after the terror attack in Charleston, South Carolina, that same year. The 1890 and 1995 controversies were designed to be read together to inform a response to the following: "Why have Confederate monuments been controversial at different times? How have those controversies changed over time?" (Gibson & Reich, 2017, p. 361). The 2015 controversy was framed around a history-in-use question: "What do today's community activists and thought leaders believe should be done with Confederate monuments?" (p. 361). At the end of the lesson, students were asked to research who has jurisdiction over the monuments on Monument Avenue (or in their own city) and to write letters that represent their position on the compelling question and address that letter to the appropriate official(s).

## A RACIALLY LITERATE CURRICULUM?: SELF-CRITIQUE AND THE PRAXIS OF RACIAL LITERACY

To what extent does this lesson engage students in the opportunity for dialectical thinking described in the previous sections? To what extent is it likely to help students become more racially literate? The theoretical literature discussed earlier suggests several dialectic relationships that teachers can explore with their students. The dialectics revolve around the meta-issue of truth at different scales, such as the relationship between an individual historical case and the larger changes and social structures of that time, between individuals and larger collectives, and between historical agents and the constraints placed on their actions by their historical context.

There are several aspects of the inquiry that address issues of scale as well as other aspects of racial literacy. The overall inquiry is designed as an in-depth look at a specific geography in which neo-Confederate memory of the Civil War has been contested at three points in time. The main inquiry question, "What criteria should be considered when deciding the future of controversial public monuments?" (Gibson & Reich, 2017, p. 361), however, asks a more general question about the practice of memorialization that can be applied in other locales. Additionally, the summative performance task asks students to take civic action in response to the monuments, a praxis that follows critical analysis with action. Racial literacy employs race and racism as a transhistorical analytical lens that is evident and significant in historical cases. Elements of this inquiry support that praxis as well. The specific assumptions about race and about how to confront racism reflect change and continuity at three different points in time. A racial literacy approach also eschews the tendency to simplify the diversity of perspectives within and between people socially classified in different groups. The inquiry contains documents representing a diversity of opinions about the monuments from Black and white commentators. In particular, the article presents a diversity of opinions from African American commentators, which can be used to counter the assumption that there is little diversity within the Black community. Such a presentation helps the learner to see that Black people exercise agency in collective and individual ways, and that the exercise of agency is structured, in part, by the historical context.

While the inquiry has potential as a tool for building racial literacy, it was not framed as a racial literacy exercise. Although the article invokes race, racism, and white supremacy frequently, it assumes that those terms are well understood by the readers. A teacher who does not bring a high level of racial literacy to their reading of the article and use of the materials may miss the nuanced connections between metahistorical concepts, such as racism, and the ideas expressed in the historical documents. In the section on the unveiling of the Lee statue in 1890 (Gibson & Reich, 2017), the contextual information focuses on Lee's placement as a metaphor for the restoration of white supremacy. The historical documents, however, do not directly address the issue of white supremacy, and are more concerned with the status of Lee as an avatar of Southern or United States nationalism. A more racially literate teacher who makes that connection will have to do a lot more work with their students to define race, racism, and the restoration of white supremacy after Reconstruction than the article calls for. In other words, teachers will have to invoke the universal and transhistorical truth of the salience of race and racism in American culture *and* discuss the specific case of post-Reconstruction Richmond to bring into students' consciousness that support for white supremacy was an assumption so widely shared in 1890 that it did not need to be named.

The discourse in the excerpts from 1995 present a different set of challenges for a teacher seeking to use this lesson to increase students' racial literacy. That primary document set includes two editorials by African American authors and one by a white author. The African American commentators did not agree with each other: one wanted Ashe on Monument Avenue, while the other argued that Ashe's presence among Confederate statues diminished his achievements. A teacher will have to come to the insight that the documents reflect diverse analyses of how the power of white supremacy operates, and be able to help students connect the opinions presented to that context. The piece written by a white author avoids any disparagement of Ashe or African Americans. Reading race into that author's discourse is difficult and requires both zooming in on his words and zooming out to the larger discourse about Civil War memory and the contemporary political aims such memory is often put to. A teacher with some knowledge of historical examples of backlash against racial equality that were the context of Confederate monument building after Reconstruction and during the Civil Rights Movement (Southern Poverty Law Center, 2021) can help students make those connections, while other teachers are likely to miss them and the opportunity for strengthening students' racial literacy.

In 2015, the discourse presented in the document set had changed subtly. An African American man was President of the United States, but euphoria about a postracial America had eroded in the face of continued police violence, the Black Lives Matter movement, and the reappearance of racist and far-right terrorism. That text set includes an excerpt from a blog post by the Virginia Flaggers, a neo-Confederate group that works to preserve outward displays of white Southern nationalism like Confederate flags and monuments. Their statement makes plain that the belief in Lost Cause mythology persists. The language used in the post frames the terror attack in South Carolina as "an unrelated tragedy" with no connection to Confederate monuments, which are presented as history itself. That rhetorical move frames those who want to remove such monuments as spuriously tying together unrelated incidents to present the illusion that racism is still salient to American society. In other words, they argue that in this case the particular does not reveal larger structural issues. Presenting the monuments as history means that calling for their removal is a denial of objective truth, a framework that can introduce the difficulty of parsing historical truth from the twists and turns of wishful thinking, myth, and faith. Perhaps the biggest shortcoming of this section of the article, however, is the failure to help teachers contend with the intersection of race and class, particularly for working-class white people. Guinier (2004) makes a compelling argument for such a focus when making sense of racial politics and larger economic forces that divide poor and working-class people.

In the hands of a racially literate teacher, and in a school that supports such work, the lesson presented in the article (Gibson & Reich, 2017) might provide useful materials for an exploration of Confederate monuments as a racially literate historical and civic praxis. The extent to which, even in that circumstance, the lesson might be successful as measured by the criteria presented by Guinier (2004) and King (2019) depends largely on the extent to which issues of race have been woven into (Leinhardt, 1993) explanations about change and continuity over time in a U.S. history course, with considerable attention given to the scale—local/regional/national—of those developments. That is quite a tall order for teachers and for students, and evidence from classrooms paints a picture of mixed success at best (Epstein et al., 2011). Thus, we will need to employ racial literacy as a praxis of historical thinking more intentionally in our published curricula and historical inquiry materials if we want to further the goals of developing a more racially literate citizenry.

## CONCLUDING THOUGHTS

The aims of the racial literacy project are vast, and achieving them is a highly ambitious goal. We would be wise to focus not on an end state (i.e., student achievement of racial literacy), but rather on the goal of creating the experience of racially literate praxis for young people, in the hopes that such praxis is continued in the future. To improve our efforts in that direction, we should heed the advice of Richard Milner IV (2017), who called for research "that dialogically examines micro and macro interplay" (p. 24). Milner was primarily interested in the relationship between classroom practice and education policies. I believe that a similar research focus is needed to explore the ways in which the dialectics of scale are dialogically traversed by teachers and learners as they relate to content.

The parallels to the challenge of creating a more historically conscious citizenry are worth reflecting on. The challenges are similar in that the goal of nuanced understanding of continuity and change, context and agency, requires detailed knowledge, a facility with dialectical thinking, and an ability to juggle more than one truth when making sense of past and present. The argument for focusing on racial literacy as a goal is compelling from ethical and intellectual standpoints. A more racially literate citizen will also be a more historically conscious one, but the opposite is not necessarily true. To get better at this, the research community will need to be more conscious of the tension between the general and the particular. That will require more research on student learning that focuses on the intellectual challenges delineated in this chapter. I believe that it will also require a more robust dialogue between theory and empirical studies of teaching and learning. In the spirit of Guinier (2004), one should not take precedence over the other. That is the work.

## REFERENCES

Bell Jr., D. A. (1980). *Brown v. Board of Education* and the interest-convergence dilemma. *Harvard Law Review, 93*(January), 518–533.

*Brown v. Board of Education*, 347 U.S. 483 (1954).

Clark, A., & Grever, M. (2018). Historical consciousness: Conceptualizations and educational applications. In S. A. Metzger & L. McArthur Harris (Eds.), *The Wiley international handbook of history teaching and learning* (pp. 177–202). Wiley.

Coleman, C., Kimball, G., Ayers, E. L., Hayter, J., Driggs, S., Lee, L., Burrs, S., Butler Rodriguez, C., Addison, A., & Gray, K. (2018). Monument Avenue commission. https://www.monumentavenuecommission.org/

Doss, E. (2010). *Memorial mania: Public feeling in America*. University of Chicago Press.

Epstein, T., & Gist, C. (2015). Teaching racial literacy in secondary humanities classrooms: Challenging adolescents' of color concepts of race and racism. *Race Ethnicity and Education, 18*(1), 40–60. https://doi.org/10.1080/13613324.2013.792800

Epstein, T., Mayorga, E., & Nelson, J. (2011). Teaching about race in an urban history class: The effects of culturally responsive teaching. *Journal of Social Studies Research, 35*(1), 2–21.

Gadamer, H. G. (2004). *Truth and method* (J. Weinsheimer & D. G. Marshall, Trans.; 2nd revised ed.). Continuum.

Gibson, M. T., & Reich, G. A. (2017). Confederate monuments: Heritage, racism, anachronism, and who gets to decide? *Social Education, 81*(6), 356–361.

Guinier, L. (2004). From racial liberalism to racial literacy: *Brown v. Board of Education* and the interest-divergence dilemma. *Journal of American History, 91*(1), 92–118. https://doi.org/10.2307/3659616

King, L. J. (2016). Teaching Black history as a racial literacy project. *Race Ethnicity and Education*, 1303–1318. https://doi.org/10.1080/13613324.2016.1150822

King, L. J. (2018). Interpreting Black history: Toward a Black history framework for teacher education. *Urban Education, 54*(3), 368–396. https://doi.org/10.1177/0042085918756716

King, L. J. (2019). What is Black historical consciousness? In A. Clark & C. Peck (Eds.), *Contemplating historical consciousness: Notes from the field* (pp. 163–174). Berghahn Books.

King, L. J., Vickery, A., & Caffrey, G. (2018). A pathway to racial literacy: Using the LETS ACT framework to teach controversial issues. *Social Education, 82*(6), 316–322.

Leinhardt, G. (1993). Weaving instructional explanations in history. *British Journal of Educational Psychology, 63*, 46–74.

Levin, K. (n.d.). Confederate monuments syllabus. *Civil war memory.* http://cwmemory .com/civilwarmemorysyllabus/

Millner IV, H. R. (2017). Where's the race in culturally relevant pedagogy? *Teachers College Record, 119*(1), 1–32.

Nordgren, K. (2016). How to do things with history: Use of history as a link between historical consciousness and historical culture. *Theory and Research in Social Education, 44*(4), 479–504.

Pew Research Center. (2011, April 8). *Civil War at 150: Still relevant, still divisive.* The Pew Research Center for People and the Press. https://www.people-press.org /2011/04/08/civil-war-at-150-still-relevant-still-divisive/

Rüsen, J. (2004). Historical consciousness: Narrative structure, moral function, and ontogenetic development. In P. Seixas (Ed.), *Theorizing historical consciousness* (pp. 63–85). University of Toronto Press.

Rüsen, J. (2005). *History: Narration, interpretation, orientation.* Berghahn Books.

Seixas, P. (2017). Historical consciousness and historical thinking. In M. Carretero, S. Berger, & M. Grever (Eds.), *Palgrave handbook of research in historical culture and education* (pp. 59–72). Palgrave Macmillan.

Simmons, G. D., King, L. J., & Adu-Gyamfi, M. (2019). Developing a Black history and Black studies course using a Black historical consciousness framework. *The Oregon Journal of the Social Studies, 7*(1), 52–66.

Smith, W. L., & Crowley, R. (2018). Barack Obama, racial literacy, and lessons from "a more perfect union." *The History Teacher, 51*(3), 445–476.

Southern Poverty Law Center. (2021). Whose heritage? Public symbols of the Confederacy. https://www.splcenter.org/20160421/whose-heritage-public-symbols-con federacy. https://www.splcenter.org/presscenter/splc-reports-over-160-confederate -symbols-removed-2020#:~:text=The%20Whose%20Heritage%3F%20report %20found%20that%20168%20Confederate,Confederate%20monuments%20 were%20removed%20between%202015%20and%202019.

## CHAPTER 5

# "We Gotta Make a Change"

## Developing Racial Literacy With Elementary Preservice Teachers Through Angie Thomas's *The Hate U Give*

*Noreen Naseem Rodríguez*

When individuals hold different racial realities, conversations around race may engender feelings of discomfort, anger, and anxiety; consequently, most people would rather avoid the topic and remain silent (Sue, 2016). Research has found this is particularly true for the white, middle-class women who make up the overwhelming majority of elementary teacher candidates (Picower, 2021; Sleeter, 2001) and current elementary educators (National Center for Education Statistics, 2017). Teacher preparation programs across the United States have been mostly ineffective in preparing white teachers to teach diverse students (Goldenberg, 2014), resulting in the perpetuation of stereotyping and deficit myth-making of children of color and an avoidance of whiteness and white supremacy. Love (2019) describes this disparity as the teacher education gap, existing between the deficit frames that many white teacher candidates are taught in preparation programs and the lived realities and dynamic cultures of students of color.

The teacher education gap reveals the lack of common knowledge around the simple fact that racist policies have driven the history of racist ideas in the United States and persist in the present day, despite uneven progress toward racial equity and justice (Kendi, 2017; Love, 2019). This gap explains why white preservice teachers often enter classrooms intent on saving students of color from failure, yet may maintain the white supremacist status quo by pathologizing students of color without recognizing their own complicity in racism (DiAngelo, 2018; Love, 2019). While efforts to explore notions of equity, diversity, social justice, and whiteness are beginning to permeate progressive teacher preparation programs across the United States, these efforts often center white privilege and rarely move beyond acts of "confession" of white preservice teachers' privilege toward more necessary visions of antiracist action (Lensmire et al., 2013).

In my eight years as a social studies teacher educator in historically and predominantly white institutions (PWIs), the topic of race has consistently been contentious among the elementary teacher candidates with whom I work and learn. After several years of relying on the same texts and activities for my elementary social studies methods course, I revamped the course in the fall of 2018 to foreground anti-Black racism in the United States through a guided inquiry of Black history and contemporary issues of racism. Essential to this effort was the assignment of Angie Thomas's (2017) *The Hate U Give,* a New York Times bestselling young adult novel about a Black teenager who witnesses the senseless murder of her childhood friend at the hands of a white police officer. Thomas's book is both an indictment of the racial profiling, police brutality, and other injustices faced by Black communities and a call to action. As such, it achieved immense popularity, becoming widely read in secondary classrooms and book clubs for both youth and adults, and was adapted into a major motion picture soon after its release. *The Hate U Give* served as a vehicle for future teachers to engage with concrete examples of anti-Black racism and violence in the past and present. Paired with a practitioner text to guide preservice teacher application of sensitive topics with young children, the social studies methods course aimed to develop preservice teachers' racial literacy.

Guinier (2004) theorized racial literacy as a means to "rethink race as an instrument of social, geographic, and economic control" (p. 114) rather than as acts of individual prejudice, absent the influence of class and geographic interests. In teacher education, racial literacy can enhance preservice teachers' racial knowledge by exposing how the structural components of race and racism are interwoven in the United States and in global contexts (King, 2016). For social studies educators in particular, the cultivation of racial literacy can be a starting point to help preservice teachers develop inclusive, multicultural, and equitable history curriculum (King, 2016). This qualitative case study examines the coursework of seven white preservice teachers who participated in the revamped elementary social studies methods course to consider the opportunities offered by young adult literature toward the development of racial literacy in preservice teacher programs.

## LITERATURE REVIEW

### Racial Literacy

Literacy is most often associated with the traditional practices of reading and writing. However, scholars have argued for a far more expansive definition of literacies. For example, Kellner (2000) describes literacies as the attainment of competencies "in contexts that are governed by rules and conventions . . . socially constructed in educational, governmental, and cultural practices involved in various institutional discourses and practices" (p. 197), which evolve and shift in response to cultural and social change. The notion of racial literacy embraces this more expansive understanding of literacy as socially constructed competencies that can be realized. In her analysis of the landmark *Brown v. Board* decision, Guinier (2004) proposed a racial literacy framework to develop an understanding of American racism. Her framework consists of three principles: racism is contextual rather than universal; the relationship between race and power must be emphasized to understand systems; and intersectionality must be recognized, such that the focus is not exclusively on race. Although Guinier's work dealt with a landmark legal decision, education scholars have taken up Guinier's racial literacy framework in a number of ways, ranging from implementation in traditional pre-K–12 spaces to teacher preparation coursework in university settings.

### Racial Literacy in Teacher Education

As American society faces ongoing and elevated racial discord in the Trump era, racial literacy is a useful tool for educators tasked with the preparation of the country's next generation of citizens. The well-documented overwhelming whiteness of teacher education and schooling spaces (Sleeter, 2001) continues to challenge those who prepare future educators. These predominantly white, segregated spaces often feel comfortable and natural to white students schooled in contexts with little racial diversity, leading white students "to understand themselves as racially innocent and as neutral observers of race and racism that they perceive to be located elsewhere" (Winans, 2010, p. 487). Sealey-Ruiz and Greene (2015) argue for the need to address the racist divide in teacher education through the development of racial literacy in preservice teacher education, thus allowing preservice teachers to examine, discuss, challenge, and take anti-racist action. Such work demands the creation of spaces for preservice teachers to talk about their fears and uncertainties related to discussions about race (Sealey-Ruiz & Greene, 2015). This process must always be interactive, for, as Guinier (2004) emphasized, racial literacy "is about learning rather than knowing" (p. 115), and the development of racial literacy may offer two essential outcomes: the adoption of an anti-racist stance by members of the dominant racial category and the resistance of a victim stance by persons of color.

Flynn, Worden, and Rolón-Dow (2018) describe racial literacy in the teacher education context as "the ability to read and interpret materials and curricula as well as having the ability to ask questions and think carefully—embodying a stance as well as skills" (p. 241). Although racial literacy has been examined extensively in literacy education in both pre-K–12 and teacher preparation contexts (Rogers & Mosley, 2006; Skerrett, 2011; Skerrett et al., 2015; Winans, 2010), social studies education has rarely been documented as a site for racial literacy development among elementary teacher candidates (Epstein & Gist, 2015; King, 2016). In this chapter, I outline the pedagogical decisions that reframed an elementary social studies methods course around racial literacy as well as preservice teachers' responses to class assignments and readings.

### The Hate U Give as Racial Literacy Text

*The Hate U Give* (Thomas, 2017) has achieved remarkable mainstream popularity, with over 219 weeks on the *New York Times* bestsellers list for Young Adult Hardcovers and the receipt of multiple honors and recognitions. The response to *The Hate U Give* has been largely positive, as educators have dubbed the text an example of "literatures of resistance" (Ebarvia et al., 2018) that exposes societal injustices through multiple perspectives. Like any popular trade book, *The Hate U Give* also has detractors, mostly school of-ficials and parents who have banned or fought for the banning of the book due to its purported offensive language (Gomez, 2018). Despite this push-back, *The Hate U Give* is unique among contemporary young adult fiction due to its massive popular appeal as well as its explicit references to the Black Panther Party and recent murders of Black people at the hands of police. These references to racial injustice in the past and present were the primary reasons for its use in the elementary social studies methods course in the fall of 2018. Additionally, the film adaptation was released in the middle of the fall semester, and students were invited to attend a private screening of the film after independently reading the book.

## METHOD OF STUDY

### Reimagining Elementary Social Studies Methods

The context of this study is a required social studies methods course in an undergraduate elementary teacher preparation program at a Midwestern PWI during the fall semester of 2018. Like many PWI teacher preparation pro-grams, the vast majority of teacher candidates, as well as the teacher educa-tors who prepare them, are white, cishet, middle-class Christian females, most of whom were born, raised, and educated in the Midwest. The state in which this PWI is located has witnessed an ongoing demographic shift in the last half-century, as increasing populations of Latinxs, Asians/Asian Americans, Pacific Islanders, and Africans have settled across the state. This resulted in growing populations of students of color in the state's public schools, re-flective of national demographic changes. The dichotomy between student and teacher demographics in public schools across the state and nation is ad-dressed to varying degrees within the teacher preparation program, but the centering of whiteness is an undeniable aspect of the program that remains largely unproblematized.

Much of the existing scholarship on racial literacy practices in teacher edu-cation centers on, and is authored by, white educators. As a woman of color working at a PWI in a state that was over 90% white, I found myself in a precarious position when it came to issues of race: Do I risk being accused of obsessively talking about race as my white colleagues minimize my concerns about teacher candidates' discomfort and obliviousness regarding race? Do I have the hard conversations with white preservice teachers anyway and deal with the repercussions that undoubtedly arise during student evaluations? Or do I conserve my energy for other work to preserve my image as a well-liked colleague and educator to build alliances for the future? I often vacillated between these various stances, particularly as a tenure-track, early-career scholar.

However, in the fall of 2018, I was not only determined to implement course changes to explicitly develop racial literacy, I was also financially supported by my institution: I received a substantial internal grant to improve the quality of undergraduate student learning about race and immigration in my course. This grant would fund the purchase of hundreds of trade books for student use. For once, institutional claims of equity and diversity did not seem like lip service, as the institution offered significant financial support for me to emphasize these ideals in my course. I redesigned my social studies methods course in earnest, introducing a new text and struggling to balance the most essential components of the methods course with the content about anti-Black racism.

The course redesign reflected my focus on racism within U.S. institutions as well as my apprehension at embarking upon this topic as one of few teacher educators of color in a teacher preparation program that was 95% white, female, and English monolingual. In addition to the historical primer *A Different Mirror for Young People* (Takaki, 2012) that I had used in multiple prior semesters, I added Sara Ahmed's (2018) *Being the Change* as a required text. Ahmed's text is rich with examples of how elementary students engage in conversations around identity and race, with particular attention to the management of comfort during moments of disagreement. Moved by her work as a teacher of color, I selected this book hoping that by foregrounding how to do equity work with children, my students would better understand both the need and the possibilities for such approaches and would therefore be more willing to take risks with each other in class. Moreover, I hoped that Ahmed's clear examples of microaggressions and labels imposed by others would resonate deeply with my students as they began to read *The Hate U Give*. However, as a teacher educator in a purple state during the Trump era, I also structured this pedagogical approach to protect myself professionally from the white rage (Anderson, 2016) and fragility (DiAngelo, 2018) that often accompany situations that demand emotional vulnerability and reflexivity around racial violence and injustice.

### Study Participants and Data Sources

All but one of the 23 undergraduate students enrolled in my required elementary social studies methods course self-identified as white. Although this study was declared exempt from Institutional Review Board (IRB) review due to its course-based nature, students were given the option to participate, and three students declined. Therefore, this case study consists of multiple data sources from 20 students: responses to questions posed by the instructor before and after class based on assigned readings and in-class activities and discussions; students' reading reflection journals for the young adult novel *The Hate U Give* (2017); small-group inquiry projects; pre- and post-Likert surveys about their levels of comfort and knowledge regarding the teaching of race and racism; and other class artifacts. We met twice a week for a total of 11 weeks, plus a final class meeting in which students presented their last major group assignment. As the instructor for the course, I took notes on student conversations and recorded analytic memos each week that reflected on how students took up class content.

At the end of the fall 2018 semester, I compiled coursework from all 20 consenting students, replacing names with pseudonyms, and began the process of coding data. First-cycle codes (Saldaña, 2015) focused on codes related to the theoretical framework of racial literacy, drawing from Guinier's (2004) guiding principles and Flynn et al.'s (2018) pedagogical objectives for developing racial literacy, as well as descriptive and *en vivo* codes. Second-cycle codes examined broader themes related to race, history, and students' shifting pedagogical perspectives.

This chapter highlights data from seven white women students who exemplify a range of positions related to their growth, or lack thereof, regarding issues of race and racism as self-reported in surveys completed at the beginning and end of the semester. On their end-of-semester Likert surveys, Grace and Alexandra reported high confidence and comfort in understanding and teaching issues about racism; Olivia, Piper, and Teri reported significant growth in their confidence and comfort in discussing racism; and Mel and Maggie reported a decrease or no growth in their confidence and comfort in teaching and discussing racism after our course ended.

## FINDINGS

### Exploring Identities and Listening With Love

In any course that asks students to consider perspectives different from their own, building community, trust, and respect is essential. In the first week of class, students read the first chapter, "Exploring Our Identities," of *Being the Change* and created and shared identity webs in an effort to "help us find commonalities which springboard us to notice, wonder, and see the humanity in one another" (Ahmed, 2018, p. 5). In the second week of class, we focused on Ahmed's (2018) notion of "listening with love," which she describes as active, empathetic listening to facilitate reflective communication. The second chapter of *Being the Change* details how to teach active, empathetic listening skills to children, with an array of student examples and Ahmed's instructional missteps and strategies. After reading this chapter, my students worked in small groups to establish common ground rules for listening to one another during discussions, particularly regarding controversial issues. After class, students were asked to provide a written reflection of what they had learned about the role of racism in U.S. history from previous classes.

The reflections written by Grace and Alexandra showed a great deal of thoughtfulness about the active, empathetic listening described in the chapter and discussed in class. Grace suggested that listening with love "might be challenging because people are afraid of offending someone or just don't accept other perspectives other than their own." Alexandra proposed,

> Adults tend to be more set in their ways, and part of this is due to our age, and part of it is due to the way we were taught . . . I think this can be challenging for some of us still today to challenge and questions [sic] the beliefs we have heard since the cradle. Therefore, discussions sometimes become less fluid when we only discuss what we know and don't acknowledge the chance of being wrong or open to new ideas.

Both teacher candidates showed an awareness of the challenges in Ahmed's approach as well as an understanding of the need for teachers *and* students to "listen with love." Similarly, the other five students' reflections emphasized the importance of managing discomfort and disagreement during classroom conversations.

Of the seven focal students in this study, Mel and Maggie expressed the most discomfort when asked about facilitating conversations about race and racism after reading the listening with love chapter. Both described being raised in homogenous white communities and never discussing race or racism in school. Maggie described race and racism as "sensitive and heated subjects," while Mel repeatedly stated they were topics that were "very hard to talk about." Mel explained,

> It's hard to talk about different perspectives of racism since white people have only played one role in this topic in the past and present. So it's hard to talk about what others went through in the past and what it's like for others now when I have no idea.

At the beginning of the fall semester, Mel claimed to not have any knowledge of the historical experiences of people of color and suggested that white people only had "one role" in the history of racism. While I anticipated that students would have limited understandings of racism in American history, I was surprised to read Mel's statement that she had "no idea" about either past or present examples. Fortunately, I had prepared for this situation by ensuring that students would receive an overview, albeit brief, about anti-Black racism in the United States the following week.

## Developing Racial Literacy Through *The Hate U Give*

As I prepared to read *The Hate U Give* during the third week of the course, I knew that providing students with information about the Black Panther Party prior to reading would be essential to ensure their understanding of those references. I asked a colleague who studies Black history to serve as a guest speaker for my class, asking if she could attempt to draw a throughline from the 13th Amendment to Black Lives Matter, covering the murder of Emmett Till as well as the Black Panther Party's Ten-Point Program. This colleague was masterful at weaving together powerful historical narratives and contemporary events, and conducted a dynamic presentation that described everything from public lynchings to the murder of beloved school cafeteria worker Philando Castile. Every focal student reported learning a wealth of new information; only Grace described learning about the Black Panther Party and Emmett Till prior to this lecture.

After this powerful session, students finally began reading *The Hate U Give*. However, still concerned that I had not yet adequately prepared them with enough context, I assigned their reading strategically for the following class. They would read Baldwin's (1985) "A Talk to Teachers," then the first two chapters of *The Hate U Give* (in which the main character's childhood friend, a Black teenage boy, is murdered by a white police officer), and last, the chapter from *Being the Change* about the labels that people impose on others based on stereotypes and assumptions. Their entry tickets for the next class session asked them to reflect on each reading and to also add a layer to their existing identity webs, one that mirrored the imposed labels described in the assigned Ahmed chapter. Students' entry tickets for this initial reading of *The Hate U Give* demonstrate notable shifts in their understanding of racialized experiences in the United States.

After reading about the character Khalil's murder in the first chapters of *The Hate U Give*, Grace wrote, "This just astonishes me that these type of events go on in society and no one does anything about them."

Piper added an explicitly racial dimension to Grace's astonishment:

> To think that situations like that actually happen really opens your eyes. It is awful to think that a lot of times these situations just get laid to rest and nothing more ever becomes of them because the shooter or attacker is white.

Alexandra, the mother of a biracial child, stated, "Personally, I am afraid daily for my boyfriend, his family, my friends, and of course, what the reality will be for my son someday." Unlike many of her peers, she possessed intimate and familial relationships that exposed her to the realities of being Black in America; consequently, her response was more nuanced than her peers. Unsurprised by the events of the book and thinking about her own biracial son's future, she added, "an appropriate and relevant topic like police brutality in the classroom could have saved [Khalil's] life."

Alexandra was the sole white student in class who was a mother and the only one who described having intimate relationships with people of color. These aspects of her identity and personal experience deeply impacted her understanding of race in unique ways.

In the four weeks that followed, students independently completed a reflection journal for *The Hate U Give*. The reflection journals were highly structured, asking students to integrate ideas from class readings and consider connections between events in the book and current events. While our classwork was still connected to the content of *The Hate U Give*, class time was dedicated to discussions around inquiry and lesson design. After the fifth week of class, we had a four-week hiatus while students went to field placements, after which students submitted their completed reflection journals.

The seven teacher candidates in this study had especially compelling answers to two sets of questions in the reflection journal, illustrative of patterns across the larger class. The first question connected to a scene in the book in which the main character's father is accosted by the police. Thomas (2017) illustrates the ways in which an interaction with police changes the body language and tone of the conversation between two older Black men who were in the midst of an argument on the sidewalk. When police officers pass by and sound their patrol siren, the two men make their arms visible at their sides and soften their voices.

"His parents must've had the talk with him" (p. 191), muses the narrator.

"The talk" refers to conversations between children and parents of color regarding police interactions; in their reflection journals, teacher candidates were provided video links that detailed "the talk," then were asked to describe how they felt after watching and whether they had experienced a similar talk with their family.

Grace was the only white student in the class who described having a similar talk with her family, explaining that they "believed that I needed to know that sometimes society is not always positive or good."

Although Alexandra had not had such a talk with her family, she knew that she would have to have it with her biracial son, and recognized the challenges of doing so as a white woman:

I felt sad when I was watching the video. I will never know what it is like to be [B]lack in America. There will be a difference in experiences, as much as I educate myself on this issue, between me and this understanding of living it. My son's father isn't around and that makes the conversation that much harder. I have a lot of questions and few answers. Empathy, knowledge? Yes. Personal experiences? No. It's hard to hear my peers in this class and [others] discuss how these issues can't be brought into a classroom, or rather that they won't.

Unlike the majority of their peers, Grace and Alexandra had parents, extended family, friends, and intimate partners who spoke frankly with them about the differential treatment of people of color in American society. Their

reflection journal responses and comments in class reflected their open atti-
tude to discussing these and other "tough" topics with young children.

The other students expressed surprise and unfamiliarity with "the talk."

Mel, Olivia, Piper, and Teri found it sad and heartbreaking, but, as Teri
described, "it is also extremely important and could potentially save their
lives."

Mel stated, "This film really made me think about how lucky I am . . . To
officers I have not been considered a threat based on what I look like."

Maggie described feeling mixed emotions, however. While she was sad-
dened by the emotions expressed by the young Black girls in the video, she
felt the video "paint[ed] a negative picture of all cops, and that they are evil."
While Maggie's comment is reminiscent of Blue Lives Matter arguments that
uphold the value of police lives over critiques of racial profiling and police
brutality, she later wrote, "Basically, you are only worth something if you are
white or if you weren't involved in any trouble, which is a systematic flaw in
this country."

These conflicting statements demonstrate her emerging understandings of
systemic injustice alongside her pre-existing conceptions of race and justice.
An earlier section of the reflection journal asked students to consider the
unique positioning of the protagonist's Uncle Carlos, a Black police officer
whose colleague shot Khalil. While Mel, Piper, and Alexandra noted Uncle
Carlos's race, Grace, Olivia, Teri, and Maggie did not note how his position
as a *Black* policeman counters the simplistic positioning of all cops as evil.

The second set of questions that elicited powerful responses from the sev-
en teacher candidates focused on the book's theme of voice: *After reading this
book, how can you use your voice to promote social justice? How can you
begin discussing inequality in your own communities?* Alexandra, Maggie,
Olivia, Grace, Piper, and Teri responded to these questions by centering their
future roles as teachers. Piper emphasized taking advantage of conversations
around inequality when they arise naturally as well as bringing up issues for
students to consider. Teri described needing to talk about social justice while
children are young to bring more awareness to the issue. Similarly, Maggie
discussed the need to have these conversations in the classroom even if it is
difficult and uncomfortable. Alexandra and Mel also described their ability
to discuss inequality with the people around them, to provide information via
social media and in person in an effort to foster social change.

## DISCUSSION

Overall, the preservice teachers reported learning a great deal about Black history and the contemporary Black experience in the United States over the
course of the fall 2018 semester. However, the surveys they completed at the
beginning and end of the semester revealed distinct differences in not only
their self-reported levels of expertise on issues related to race and racism, but

also their comfort and confidence regarding the teaching of these topics. The preservice teachers' self-reported ratings, in tandem with the wealth of qualitative data collected from their class assignments, suggest that their white racialized lived experiences are deeply influential but are not necessarily barriers to their understanding of systemic injustice and inequity. The findings from this study suggest that racial literacy development occurred to varying degrees over the course of the semester for all participants, but many sociohistorical gaps in content knowledge remained, and further racial literacy development was needed.

Prior to the social studies methods course, all teacher candidates had taken required courses in foundations of education and multicultural education. Although these classes attended to a range of societal oppressions, students arrived in my methods class with little knowledge of non-white histories in the United States. Some, like Maggie and Mel, began the semester still uncomfortable even engaging in conversations related to race and racism. The lack of concrete historical examples in their education made it difficult for these and other students to fully conceive of American society as fundamentally racist, and of American schooling as an institution that perpetuates racism and other oppressions.

While the efforts made to center anti-Black racism and Black history in my class certainly provided the teacher candidates with meaningful, important examples of anti-Black racism in the past and present, it was undoubtedly not enough. Moreover, within the context of our specific teacher preparation program, it was likely the last time they received such explicit instruction around issues of anti-Black racism and social justice. For individuals whose experiences are always centered and regarded as the norm, clear and continuous conversations around bias, microaggressions, and macroaggressions are essential. Simply attending to privilege, stereotypes, and discrimination in a single multicultural education class will not adequately prepare prospective teachers to engage in anti-racist and decolonial practices. Until teacher preparation programs more deliberately weave anti-racist foci into all aspects of coursework and field placements, the teacher education gap will remain intact.

## STUDY IMPLICATIONS

Elementary teacher candidates have few opportunities to build their content knowledge across social studies disciplines and to witness social studies teaching and learning in the classroom (Bolick et al., 2010; Hawkman et al., 2015), and therefore are likely to rely on textbooks, peers, and memories from their own schooling experience to guide their approach to social studies. As the official narrative of American history taught in schools is centered on themes of American progress and exceptionalism and ignores moments of conflict, racism, and injustice (VanSledright, 2008), elementary teacher candidates may consider contemporary U.S. society to be postracial, with the Civil Rights Movement as a period during which racial injustice was largely resolved. To this effect, elementary preservice teachers must have opportunities to learn about and discuss contemporary racism, across a range of contexts and racial groups, as well as ways in which white supremacy is maintained institutionally, particularly in educational settings (Rodríguez & Swalwell, 2021).

White preservice teachers often struggle with the very idea of whiteness, resulting in color-evasive racism in which they claim to not see race while simultaneously acting out racist practices (Annamma et al., 2017; Bonilla-Silva, 2010). While there exists a wealth of data demonstrating the vastly inequitable educational outcomes for students of color, teacher candidates may more acutely understand the material impacts of race on educational experiences by exploring individual counternarratives. Young adult fiction like *The Hate U Give* can provide teacher candidates with an in-depth exploration of racialized experiences and perspectives that may be radically different from their own. In addition, complementary picture books can help preservice teachers begin to envision how they might broach issues of race and racism such as those that occur in the young adult novels with young children, particularly in connection to current events that may provide real-world examples of topics present in the texts (Rodríguez & Vickery, 2020; Vickery & Rodríguez, 2020). However, teacher educators must be careful not to sensationalize or exoticize communities of color through this work, and should take time to contextualize relevant histories and allow students multiple opportunities for reflection and connection to other topics in education (Rodriguez et al., 2020).

The ongoing, interactive nature of racial literacy (Guinier, 2004) should demand that all of us—teacher candidates, inservice teachers, and teacher educators alike—are constantly becoming more literate in our understandings of race and experiential positioning. Ultimately, racial literacy must be coupled with anti-racist pedagogy to achieve the kinds of dispositions needed for future and current teachers to interpret racialized practices and imagine possibilities for racial justice (Falkner, 2019). In the words of Tupac Shakur, whose music and poetry flow throughout *The Hate U Give*, we gotta make a change.

This study was funded by the Iowa State University College of Human Sciences Miller Faculty Fellowship.

## REFERENCES

Ahmed, S. K. (2018). *Being the change: Lessons and strategies to teach social comprehension*. Heinemann.

Anderson, C. (2016). *White rage: The unspoken truth of our racial divide*. Bloomsbury.

Annamma, S. A., Jackson, D. D., & Morrison, D. (2017). Conceptualizing color-evasiveness: Using dis/ability critical race theory to expand a color-blind racial ideology in education and society. *Race Ethnicity and Education, 20*(2), 147–162.

Baldwin, J. (1985). *The price of the ticket: Collected nonfiction, 1948–1985*. Macmillan.

Bolick, C. M., Adams, R., & Willox, L. (2010). The marginalization of elementary social studies in teacher education. *Social Studies Research and Practice*, *5*(2), 1–22.

Bonilla-Silva, E. (2010). *Racism without racists: Color-blind racism and the persistence of racial inequality in the United States* (Vol. 3). Rowman & Littlefield.

DiAngelo, R. (2018). *White fragility: Why it's so hard for white people to talk about racism*. Beacon Press.

Ebarvia, T., Parker, K., & Schmidt, P. S. (2018). Carpe librum: Seize the (YA) book. *English Journal*, *107*(5), 92–95.

Epstein, T., & Gist, C. (2015). Teaching racial literacy in secondary humanities classrooms: Challenging adolescents' of color concepts of race and racism. *Race Ethnicity and Education*, *18*(1), 40–60.

Falkner, A. (2019). "They need to say sorry": Anti-racism in first graders' racial learning. *Journal of Curriculum, Teaching, Learning and Leadership in Education*, *4*(2), 37.

Flynn, J. E., Worden, L. J., & Rolón-Dow, R. (2018). The responsibilities of white teacher candidates and teacher educators in developing racial literacy. *Multicultural Perspectives*, *20*(4), 240–246.

Goldenberg, B. M. (2014). White teachers in urban classrooms: Embracing non-white students' cultural capital for better teaching and learning. *Urban Education*, *49*(1), 111–144.

Gomez, B. (2018, September 6). Banned spotlight: *The hate u give*. https://banned booksweek.org/banned-spotlight-the-hate-u-give/

Guinier, L. (2004). From racial liberalism to racial literacy: *Brown v. Board of Education* and the interest-divergence dilemma. *The Journal of American History*, *91*(1), 92–118.

Hawkman, A. M., Castro, A. J., Bennett, L. B., & Barrow, L. H. (2015). Where is the content?: Elementary social studies in preservice field experiences. *The Journal of Social Studies Research*, *39*(4), 197–206.

Kellner, D. (2000). New technologies/new literacies: Reconstructing education for the new millennium. *Teaching Education*, *11*(3), 245–265.

Kendi, I. X. (2017). *Stamped from the beginning: The definitive history of racist ideas in America*. Random House.

King, L. J. (2016). Teaching black history as a racial literacy project. *Race Ethnicity and Education*, *19*(6), 1303–1318.

Lensmire, T., McManimon, S., Tierney, J. D., Lee-Nichols, M., Casey, Z., Lensmire, A., & Davis, B. (2013). McIntosh as synecdoche: How teacher education's focus on white privilege undermines antiracism. *Harvard Educational Review*, *83*(3), 410–431.

Love, B. L. (2019). *We want to do more than survive: Abolitionist teaching and the pursuit of educational freedom*. Beacon Press.

National Center for Education Statistics. (2017). *Number, highest degree, and years of teaching experience of teachers in public and private elementary and secondary schools, by selected teacher characteristics: Selected years, 1999–2000 through 2015–16*. https://nces.ed.gov/programs/digest/d17/tables/dt17_209.20.asp

Picower, B. (2021). *Reading, writing, and racism: Disrupting whiteness in teacher education and in the classroom*. Beacon Press.

Rodríguez, N., Brown, M., & Vickery, A. (2020). Pinning for profit? Examining elementary preservice teachers' critical analysis of online social studies resources about Black history. *Contemporary Issues in Technology and Teacher Education, 20*(3).

Rodríguez, N. N. & Swalwell, K. (2021). *Social studies for a better world: An anti-oppressive approach for elementary educators.* W. W. Norton.

Rodríguez, N. N. & Vickery, A. E. (2020). Much bigger than a hamburger: Problematizing picturebook depictions of youth activism in the Civil Rights Movement. *International Journal of Multicultural Education, 22*(2), 109–128.

Rogers, R., & Mosley, M. (2006). Racial literacy in a second-grade classroom: Critical race theory, whiteness studies, and literacy research. *Reading Research Quarterly, 41*(4), 462–495.

Saldaña, J. (2015). *The coding manual for qualitative researchers.* Sage.

Sealey-Ruiz, Y., & Greene, P. (2015). Popular visual images and the (mis)reading of Black male youth: A case for racial literacy in urban preservice teacher education. *Teaching Education, 26*(1), 55–76.

Skerrett, A. (2011). English teachers' racial literacy knowledge and practice. *Race Ethnicity and Education, 14*(3), 313–330.

Skerrett, A., Pruitt, A. A., & Warrington, A. S. (2015). Racial and related forms of specialist knowledge on English education blogs. *English Education, 47*(4), 314–346.

Sleeter, C. E. (2001). Preparing teachers for culturally diverse schools: Research and the overwhelming presence of whiteness. *Journal of Teacher Education, 52*(2), 94–106.

Sue, D. W. (2016). *Race talk and the conspiracy of silence: Understanding and facilitating difficult dialogues on race.* John Wiley & Sons.

Takaki, R. (2012). *A different mirror for young people: A history of multicultural America.* Seven Stories Press.

Thomas, A. (2017). *The hate u give.* HarperCollins.

VanSledright, B. (2008). Narratives of nation-state, historical knowledge, and school history education. *Review of Research in Education, 32*(1), 109–146.

Vickery, A. E. & Rodríguez, N. N. (2020). "A woman question and a race problem": Attending to intersectionality in children's literature about women in the long civil rights movement. *The Social Studies,* 1–6.

Winans, A. E. (2010). Cultivating racial literacy in white, segregated settings: Emotions as site of ethical engagement and inquiry. *Curriculum Inquiry, 40*(3), 475–491.

# Part III

# RACIAL LITERACY AND STUDENT LEARNING

## CHAPTER 6

# The National Curriculum of Whiteness Created by Our Public Spaces

*Karen L. B. Burgard*

Trips to historic sites and museums that are outside of the traditional class-room often provide meaningful learning experiences that are hands-on, engaging, and experiential in nature. The visitors to these sites can spend a few hours traveling back in time through personal letters and records, artifacts, photographs and images, newspapers, audio recordings, and a host of other primary sources they may encounter. Much has been written about the positive impact museum learning can have (Bidgood et al., 2017; Bromwich, 2017; Fischer et al., 2017; Foner, 2017; Forest et al., 2004; Glassberg, 1996; Handler & Gable, 1997; Hollaway, 2017; Inwood, 2012; Inwood & Alderman, 2016; Kutner, 2017; Mahoney, 2015; McCrummen & Izadi, 2015; Namakkal, 2015; National Trust for Historic Preservation, 2017; Rockeymoore, 2017; Silverman, 2011; Tyner et al., 2014), but while these sites present important nontraditional learning spaces, the story typically presented perpetuates whiteness to the diminishment or exclusion of all others who contributed to the history presented (Inwood, 2012; Inwood & Alderman, 2016). As stated in previous work, when taken in their totality, America's public heritage sites, including historic museums, landmarks, monuments, and commemoration sites, create spaces where national historic memory is passed on for decades. However, these sites also present a unified curriculum of whiteness; specifically, white male supremacy, white innocence, whiteness as civilization, continual American advancement, and white normality (Burgard & Boucher, 2016).

This curriculum plays out in most public spaces but is expressed in its most aggressive stance in the monuments to Confederate soldiers and generals and the Lost Cause narratives (for example, that the Civil War was not fought over slavery, but rather a stand against an oppressive government) in those public spaces. This chapter explores the origins, implementation, and impact of that curriculum. By deconstructing these spaces and their artifacts as curriculum, educators can teach students to view them more critically and recognize the need to dismantle and replace them with a more holistic, au-thentic, and accurate narrative.

To understand the significant impact historic sites and museums have on our national narrative, we must first begin to view the material presented there as *curriculum*. When confined to a classroom in a school building, it is understood that there is a particular curriculum presented to the students. This curriculum appears in the textbooks students receive, the selected readings for the course, the curricular and pedagogical choices each teacher makes, and even the stories teachers choose to use as examples in their classroom. Acknowledging there is indeed a definite curriculum within a classroom is not difficult for most to accept. Scholars and the public conceptually grasp that curriculum is taught in a school. When that concept of curriculum shifts to a public space open to all, however, that complicates the facile definition of what curriculum is and what it does.

## HOW WE SEE THE PAST IS HOW WE SEE OURSELVES

Throughout the American South, there are currently over 100 schools named after Robert E. Lee and other Confederate generals. What makes this even more troubling is that in many cases, the student populations in these schools are comprised largely of students of color. These students are subjected to icons promoting generals and soldiers who fought to keep the institution of slavery and inflicted cruelty and horrors on enslaved African Americans. The Southern Poverty Law Center (SPLC) found, ". . . there are at least 109 public schools named after Robert E. Lee, Jefferson Davis or other Confederate icons in the United States. Of those, 27 have student populations that are majority African-American, and 10 have African-American populations of over 90 percent" (Holland, 2017). This cognitive dissonance by school administrators, or perhaps more aptly a genuine denial that the naming of these schools presents any problems for their students, is forcing the issue to the forefront.

### The School Name Debate

The debate around the use of Confederate names is deeper than just who should or should not be named in a community. Throughout history, the act of naming a building is a placement of an identification marker meant to show the world what a community values, its identity, and who it aspires to be. These markers are icons used to teach future generations the remembrances of the builders. Those whom we revere and emulate are memorialized in our public spaces. When those memorials are created specifically to suppress the truth and lift up oppressors, a community must decide what matters—the people or the icon. Memorials to the Confederacy are now under scrutiny and communities are faced with decisions. As Taft explained,

> Though the particulars differ, the fundamental issues at stake in each community are the same. How should we evaluate historical figures? Who is entitled to make

those evaluations? Where is the line between remembering and commemorating? Can society repudiate the Confederacy but still decorate public spaces with allusions to its heroes? And in every case, battles over school name changes have been fraught and emotional, sometimes leading to allegations on both sides of bullying, rescinded birthday party invitations and grocery store parking lot confrontations. (Taft, 2016)

In the fall of 2018, after years of debate and several attempts, Legacy of Educational Excellence (L.E.E.) High School welcomed students for a new school year. To an outside observer, this might have looked like a typical first day of the fall semester in an American high school. Students' cars and school buses were in the parking lot, hallways were filled with hundreds of students with backpacks moving to their lockers, and teachers anxiously awaited their new students. What that observer might not know is that the name L.E.E. High School had gone through quite a transformation over the past decade, with San Antonio community members engaged in almost always emotional, sometimes heated, debates on whether to change the original name of the school, Robert E. Lee High School, named after the Confederate general.

Robert E. Lee High School, one of over three dozen schools within the state of Texas named after Confederate soldiers and generals, was founded in 1958 on the north side of the multiracial, multi-ethnic city of San Antonio. Each day Black and Brown students entered through the front doors and walked past an 8-foot bronze statue of Lee and mosaics and memorabilia commemorating the Confederate general. Each day was a renewed reminder that commemorating the story of the Lost Cause was more important than being a welcoming place where all students felt safe and valued. In 2016, when the topic of changing the name of the school was discussed, many San Antonio citizens had strong opinions.

> Oliver Hill, 81, grew up in segregated San Antonio. He graduated in 1952 from the all-black Phillis Wheatley High School, named for the famous poet who was brought to America as a slave. When Robert E. Lee High School opened across town in 1958 honoring the Confederate general, Hill viewed the name as a deliberate reminder to black San Antonians that the city did not belong to them . . . "They haven't walked in my shoes," Hill said of those who wanted to keep Lee's name. "They don't understand what I go through when I walk past those things." (Taft, 2016)

However, there were many within the district who wanted to keep the name in its original form, arguing that Lee was a part of Texas history, as Texas was a member of the Confederacy, and thus changing the name would be denying their state's past:

> Watching her son play on the field below, Tiffany Laney said she didn't have a problem with his school being called Robert E. Lee. "Personally, I felt like the

name change shouldn't have even took place. I mean, the money could have went to better resources . . . I see where people thought it was kind of inappropriate because the south owned the slaves and everything. But I also think they shouldn't have changed the name to begin with because it's part of history. You can't change it." (Phillips, 2018)

Emotions ran high throughout the years-long debate, but when the dust finally settled, the decision to finally change the name did little to change much at all. Instead of opting for a completely new name, with no connection or remembrance to the previous one, the school decided on the name Legacy of Educational Excellence (acronym L.E.E.), essentially leaving the school's name, and how it was identified in the community, the same. To many, this demonstrated a weak compromise by the school board and district personnel that still provided a painful reminder of the original man commemorated at that site. The administration, however, argued that the new L.E.E. High School had a completely new focus, changing their mascot and dance team names, removing the Lee statue and other Lee commemorative items from the entryway, housing them in a school museum, and auctioning off surplus Robert E. Lee High School memorabilia (Donaldson, 2018; Karacostas, 2018; Phillips, 2018; Sauers, 2019; Toppo, 2017).

## The Fight Around Monuments Turns Deadly

The fight around the memories and who should be lifted up as heroes has escalated over the past few years. Currently, schools and public buildings with names and references to Confederate generals are eclipsed only by the number of Confederate monuments and statues dedicated to the same people. These monuments are scattered throughout the United States, but most visibly in the American South. In 2017, Heather Heyer fell victim to this extreme devotion to white supremacy. Heyer, a white, unarmed anti-racist protester in Charlottesville, Virginia, was murdered, and several others were beaten and injured, by admitted white supremacists seeking to defend a statue. This was the horrific conclusion to a shocking rally that was termed Unite the Right by a collection of white nationalist groups hoping to pull together as a political and social movement.

The University of Virginia (UVA), located in Charlottesville, was established and designed by Thomas Jefferson, the writer of the Declaration of Independence and third president of the United States. However, despite Jefferson's foundational pronouncement that it was self-evident that "all men are created equal," his university also stood in Virginia, the state that propagated the very general who fought against his countrymen in the hope that Jefferson's ideals would never be a reality for all. Since its early years, UVA has been a center of defiance against racial equality. UVA's history of segregation and identity as a defender of the Lost Cause is deeply embedded in the ethos of the university (Schmidt & von Daacke, 2019). For example, a survey of the University of Virginia publication, *UVA Today*, showed that the campus has a history steeped in racism and that racist incidents and mentality have continued into the 21st century:

> Contemporary news headlines show that these old models of racist expression did not disappear at the University in the middle of the 20th century. They remained a recurring theme in social events, if not printed regularly in student publications as they had been in earlier years. Fraternities and sororities continued to hold parties honoring an imagined "plantation" past steeped in Lost Cause mythologizing for decades. In 1959 and again in 1971, staged protest lynchings-in-effigy that included blackface appear in student publications. As recently as 2002, a costume party at the University involved students appearing in blackface. Other forms of racial or ethnic stereotyping and cultural appropriation have occurred as recently as the beginning of the 2019 spring semester, when images circulated depicting students inappropriately wearing Native American and other attire. These serve as a powerful reminder that modes of expression rooted in older white supremacist ways of thinking persist even today. (Schmidt & von Daacke, 2019)

The university curriculum of the Lost Cause and white supremacy is seen throughout campus, including reenactments, themed parties, names on buildings, plaques, and public art. These icons keep the myth of an enlightened, civilized Confederacy alive generation after generation, obscuring the truth and celebrating what should be shameful. And while the events of 2017 did not happen expressly on the UVA campus, the longstanding history of both overt and covert racism that exists on the campus even today provide a window into the larger surrounding Charlottesville community.

In 2016, Charlottesville's city leadership tried to come to a reckoning with its past. In Charlottesville, a statue of Robert E. Lee astride a horse towered 26 feet in the air, centering a park that also bore his name. The statue was dedicated in 1924 and was placed on the National Register of Historic Places in 1997. The city council voted unanimously to remove the Lee statue and rename the park Emancipation Park. The white nationalists' response became the coalescing force for the Unite the Right rally a year later. To kick off the event, a nighttime Nazi-style torchlit parade was held on August 11, 2017. The participants marched around the statue of Lee declaring, "Jews will not replace us" (Gray, 2017). The next day was to be a daytime parade, but this time, Americans from all over the country came to Charlottesville to stand up to the white nationalists. The battle that ensued between anti-racists, antifa (an anti-fascist organization that is not committed to nonviolence), and other motivated citizens against armed white nationalists clad in military gear and carrying various flags including swastikas and the Confederate battle flag ended with multiple injuries and the death of Ms. Heyer, who was run over by a car driven at high speed into the crowd by a Unite the Right participant.

After prodding from the media, Donald Trump spoke empathetically, not about those hurt and killed, but rather about the Nazis and white supremacists who perpetrated the crimes. He said that the marchers had valid reasons for wanting to defend Confederate monuments, as they were merely protecting history and that "the press has treated them absolutely unfairly" (Gray, 2017). He then added a caveat intended to show his even-handed treatment befitting the office, stating, "You also had some very fine people [pause] on both sides" (Gray, 2017).

The message from our highest office in the land was that the actions of white supremacists are well intentioned and well reasoned, and therefore acceptable, even when they brutalize and kill. The Trump administration's failure to immediately reproach the actions of the Unite the Right members placed substantial weight behind the white supremacist narrative of history they were aiming for.

In both examples, L.E.E. High School and Charlottesville, people clung to the historic myth of Robert E. Lee and commemorated him, further crystalizing the curriculum of white supremacy into our national memory. The significance of this school naming debate highlights the larger discussion concerning public memory and historical narratives—whose history is told and whose history is preserved in a local community. In San Antonio, removing the statue and artifacts and changing the mascot were movements toward healing wounds inflicted upon communities of color, but keeping the name of the school itself as L.E.E. High School allowed the white supremacist narrative to continue. Cowing to outside pressures permitted the community to continue calling the school, in essence, Lee and allowed the commemoration of the general to persist. The events in Charlottesville—the rally itself with the expressed mission of protecting the Confederate general's statue, the terrorizing and threatening behavior by rally participants, and the president providing legitimacy and credibility to white supremacists—provided a national stage for the support of a national whiteness curriculum (Serwer, 2017).

## WHITENESS CURRICULUM AND PUBLIC HISTORY

Historic sites and public spaces have a curricular purpose. The artifacts and primary documents selected become our national story, with heroes and villains, challenges and conquests. More than any book or documentary, the history presented at historic sites and museums becomes our inherited national curriculum, passed down through generations. It becomes *our nation's story*.

All public heritage sites—be they historical museums, historic landmarks and markers, or commemoration sites—provide a framed image of the past. All sites focus on some aspects and exclude others to orient the viewer to the narrative provided by the curators, donors, or creators of the site. The intent of these spaces is to craft and cultivate the national historical memory. They provide a curriculum that teaches the visitors about the past and therein helps to create the historical constructs they hold regarding our national narrative. Curricular choices made by museum personnel present the historical narratives to further a framed story of the past. Taken in sum, these sites weave a tapestry that portrays the nation's memory. Historians and public heritage researchers have long understood this; however, these scholars are often missing the pedagogical and curricular context in these sites and the importance of evaluating the sites and challenging the narratives therein (Burgard, 2019, 2020a, 2020b; Burgard & Boucher, 2018). To see how this national curriculum operates, we must investigate how people understand history as a discipline.

## Making Sense of the Past

The ways in which people make sense of history, the development and deepening of their historical understanding, has more than three decades of examination (Barton, 2001a, 2001b, 2004, 2005; Barton & Levstik, 2004; Marcus, 2007; Mayer, 2006; Schocker, 2014; Seixas, 1994, 2000; Stearns et al., 2000; Vansledright, 2004; Vansledright & Afflerbach, 2000; Wineburg, 2001). Viewing the basic tenets of historical understanding through the lens of race, culture, ethnicity, and heritage provides us with an even more nuanced and complex understanding of our nation's historical narrative. Current research has found that our personal experiences, background, cultural and ethnic heritage, and racial identity all play a role in how we view the past (Burgard & Boucher, 2016, 2018; Epstein, 1998, 2000, 2001, 2009; Epstein & Shiller, 2015; Howard, 2004; Terzian & Yeager, 2007; Trainor, 2005). This racialized historical understanding is particularly important as it extends to historic sites, monuments, and other public spaces. Over the past 15 years, researchers have noted that meaningful learning can and does take place in historical sites and museums (Baron, 2012; Dean, 2013; DeWitt & Hohenstein, 2010; Evans, 2013; Falk & Dierking, 2000; Foreman-Peck & Travers, 2013; Gallas & Perry, 2015; Hooper-Greenhill, 2007; Lewis, 2005; Loewen, 2007a; Marcus & Levine, 2011; Marcus et al., 2012; Marcus et al., 2017; Rose, 2016; Segall, 2014; Wood & Wolf, 2008; Woods, 1995; Wunder, 2002). It has been established that visitors *are* learning. Now it is time to look at *what* they are learning and how to deconstruct that learning. By extension, people of color and other marginalized groups will interpret the information they see, read, and hear at public history sites in ways markedly different than those of their white counterparts (Burgard & Boucher, 2016).

If we make the argument that our historical museums, historic sites, national monuments, national landmarks, and markers all contribute to our national memory and help to create our national narratives, then we must also make the argument that this memory is being constructed using an incomplete and inadequate view of the past. Consequently, the whitening of our past and the erasure of all others hurts every visitor to historic sites in that the contributions of marginalized people are missing in these narratives, perpetuating stereotypes, biases, and ignorance. Using a racial literacy lens and building upon the work of racial literacy educational scholars (Epstein & Gist, 2015; King, 2016; King et al., 2018; Smith & Crowley, 2018), we have a responsibility to challenge these public sites and acknowledge that historical erasure is as present in these spaces as it is in classroom textbooks. At public heritage sites, people of color often do not hear their history told, or if they do, the story is one of an add-on or ancillary roles, making the national curriculum of whiteness all the more salient.

## Historical Erasure in the Discipline of History

Historical erasure is often present in classroom narratives the teachers provide, classroom curriculum materials, and the stories in our school textbooks (Alridge, 2006; Foster, 1999; Garcia, 1993; Hall, 2008; Hawkman, 2018; Lee, 2017; Loewen, 2007b; Santiago, 2017; Sehgal, 2016; Takaki, 2008; Woodson, 2015, 2017; Zinn, 2005). These studies show that students view classroom textbooks as authoritative and therefore do not question the information presented there, so when whiteness becomes the norm in the classroom, and the decisions and choices of white people become the example for progress and advancement, others are erased from the story altogether.

A key component to creating and perpetuating a white supremacist curriculum is to establish the narrative that only white men of power are worthy of having their history told and that all others are merely background or scenery to their exploits. Historical erasure organizes our historical narratives to perpetuate the idea that the contributions of white people, and even more specifically white males, are more significant than those of all other groups. It intentionally diminishes the contributions of people of color, Indigenous peoples, women, and all other marginalized groups (Burgard & Boucher, 2016, 2018; Sehgal, 2016). However, historical erasure is more than simply eliminating the stories of others and amplifying the stories of white people. It is the intentional design of centering white people in all narratives. It associates the experiences of white people as the norm and all others as diverse. Erasure establishes whiteness, defines normalcy, and decides that what is not white is unworthy of historical memory.

Sehgal (2016) explained that "'Erasure' refers to the practice of collective indifference that renders certain people and groups invisible . . . to dismiss inconvenient facts and is increasingly used to describe how inconvenient people are dismissed, their history, pain and achievements are blotted out" (para. 3).

Erasure also establishes a white progressive narrative that defines progress as white dominance over people of color and their lands. Settlement is the creation of white spaces. Civilization is the creation of white-run governments and economies where people of color are excluded. Colonization, settlement, and civilization, then, are all perceived as the progression of white people across the land and the establishment of whiteness. The erasure of others in the narrative emphasizes white goodness, inherent honesty, responsibility, hard work, and/or preferential treatment in all spaces. It also demands counterfactual narratives of white innocence and erases white complicity in historical conflicts.

Erasure does immense damage to students of color. Not seeing or reading about the history of their community and their culture can have a profoundly negative impact on their self-esteem and can affect their overall engagement in school. Historical erasure also damages the white students, making them oblivious to the contributions of their classmates and fellow citizens. For too many, that ignorance follows them for the rest of their lives.

## THE WHITE SUPREMACIST CURRICULUM
## OF CONFEDERATE SITES

The curriculum of white supremacy is seen in many of our national historic sites and landmarks, but perhaps none more belligerently than the Confederate monuments and sites erected to commemorate Confederate soldiers and generals. From the extant literature, we can discern the themes across sites pointing to their purpose: to provide a perspective based on white supremacy and white normality (Southern Poverty Law Center, 2019).

### Original Purpose and Construction of the Sites

In a nationwide survey, the Southern Poverty Law Center (SPLC) identified an extraordinary 1,747 Confederate monuments, place names, and other symbols in public spaces, both in the South and across the nation, even in places outside the former confederacy. These include:

> 780 monuments, more than 300 of which are in Georgia, Virginia or North Carolina; 103 public K–12 schools and three colleges named for Robert E. Lee, Jefferson Davis or other Confederate icons; 80 counties and cities named for Confederates; 9 observed state holidays in five states; and 10 U.S. Military bases. (SPLC, 2019)

Most of the monuments were placed by groups who sought to reclaim and reshape the history of the Civil War, not as a war to oppress and keep others in bondage, as was the reason stated in several declarations of independence by Southern states, but as a glorious fight for freedom in the best spirit of Americanism.

***United Daughters of the Confederacy.*** One group that had the purpose and function of reifying the white supremacist lens at the past and attempted to shape how the Civil War was presented in history books was the United Daughters of the Confederacy (UDC). They worked to establish a historical narrative that presented the Confederate states during the Civil War in a positive light, and those who fought for the Confederacy as noble warriors fighting for a meaningful cause as seen in manuals (referred to as a catechism) for young children that honored Confederate generals and soldiers and championed the Lost Cause (Encyclopedia Virginia, 2018). In addition to this explicit mode of passing on an intentionally distorted view of the South during the Civil War, one that directly perpetuated white supremacist ideology, the UDC also raised funds to establish numerous Confederate monuments around the country commemorating Confederate generals and soldiers and championing their cause.

As historian Karen Cox explained:

> The UDC and other like-minded heritage organizations were intent on honoring the Confederate generation and establishing a revisionist history of what they called the War Between the States. According to this Lost Cause mythology, the South went to war to defend states' rights, slavery was essentially a benevolent institution that imparted Christianity to African "savages," and, while the Confederates were defeated, theirs was a just cause and those who fought were heroes. The Daughters regarded the Ku Klux Klan, which had been founded to resist Reconstruction, as a heroic organization, necessary to return order to the South. Order, of course, meant the use of violence to subdue newly freed blacks. (Cox, 2021)

As the 20th century began, the United Daughters of the Confederacy began a successful campaign to build monuments throughout the South and to reshape the American memory around the Civil War (Cox, 2021).

**Intimidation and Fear.** In addition to those wishing to write a very particular and self-congratulatory version of history, the Confederate monuments and statues were also used as a tool for intimidation and fear.

> Almost none of the monuments were put up right after the Civil War. Some were erected during the civil rights era of the early 1960s, which coincided with the war's centennial, but the vast majority of monuments date to between 1895 and World War I. They were part of a campaign to paint the Southern cause in the Civil War as just and slavery as a benevolent institution, and their installation came against a backdrop of Jim Crow violence and oppression of African Americans. The monuments were put up as explicit symbols of white supremacy. (Cox, 2021)

The statues provided a visual reminder to all African Americans that their town's leaders believed they should be oppressed and marginalized and that their rights and humanity would not be honored or protected. As African Americans walked past these numerous statues, erected in city squares, in parks, and in city buildings and state houses, they were acutely aware of the message intended.

## The Current Calls for Removal

Recently, we have seen a national call for the removal of statues and monuments dedicated to Confederate generals and all those who fought for the South during the Civil War grow stronger every year. The national conversation regarding race, race relations, and the treatment of people of color in America has brought about this change. After the 2015 Charleston, South Carolina massacre where nine African Americans churchgoers were gunned down during Bible study by white nationalist Dylan Roof at the historic Mother Emanuel Church, more than 100 monuments and other symbols of the Confederacy were removed from U.S public spaces. Roof had engaged in racist rhetoric on the Internet and had posed with the Confederate battle flag, the same flag that flew atop the statehouse in South Carolina and is a part of the state flag of Mississippi.

Later that year, activist Bree Newsome scaled the South Carolina statehouse with climbing gear and tore down the Confederate flag. She was arrested and her courageous action became a symbol for what many were calling for—the removal of the icons of hatred, fear, and intimidation. When asked why she did it, she explained that it was in response to the murders at the Charleston church:

> "A white man had just entered a black church and massacred people as they prayed. He had assassinated a civil rights leader. This was not a page in a textbook I was reading nor an inscription on a monument I was visiting," Newsome wrote. "This was now. This was real. This was—this is—still happening . . . You see, I know my history and my heritage," Newsome continued. "The Confederacy is neither the only legacy of the south nor an admirable one. The southern heritage I embrace is the legacy of a people unbowed by racial oppression . . . We made this decision because for us, this is not simply about a flag, but rather it is about abolishing the spirit of hatred and oppression in all its forms," Newsome added. (Phillip, 2015)

While Newsome's act of civil disobedience and protest was covered nationally, it was not the first. Cities throughout the United States have struggled for years with what to do with sites and monuments, and several are in the process of removal or had already been removed before that day Newsome climbed up to remove the flag. However, her actions and call for equality and justice inspired many to also take a stand, and this chorus has grown increasingly louder.

In statehouses and town halls across the American South, proponents argue that leaving those icons teaches the mistakes of the past. However, with few exceptions, the symbols stay in place with no critical discussion or discourse. Keeping the statues of General Lee and other Confederate generals and soldiers in public spaces and allowing their names to remain on school-house doors and public buildings further entrenches the Lost Cause national curriculum.

Texas is second to Virginia in the number of Confederate monuments. There were over 200 in the state, but 35 have been removed since 2000, mostly from the state's largest population centers, where people of color have brought the issue to officials (SPLC, 2019). In reaction to calls for their removal, states legislatures took up bills to protect all monuments from destruction unless the state legislature approved it. In 2019, the Texas legislature approved such a bill, and the debate took a turn toward acknowledging that the statues are meant to be curriculum. Brandon Burkhart, president of This Is Texas Freedom Force, argued that taking down monuments would be tantamount to an "assault on Texas history." He said that "The monuments are there for us to learn from. It's part of our history, no matter how you want to teach your child or teach future generations from it. History isn't always glorious. It can be ugly and violent at times, but it's still our history" (Samuels, 2019).

Even if we take Mr. Burkhart and others who oppose the removal of Confederate monuments at their word, that they are genuinely interested in preserving history, one must ask, "What history is intended to be preserved?" The Confederate monuments celebrate and honor soldiers and generals who fought for the practice of owning other human beings, and the sites were constructed to intimidate Black men and women seeking justice.

Other cities have also faced removing Confederate icons. In March 2017, the New Orleans City Council voted to remove four Confederate statues, declaring them a public nuisance (Wendland, 2017). The removals included the Liberty Place monument commemorating the Reconstruction Era, a bronze statue of Jefferson Davis, a statue of General P. G. T. Beauregard, and the final statue of General Robert E. Lee (Wendland, 2017).

"Statue supporters say they represent an important part of the state's identity and culture—but in a city where 60 percent of the residents are African-American, many see the monuments as an offensive celebration of the Confederacy and the system of slavery it sought to preserve" (Wendland, 2017, para. 4).

Later that same year, in the summer of 2017, after the horrors that transpired in Charlottesville, Baltimore mayor Catherine Pugh ordered the removal of Confederate monuments, stating that doing so was "in the best interest of my city" (Fandos et al., 2017). Many other city leaders throughout the United States, in particular cities in the South, are faced with these same challenges.

This nationwide movement to trouble and disrupt the national whiteness curriculum has undeniably been transferred to buildings named after the Confederacy (Bradham, 2018; Fink, 2019; Holland, 2017; Little, 2018; Remnick, 2017; Selk, 2017; Taft, 2016; Thomsen, 2015; Wang & Svrluga 2017, *Yale News*, 2017). Parents, students, and local community members are challenging the notion that places where Confederate generals are celebrated and commemorated should be places and structures of learning. People are coming forward to argue that to create a safe, embracing, and welcoming place for all students, we must first look at the name on the front of the building. By having our students of color walk into a building named after, and walk past a statue erected to honor, avowed white supremacist Confederates, we are subjecting them not only to unjust treatment and an unwelcome environment, but also teaching them that American history is done to them, not with them, and that the losers still become the winners if they are white.

## CHALLENGING THE CURRICULUM PRESENTED AT HISTORIC SITES

It is our responsibility as educators, as public intellectuals, as citizens of democracy, to understand the power that the curriculum of public spaces has on our national story. Those public sites create the historical narrative that tells the story of our nation and its peoples. If that story perpetuates a white supremacist narrative and omits the contributions of all other peoples, educators have a responsibility to challenge that narrative and present a more accurate and inclusive story. Questioning accepted narratives can increase historical understanding. This is crucial if students are to trouble white supremacist narratives. To do so, they will be challenging the narratives that are taught through these spaces and going against the accepted versions of events in some cases. Curriculum is not neutral, but ideological in nature, and laden with unquestioned suppositions about how the world works. We can challenge the narrative. We can write a different story, a more complete story. This is true of statues, monuments, and other historic sites and public spaces, but it is also true of the names on school buildings, parks, and other places where people gather and share common space.

## REFERENCES

Alridge, D. (2006). The limits of master narratives in history textbooks: An analysis of representations of Martin Luther King, Jr. *The Teachers College Record*, *108*(4), 662–686.

Baron, C. (2012). Understanding historical thinking at historic sites. *Journal of Educational Psychology*, *104*(3), 833–847. https://doi:10.1037/a0027476

Barton, K. C. (2001a). A picture's worth: Analyzing historical photographs in the elementary grades. *Social Education*, *65*(5), 278–283.

Barton, K. C. (2001b). A sociocultural perspective on children's understanding of historical change: Comparative findings from Northern Ireland and the United States. *American Educational Research Journal*, *38*(4). 881–913.

Barton, K. C. (2004). Research on students' historical thinking and learning. *Perspectives*, 19–27.

Barton, K. C. (2005). Best not to forget them: Secondary students' judgments of historical significance in Northern Ireland. *Theory & Research in Social Education*, *33*(1), 9–44. https://doi:10.1080/00933104.2005.10473270

Barton, K. C., & Levstik, L. S. (2004). *Teaching history for the common good.* Routledge.

Bidgood, J., Bloch, M., McCarthy, M., & Stack, L. (2017, August 16). Confederate monuments are coming down across the United States. Here's a list. *New York Times.* https://www.nytimes.com/interactive/2017/08/16/us/confederate-monuments-removed.html

Bradham, B. (2018, December 1). Duke to rename Carr Building. *Duke Chronicle.* https://www.dukechronicle.com/article/2018/12/duke-university-renames-carr-building-julian-carr-white-supremacist

Bromwich, J. E. (2017, August 21). University of Texas at Austin removes confederate statues in overnight operation. *New York Times.* https://www.nytimes.com/2017/08/21/us/texas-austin-confederate-statues.html

Burgard, K. (2019). Making the most of field trips to historic museums. *Middle Level Learning, 66,* 19–24.

Burgard, K. (2020a). Constructing deeper meaning: A museum curriculum evaluation framework for students. *Kappa Delta Pi Record, 56*(2), 58–63.

Burgard, K. (2020b). Framework for de-centering whiteness in social studies field trips: Evaluating museums and public sites and the whiteness curriculum. In A. Hawkman & S. Shear, *Marking the invisible: Articulating whiteness in social studies education and research* (pp. 363–385). Information Age Publishing.

Burgard, K., & Boucher, M. L. (2016). Same story; different history: Students' racialized historical understanding of historic sites. *The Urban Review, 48*(5), 696–717. https://doi:10.1007/s11256-016-0374-9

Burgard, K., & Boucher, M. L. (2018). The special responsibility of public spaces to dismantle White supremacist historical narratives. In A. Labrador & N. A. Silberman (Eds.), *The Oxford handbook of public heritage theory and practice* (pp. 239–256). Oxford University Press. https://doi:10.1093/oxfordhb/9780190676315.001.0001

Cox, K. L. (2021, October 28). The whole point of Confederate monuments is to celebrate white supremacy. *The Washington Post.* https://www.washingtonpost.com/news/posteverything/wp/2017/08/16/the-whole-point-of-confederate-monuments-is-to-celebrate-white-supremacy/

Dean, D. (2013). Museums as sites for historical understanding, peace, and social justice: Views from Canada. *Peace and Conflict: Journal of Peace Psychology, 19*(4), 325–337.

DeWitt, J., & Hohenstein, J. (2010). Supporting student learning A comparison of student discussion in museums and classroom. *Visitors Studies, 13*(1), 41–66.

Donaldson, E. (2018, April 03). With name change looming, Lee High School adopts new mascot. *The San Antonio Report.* https://sanantonioreport.org/with-name-change-looming-lee-high-school-adopts-new-mascot

Encyclopedia Virginia. (2018). Primary resource: U.D.C. catechism for children (1904). https://www.encyclopediavirginia.org/Children_U_D_C_Catechism_for_1904

Epstein, T. (1998). Deconstructing differences in African-American and European-American adolescents' perspectives on U.S. history. *Curriculum Inquiry, 28*(4), 397–423.

Epstein, T. (2000). Adolescents' perspectives on racial diversity in U.S. history: Case studies from an urban classroom. *American Educational Research Journal, 37*(1), 185–214.

Epstein, T. (2001). Racial identity and young people's perspectives on social education. *Theory into Practice, 40*(1), 42–47.

Epstein, T. (2009). *Interpreting national history: Race, identity, and pedagogy in classrooms and communities*. Routledge.

Epstein, T., & Gist, C. (2015). Teaching racial literacy in secondary humanities classrooms: Challenging adolescents' of color concepts of race and racism. *Race Ethnicity and Education, 18*(1), 40–60.

Epstein, T., & Shiller, J. (2015). Race, gender, and the teaching and learning of national history. In W. Parker (Eds.), *Social studies today: Research and practice*
(2nd ed., pp. 113–119). Routledge.

Evans, S. (2013). Personal beliefs and national stories: Theater in museums as a tool
for exploring historical memory. *Curator: The Museum Journal, 56*(2), 189–197.
https://doi:10.1111/cura.12019

Falk, J. H., & Dierking, L. D. (2000). *Learning from museums: Visitor experiences
and the making of meaning*. AltaMira Press.

Fandos, N., Goldman, R., & Bidgood, J. (2017, August 16). Baltimore mayor had
statues removed in "best interest of my city." *New York Times*. https://www
.nytimes.com/2017/08/16/us/baltimore-confederate-statues.html

Fink, J. (2019, April 16). Rhodes College renames building honoring confederate pas-
tor who used Bible to justify slavery. *Newsweek*. https://www.newsweek.com
/rhodes-college-renames-building-confederate-pastor-bible-slavery-1398229

Fischer, D., Anali, S., & Moore, P. (2017). Coming together to address systemic racism in museums. *Forum, 60*(1), 23–31.

Foner, E. (2017, August 20). Confederate statues and "our" history. *New York Times*.
https://www.nytimes.com/2017/08/20/opinion/confederate-statues-american
-history.html

Foreman-Peck, L., & Travers, K. (2013). What is distinctive about museum pedagogy and
how can museums best support learning in schools? An action research inquiry into
the practice of three regional museums. *Educational Action Research, 21*(1), 28–41.

Forest, B., Johnson, J. E., & Till, K. (2004). Post-totalitarian national identity: Public
memory in Germany and Russia. *Social and Cultural Geography, 5*(3), 357–580.

Foster, S. J. (1999). The struggle for American identity: Treatment of ethnic groups in
United States history textbooks. *History of Education, 28*(3), 251–278. https://
doi:10.1080/004676099284618

Gallas, K. L., & Perry, J. D. (2015). Developing a comprehensive and conscientious
interpretation of slavery at historic sites and museums. In M. A. Van Balgooy (Ed.),
*Interpreting African American history and culture at museums and historic sites*
(pp. 13–26). Rowman & Littlefield.

Garcia, J. (1993). The changing image of ethnic groups in textbooks. *The Phi Delta
Kappan, 71*(1), 29–35.

Glassberg, D. (1996). Public history and the study of memory. *The Public Historian,
18*(2), 7–23. https://doi:10.2307/3377910.

Gray, R. (2017, August 15). Trump defends white nationalist protesters: "Some very
fine people on both sides." *The Atlantic*. https://www.theatlantic.com/politics
/archive/2017/08/trump-defends-white-nationalist-protesters-some-very-fine
-people-on-both-sides/537012

Hall, L. (2008). Strategies for erasure: U.S. Colonialism and native Hawaiian feminism. *American Quarterly, 60*(2), 273–280.

Handler, R., & Gable, E. (1997). *The new history in an old museum: Creating the past at Colonial Williamsburg*. Duke University Press.

Hawkman, A. (2018). Exposing whiteness in the elementary social studies methods classroom: In pursuit of developing antiracist teacher education candidates. In S. Shear et al. (Eds.), *(Re)Imagining elementary social studies: A controversial issues reader* (pp. 49–71). Information Age Publishing.

Holland, J. J. (2017, August 30). US high schools named after Confederate generals could be forced to rebrand. *The Independent*. https://www.independent.co.uk/news/world/americas/us-high-schools-confederate-generals-identity-new-academic-year-robert-e-lee-stonewall-jackson-a7919676.html

Holloway, K. (2017, May 27). Georgia Civil War museum shuts down rather than surrender its Confederate flags. Salon.com. https://www.salon.com/2017/05/27/georgia-civil-war-museum-shuts-down-rather-than-surrender-its-confederate-flags_partner

Hooper-Greenhill, E. (2007). *Museums and education: Purpose, pedagogy, performance*. Routledge.

Howard, T. C. (2004). "Does race really matter?" Secondary students' constructions of racial dialogue in the social studies. *Theory & Research in Social Education, 32*(4), 484–502.

Inwood, J. F. (2012). The politics of being sorry: The Greensboro truth process and efforts at restorative justice. *Social and Cultural Geography, 56*(1), 9–15.

Inwood, J. F., & Alderman, D. (2016). Taking down the flag is just a start: Toward the memory-work of racial reconciliation in White supremacist America. *Southeastern Geographer, 56*(1), 9–15. https://doi:10.1353/sgo.2016.0003

Karacostas, C. (2018, July 10). NEISD to auction off Robert E. Lee High School memorabilia. *mySA*. https://www.mysanantonio.com/news/local/article/NEISD-to-auction-off-Robert-E-Lee-High-School-13063330.php#photo-8713384

King, L. J. (2016). Teaching black history as a racial literacy project. *Race Ethnicity and Education, 19*(6), 1303–1318.

King, L. J., Vickery, A., & Caffrey, G. (2018). A pathway to racial literacy: Using the LETS ACT framework to teach controversial issues. *Social Education, 82*(6), 316–322.

Kutner, M. (2017, August 16). *Newsweek*. Where do Confederate statues go after they're removed? http://www.newsweek.com/where-do-confederate-statues-go-when-theyre-removed-650698

Lee, E. (2017, March 16). Why are Asian Americans missing from our textbooks? *Pacific Standard*. https://psmag.com/news/why-are-asian-americans-missing-from-our-textbooks

Lewis, C. M. (2005). *The changing face of public history: The Chicago Historical Society and the transformation of an American museum*. Northern Illinois University Press.

Little, B. (2018, June 21). *Not just monuments: Schools named after Confederates are rebranding*. The History Channel. https://www.history.com/news/confederate-school-names-changing

Loewen, J. W. (2007a). *Lies across America: What our historic sites get wrong*. Simon & Schuster.

Loewen, J. W. (2007b). *Lies my teacher told me: Everything your American history textbook got wrong*. Touchstone.

Mahoney, S. (2015). "Faced with courage": Interpreting and presenting sites of African American heritage to the public. *Conservation and Management of Archaeological Sites, 17*(1), 56–66.

Marcus, A. (2007). *Celluloid blackboard*. Information Age Publishing.

Marcus, A. S., & Levine, T. H. (2011). Knight at the museum: Learning history with museums. *The Social Studies*, *102*(3), 104–109.

Marcus, A. S., Levine, T. H., & Grenier, R. S. (2012). How secondary history teachers use and think about museums: Current practices and untapped promise for promoting historical understanding. *Theory & Research in Social Education*, *40*(1), 66–97. https://doi:10.1080/00933104.2012.649466

Marcus, A. S., Stoddard, J. D., & Woodward, W. W. (2017). *Teaching history with museums: Strategies for K-12 social studies*. Routledge.

Mayer, R. H. (2006). Learning to teach young people how to think historically: A case study of one student teacher's experience. *The Social Studies*, *97*(2), 69–76. https://doi:10.3200/tsss.97.2.69-76

McCrummen, S., & Izadi, E. (2015, July 10). Confederate flag comes down on South Carolina's statehouse grounds. *Washington Post*. https://www.washingtonpost.com/news/post-nation/wp/2015/07/10/watch-live-as-the-confederate-flag-comes-down-in-south-carolina

Namakkal, J. (2015, June 26). Re-naming as decolonization. *Counter Punch*. https://www.counterpunch.org/2015/06/26/re-naming-as-decolonization

National Trust for Historic Preservation. (2017, June 19). *Statement on Confederate memorials: Confronting difficult history*. https://savingplaces.org/press-center/media-resources/national-trust-statement-onconfederate-memorials

Phillip, A. (2015, June 29). Why Bree Newsome took down the Confederate flag in S.C.: "I refuse to be ruled by fear." *Washington Post*. https://www.washingtonpost.com/news/post-nation/wp/2015/06/29/why-bree-newsome-took-down-the-confederate-flag-in-s-c-i-refuse-to-be-ruled-by-fear/?utm_term=.ff2a42c0cbbe

Phillips, C. (2018, September 20). *San Antonio's LEE High School adjusting to new name*. Texas Public Radio. https://www.tpr.org/post/san-antonio-s-lee-high-school-adjusting-new-name

Remnick, N. (2017, February 11). Yale will drop John Calhoun's name from building. *New York Times*. https://www.nytimes.com/2017/02/11/us/yale-protests-john-calhoun-grace-murray-hopper.html

Rockeymoore, M. (2017, June 04). Removing Civil War statues: The first step in finally defeating the Confederacy. *The Hill*. http://thehill.com/blogs/pundits-blog/civil-rights/336276-removing-civil-war-statues-the-first-step-in-finally

Rose, J. (2016). *Interpreting difficult history at museums and historic sites*. Rowman & Littlefield.

Samuels, A. (2019, April 10). Texas legislation aimed at protecting monuments of all kinds sparks heated debate over Confederate markers. *Texas Tribune*. https://www.texastribune.org/2019/04/10/texas-confederate-monuments-debate-heats-over-proposed-protection-law/

Santiago, M. (2017). Erasing differences for the sake of inclusion: How Mexican/Mexican American students construct historical narratives. *Theory and Research in Social Education*, *45*(1), 43–74.

Sauers, C. (2019, April 20). Following subtle name change, former Robert E. Lee High School auctioning memorabilia. *San Antonio Current*. https://www.sacurrent.com/the-daily/archives/2018/07/10/following-subtle-name-change-former-robert-e-lee-high-school-auctioning-memorabilia

Schmidt, A. & von Daacke, K. (2019, September 4). UVA and the history of race: Blackface and the rise of a segregated society. *UVAToday*. https://news.virginia.edu/content/uva-and-history-race-blackface-and-rise-segregated society

Schocker, J. B. (2014). A case for using images to teach women's history. *The History Teacher*, 47(3), 421–450.

Segall, A. (2014). Making difficult history public: The pedagogy of remembering and forgetting in two Washington DC museums. *Review of Education, Pedagogy, and Cultural Studies*, 36(1), 55–70.

Sehgal, P. (2016, February 2) Fighting erasure. *New York Times*. https://www.nytimes .com/2016/02/07/magazine/the-painful-consequences-of-erasure.htm

Seixas, P. (1994). Students' understanding of historical significance. *Theory & Research in Social Education*, 22(3), 281–304. https://doi:10.1080/00933104.1994.10505726

Seixas, P. (2000). *Knowing, teaching and learning history*. New York University Press.

Selk, A. (2017, April 24). New Orleans removes a tribute to "the lost cause of the Confederacy"—with snipers standing by. *Washington Post*. https://www.washi ngtonpost.com/news/post-nation/wp/2017/04/24/new-orleans-removes-a-tribute -to-the-lost-cause-of-the-confederacy-with-snipers-standing-by

Serwer, A. (2017, June 04). The myth of the kindly General Lee. *The Atlantic*. https:// www.theatlantic.com/politics/archive/2017/06/the-myth-of-the-kindly-general -lee/529038/

Silverman, H. (2011). Contested cultural heritage: A selective historiography. In H. Silverman (Ed.), *Contested cultural heritage: Religion, nationalism, erasure, and exclusion in a global world* (pp. 1–49). Springer.

Smith, W. L., & Crowley, R. (2018). Barack Obama, racial literacy, and lessons from "a more perfect union." *The History Teacher*, 51(3), 445–476.

Southern Poverty Law Center. (2019, February 1). Whose heritage? Public symbols of the Confederacy. https://www.splcenter.org/20190201/whose-heritage-public-symbols -confederacy

Stearns, P. N., Seixas, P. C., & Wineburg, S. S. (Eds.) (2000). *Knowing, teaching, and learning history: National and international perspectives*. New York University Press.

Taft, I. (2016, August 14). 10 Texas school names honoring Confederates have changed. At least 24 haven't. *Texas Tribune*. https://www.texastribune.org/2016/08/14 /school-year-begins-communities-take-stock-confeder/

Takaki, R. (2008). *A different mirror: A history of multicultural America*. Back Bay Books.

Terzian, S. G., & Yeager, E. A. (2007). "That's when we became a nation": Urban La- tino adolescents and the designation of historical significance. *Urban Education*, 42(1), 52–81. https://doi:10.1177/0042085906294027

Thomsen, J. (2015, July 1). *As debate on Confederate flag emerges, institutions named after controversial figures also come into play*. Inside Higher Ed. https://www .insidehighered.com/news/2015/07/01/debate-confederate-flag-emerges -institutions-named-after-controversial-figures-also

Toppo, G. (2017, October 11). Texas high school gets new name L.E.E.—or does it? *USA Today*. https://www.usatoday.com/story/news/2017/10/11/texas-high-school -gets-new-name-l-e-e-does-it/754882001/

Trainor, J. S. (2005). "My ancestors didn't own slaves": Understanding white talk about race. *Research in the Teaching of English*, 40(2), 140–167.

Tyner, J., Inwood, J. F., & Alderman, D. H. (2014). Theorizing violence and the dia- lects of landscape memorialization: A case study of Greensboro, North Carolina. *Environment and Planning D: Space and Society*, 32(5), 902–914.

Vansledright, B. A. (2004). What does it mean to think historically . . . and how do you teach it? *Social Education*, 68(3), 230–233.

Vansledright, B., & Afflerbach, P. (2000). Reconstructing Andrew Jackson: Prospective elementary teachers' readings of revisionist history texts. *Theory & Research in Social Education, 28*(3), 411–444. https://doi:10.1080/00933104.2000.1050 5915

Wang, M., & Svrluga, S. (2017, February 12). Yale renames Calhoun College because of historical ties to white supremacy and slavery. *Washington Post.* https://www .washingtonpost.com/news/grade-point/wp/2017/02/11/yale-renames-calhoun -college-because-of-historic-ties-to-white-supremacy-and-slavery/?utm_term= .d72032541728

Waxman, O. (2021, March 30). A "history of exclusion, of erasure, of invisibility." Why the Asian-American story is missing from many U.S. Classrooms. *Time.* https:// time.com/5949028/asian-american-history-schools/

Wendland, T. (2017, March 20). With Lee's statue's removal, another battle of New Orleans comes to a close. *NPR.* https://www.npr.org/2017/05/20/529232823/with -lee-statues-removal-another-battle-of-new-orleans-comes-to-a-close

Wineburg, S. S. (2001). *Historical thinking and other unnatural acts: Charting the future of teaching the past.* Temple University Press.

Wood, E., & Wolf, B. (2008). Between the lines of engagement in museums: Indiana University and the Children's Museum of Indianapolis. *Journal of Museum Education, 33*(2), 121–130. https://doi:10.1179/jme.2008.33.2.121

Woods, T. A. (1995). Museums and the public: Doing history together. *The Journal of American History, 82*(3), 1111. https://doi:10.2307/2945116

Woodson, A. (2015). "What you supposed to know": Urban black students' perspectives on history textbooks. *Journal of Urban Learning Teaching and Research, 11,* 57–65.

Woodson, A. (2017). "There ain't no white people here": The master narratives of the Civil Rights Movement in the stories of urban youth. *Urban Education, 52*(3), 316–342.

Wunder, S. (2002). Learning to teach for historical understanding: Preservice teachers at a hands-on museum. *The Social Studies,* 159–163.

*Yale News.* (2017, February 27). Yale to change Calhoun College's name to honor Grace Murray Hopper. https://news.yale.edu/2017/02/11/yale-change-calhoun -college-s-name-honor-grace-murray-hopper-0

Zinn, H. (2005). *A people's history of the United States.* HarperCollins.

## CHAPTER 7

# The Refusal to Learn

## Inquiry Through Marronage in the History Classroom

*Tadashi Dozono*

Over the last two decades, I have served as an agent of the state through my role as a public school teacher. I have been dedicated to teaching in public schools in communities of color and meeting the needs of marginalized publics through my roles in the education system. However, my job simultaneously has positioned me in opposition to marginalized students of color over the years. I am unavoidably implicated as an agent of the state. This chapter addresses those moments when students of color refuse to learn in the history classroom. But instead of blaming Black and Brown students and advocating for their conformity, I argue that the problem lies with teachers' attempts to engage Black and Brown bodies and minds into an exclusionary repressive system.

What would it mean for the teacher to follow Black and Brown students' thread of refusal? What if we interpreted their refusal not as a rejection of learning, but as a refusal of this repressive state? As a teacher, I take it for granted that I have agency in my choice to work within a system that both supports my social justice activism, yet simultaneously is the very system I aim to subvert. With students of color, teachers can misinterpret those moments of student rebellion and lack the intellectual tools to support such forms of insurgency.

It makes sense that my Black and Brown students would rebel against the very system I, too, aim to rebel against. Such students rebel against me, as an agent of the state, and I ought to applaud them. So why would I try to reengage them in this system that we both know is a problem? Just because I choose to work within the system I aim to transform does not mean that my students must as well. I accept their refusal not as a refusal of my teaching, but rather as a refusal of a school system that refused them first. Their turning away is an intellectual countermove and an agentive form of engagement. What else might be hidden within apparently negative approaches to the classroom space?

This chapter asserts that studying marronage in the history classroom broadens historical inquiry to account for students' experiences and disciplinary engagements, including students who experience negation through history. Marronage refers to maroon communities that developed throughout the African diaspora in the Caribbean, South America, and the Southern regions of the United States during the systemic enslavement of African peoples. Maroon communities were communities of peoples who had been enslaved but escaped to create their own autonomous communities hidden away from the white colonial system of slavery. Some of the better-known maroon communities were the Jamaican maroons and Brazilian quilombos. The genealogical traces of marronage offer fleeting moments when people turn away from the status quo to generate something else. Marronage pushes the history classroom at two levels: on an ideal curricular level (as classroom content), and on a material spatial level (the history classroom as a contested geographic space of power and knowledge). Marronage conceptually challenges teachers to read students differently, and to create opportunities for academic inquiry based on disciplinary work from and of the margins.

Before examining the ways marronage pushes disciplinary inquiry, we must establish marronage within the context of a prior negation. The first main section situates the refusal to learn as a negation of the negation, a refusal of the refusal. I briefly contextualize marronage in relation to negative dialectics. This refusal to learn must be contextualized within a system of knowledge set up against many peoples. It is not a system that supports all publics. Rather, schooling serves the reproduction of a capitalist white supremacist state. The sections thereafter emphasize marronage as negative dialectics within three disciplinary spaces: first as epistemology, second as geography, and third as historical case studies.

Marronage as epistemology addresses the negation of bodies of knowledge. The concept of marronage allows us to read students' refusal to learn differently, and for students to have an additional epistemic thread upon which they might build. If we understand that refusal as a form of marronage, where can marronage lead us intellectually?

Marronage as a form of Black geography becomes an engagement of the abject, of dismal swamps and fallow terrain in relation to white capitalist geographies. Framing marronage as Black geography allows students and teachers to rethink the classroom and school space as a geographic space of contestation over power and knowledge.

The study of marronage through historical case studies opens up historical disciplinary work as a potentiality to disrupt the standard teleological narrative of progress. As case studies, marronage offers not necessarily models to follow, but moments that—when juxtaposed against our present condition—offer the possibility to break through the status quo into other spaces of being. The secondary source literature by historians of marronage turns to questions of narrativization, and a disciplinary honesty to the complexities of marronage beyond an idealized utopia. The historical study of marronage interrogates the negotiation between the ideal and the material, between the consequential power of the dominant state surrounding hidden spaces of autonomy and creative sovereignty.

## ORIENTATIONS

One's orientation to the world matters in learning. As Freire and Macedo (1987) put it, reading the word is intertwined with reading the world. Many of my high school students of color express that they feel like school is not for them. What if they're right? I don't mean to say that they do not have the intellectual capacity for school, but I take seriously their insight that school is not meant for them, nor serves their needs. The way school has historically been structured and continues to function does not serve all students. Instead of trying to force rebellious students into a system not of or for them, we must acknowledge that and support them in their intellectual endeavors that rebel against schooling. This does not mean we give up on students, but on the contrary, that we reorient ourselves to acknowledge how students are engaged through marginalization. Research in racial literacy accounts for how students of color read the world through and for race (Epstein & Gist, 2015; King, 2016). This chapter extends racial literacy to emphasize literacies of racial negation, the capacity to read the world through how one is negated because of one's race, and to read students' refusal to engage a system that negates them due to their race.

If the teacher has not experienced school as negation and sees school as the promise for equality and uplift, then when students refuse school, the teacher might interpret this as students refusing a universally "good" life. But if your orientation is such that schooling is linked to oppressive state systems, the school-to-prison pipeline, then the refusal might best be understood as a refusal of a prior refusal.

Schools are a part of the school-to-prison pipeline and the prison-industrial complex (Alexander, 2012; Hereth et al., 2017; Love, 2019; Rios, 2011). I do not want my classroom to be an incarceration site. Nonetheless, I am an agent of the state, and my classroom is a site of state-mandated compulsory presence. There is an inevitable contradiction in the work I claim to do, and the space where I do that work. My work implicates me in the legacies of slavery through the school-to-prison-pipeline and prison-as-continuation-of-slavery. I turn to marronage because it is linked both to the histories of the African diaspora in the Americas integral to a contemporary American historical present, and to the continuation of a repressive school-to-prison pipeline in the United States.

I acknowledge that I have no authority over marronage as an intellectual and historic space. This space is not mine. I arrive from my own position as a queer Japanese American cis-male teacher in New York City public schools, but this space is not mine. I ask permission to be present in this space, to speak from my own experience and my thinking about this space. This work is about power over space, and how we orient ourselves toward bodies of knowledge.

Growing up as a queer Japanese American cis-male in Oregon taught me that the predominantly assimilationist strategies my Japanese American community pre- and post-World War II would not work for me. My intersectional negations as a queer Japanese American cis-male overlap through internalized racism and homophobia. My experiences of negation left me angry, but queer theory was my way through that refusal, to refuse the very system that had negated me. I come to marronage through my queer lens of refusing the systems that taught me to internalize my own negation. This chapter is the result of my own orientation toward marronage as both considering an ideal of liberation and the material realities of marginalized communities having to negotiate with dominant society.

## MARRONAGE AS NEGATIVE DIALECTICS: REFUSAL OF THE REFUSAL

When students refuse to learn in the spaces we create for them, marronage challenges us to reread their refusal as a refusal to be interpellated by the police state, by the prison-industrial complex, by schools-as-prisons-as-continuation-of-slavery-through-Thirteenth-Amendment. Public schooling, as understood by Althusser (1971), is a part of the ideological state apparatus that ensures the systemic reproduction of the state's ideology (p. 143). The state coopts knowledge and learning for the sake of its own maintenance and reproduction. The state's control over knowledge and values are reproduced through school curriculum, structures, and daily rituals of conformity (McLaren, 1988). Althusser (1971) explained his notion of *interpellation* through the metaphor of being hailed by a police officer on the street. By turning around to the police officer's call of "Hey! You there!," one becomes a subject, one recognizes the authority of the state (p. 174). As a public school teacher, when I demand a student's attention, I *interpellate* them into the state's ideological system. I call out for my students to submit to the state as subjects, and to my authority granted by the state, no matter how revolutionary I might claim my curriculum to be.

Some of these students who refuse to be hailed by the system have the capacity to see the system and how it refuses them.[1] But some forms of rebellion against school's negation push students to focus on rejection alone. For example, in Paul Willis's (1977) work on the reproduction of social class through schooling in England, the rebellious group of the lads reject the school system, but they do so without a distinct direction into something else. Willis exposed how schooling succeeds in getting some students to reject intellectual endeavors and rebel against schooling, hence becoming working-class with low-wage jobs. In contrast, marronage is a distinct form of rebellion that leads one through that negative space to generate something else. Marronage offers an alternative engagement: instead of forcing students to turn their heads in the direction of the state, teachers might better serve their intellectual development by following their gaze, walking beside them, and engaging their inquiry leading away from the system.

To better understand students' refusal to learn as a refusal of a prior refusal, we must first review the classic Hegelian dialectical relationship. In Hegel's (1807/2004) "Lordship and Bondage" passage, Hegel articulated the negation of the negation. The servant is negated by the master, constructed as negative in relation to the positive and good master. The servant, however, realizes that their own negation is something that the master depends on. The servant has a certain agency to be free of that relationship, and the master does not.[2] That struggle ends when the two create a positive unity greater than existed previously. In the classroom, this translates to the teacher overcoming the students' rebellion and coercing them back into the day's lesson, for the betterment of everyone. The Hegelian dialectic reinforces a teleological narrative of progress.

Marronage can be understood as a response to Hegel here, as a negation of a prior negation, refusing to be sublated into that teleology of progress. Instead, marronage inhabits that space of negation in order to create one's own realm outside the system. This brings us through to Theodor Adorno's negative dialectics (1966/2007). Negative dialectics turns away from an idealized reconciliation where that rebellion gets folded into a narrative of progress. Negative dialectics represents the turn toward that negative space, embracing those cracks in the system as an escape hatch into invisible possibilities. Fred Moten's (2013) work in Afropessimism moved Blackness through that negation into something else: "What if the nothing that is in question here moves through to the other side of negation, in 'the real presence' of blackness, in and as another idea of nothingness altogether that is given in and as and to things?" (p. 751). Maroon societies take that negation into negated spaces, to create something out of nothingness.

Marronage as negative dialectics allows teachers and students to read history and the classroom for and through negation. Neil Roberts paired these two in framing his book *Freedom as Marronage* (2015): "If liberation is the negative dialectical release from bondage prior to the constitution of freedom, then resistance is the means through which an agent achieves this condition of emancipation" (p. 161). Rather than relying on the promise of the school system to liberate oneself, students might find their own liberation by disappearing into the cracks of negation. Given the role of schooling in the reproduction of inequality in our society, I do not blame students for fleeing from the system that negates them.

Marronage offers a way to read flight from negation through a different means than we are taught to understand it through state-sanctioned teacher education programs. "Marronage is a flight from the negative, subhuman realm of necessity, bondage, and unfreedom toward the sphere of positive activity and human freedom" (Roberts, 2015, p. 15). Some of those students turning away from the state curriculum and agents of the state might be better served if read through marronage as negative dialectics.

## MARRONAGE AS EPISTEMOLOGY

Marronage reorients inquiry in the history classroom away from the state. Marronage represents a way of knowing and being through negation, as an epistemology through negation. Epistemology is the study of how we know what we know, where knowledge comes from, and the justification for our beliefs. Whereas students might choose to rebel against the forms of knowledge forced upon them by the state, marronage offers a new relationship to epistemology grounded in student experiences of marginalization and negation. Marronage accounts for ways of thinking and being in the world that respond to a larger experience of dehumanization and marginalization.

The study of marronage provides teachers new ways to understand how their students' experiences through raced gendered bodies shape their orientation to learning and school-as-ideological-state-apparatus. Marronage moves teachers away from reading their students through deficit models that normalize students into exclusionary narratives of progress. Marronage is an epistemology of negative dialectics, as all of the other things these students could be beyond deviant, criminal, or truant: a different way to name their actions and rationality. Roberts (2015) explained, "In each episteme, the unfree experience liminality. Liminality is a fringe existence, a lack, a marginality in an order that nonetheless relies upon liminal figures to buttress a normative agent's way of life. Epistemes naturalize cultural constructs to the advantage of normative agents' structuring of rules, regulations, and laws of governance" (p. 160). The school system relies on the students who fail to prop up those who succeed (Brantlinger, 2006). Rather than students accepting being put in a position of marginalization, marronage as epistemology allows them to follow the darkened paths of inquiry obscured by the normative narrative of school success.

The aim should not be to simply move students from the margins into the mainstream. Marronage links to queer theory's and Afropessimism's consideration of what inquiry looks like from a position of abjection. Black queer scholar Darieck Scott (2010) dared to ask the question, "If we are racialized (in part) through domination and abjection and humiliation, is there anything of value or to be learned from the experience of being defeated, humiliated, abjected?" (p. 6). Scott engaged the experience of negation not as negative value, but for what value negation offers. Marronage as epistemology enables negation and abjection to be the starting point of inquiry.

Marronage breaks dominant society's hold over what legitimate inquiry looks like. Marronage is a form of flight that turns away from the Fanonian zone of nonbeing (Roberts, 2015, p. 119). In a nod to Fanon, Roberts (2015) described what he calls sociogenic marronage:

> Sociogenic marronage classifies the supreme ideal of freedom. It denotes a revolutionary process of naming and attaining individual and collective agency, nonsovereignty, liberation, constitutionalism, and the cultivation of a community that aligns civil society with political society. Flight can be both real and imagined. That pronouncement bolsters a central maxim of the theory of marronage: Freedom is not a place; it is a state of being. (p. 11)

Roberts understood marronage beyond the physical communities hidden from sight, as an embodied state of being and knowing that rejects dominant society. As an epistemology, marronage is grounded in the particular ways of knowing through racially marginalized bodies. In U.S. society, race continues to be a major structuring principle that divides how people experience the world and come to consciousness about their place in the world. One's experiences through raced and gendered bodies deeply shapes one's orientation within the world, and thus their inquiries about the world. The students' experiences become the entry point to inquiry, liberated from what the teacher and state deem legitimate intellectual engagement.

Marronage as epistemology allows teachers to see students' refusal from a different vantage point, rereading daily acts of defiance that might otherwise be punished. The simplest form of marronage is petit-marronage, which involves small acts of rebellion and escape by individuals. "By petit marronage, I mean freedom understood as fleeting ontology, a temporary flight from slavery by an individual or small group through fugitive acts of truancy away from the zone of enslavement" (Roberts, 2015, p. 98). In the classroom, this might be understood as those moments when students shut themselves off through what means they have access to. For example, students shut off their sensory inputs through putting on their hoodies and headphones. When students cut school, the truancy police hauls them back into the system, arresting their defiance. Truancy is this petit marronage against school as an arm of the state. Marronage delegitimizes the oppressive state system, validating the active decision to be truant against compulsory schooling.

Some of my brightest students have been those that see through the system and are compelled to rebel against it. Unfortunately, schooling impresses an association of success with conformity (Bowles & Gintis, 1976/2011). Marronage opens a new relationality to knowledge and learning that is possible beyond the school's monopoly over knowledge. How might we promote rebellions that move away from conformity and into intellectually creative sovereign spaces? How can experiences of negation reveal hidden paths of inquiry, and how might teachers support students along those paths of inquiry? Rather than seeing it as deviant and truant against the good of the state, what if we understand it from an orientation of refuge?

## MARRONAGE AS BLACK GEOGRAPHY

Marronage as Black geography allows readings of classroom and curricular spaces traditionally marginalized to the point of being off the map. When we consider marronage as Black geography, it challenges traditional geographic inquiry in the history classroom, pushing teachers to rethink the urban classroom as a Black geographic space. Katherine McKittrick (2006) asked, "How do geography and blackness work together to advance a different way of knowing and imagining the world? Can these different knowledges and imaginations perhaps call into question the limits of existing spatial paradigms and put forth more humanly workable geographies?" (p. xxvii). Traditional geography instruction fails to provide Black and Brown students methods for understanding what it means to move through the space of schooling as white supremacist capitalist state apparatus. How can this conflict over space, power, and knowledge in the history classroom be rearticulated through the terms of Black geographic inquiry?

McKittrick's framing of Black geography breaks the disciplined boundaries of geographic inquiry, highlighting Black knowledge production. McKittrick critiqued geography's reliance on the white male European gaze to map and make sense of the Americas. Black geography reveals "what might be called rational spatial colonization and domination: the profitable erasure and objectification of subaltern subjectivities, stories, and lands" (McKittrick, 2006, p. x). Marronage embraces terrains otherwise understood as fallow and desolate wasteland. Studying marronage through Black geography enables historical inquiries that attend to subaltern stories and alternative valuations of land.

Marronage engages geographic spaces through negation, challenging their devaluation within a normative capitalist geographic production framework (Bledsoe, 2017). Dismal swamps become sites of refuge and life when studied through marronage as Black geography (Sayers, 2014). Roberts linked epistemic negation with geographic negation through marronage. "Flight from the zone of nonbeing to zones of refuge results in keeping states at a distance. Escape from state legibility and the enactment of local forms of lawmaking, epistemology, organization, agriculture, and relations is a mechanism to avoid the appropriating dynamics of state power" (Roberts, 2015, p. 152). Maroon communities fled to spaces of negation in order to create new forms of autonomy and sovereignty, both physical and ideal. Those physical maroon communities then enabled new relationalities to knowing oneself, the land, and dominant society.

By categorizing marronage along levels of flight, Roberts (2015) provided a vocabulary for considering larger geopolitical implications. Grand-marronage is the term to describe the larger-scale form of maroon communities, and its generation through geographic spaces. "Grand marronage refers to the mass flight of individuals from slavery to form an autonomous community of freedom emphasizing physical escape, geographic isolation, rejection of property relations associated with a slavery regime, and avoidance of sustained states of war through compacts, treaties, and negotiations for political recognition" (Roberts, 2015, p. 99). Political recognition here aims more at autonomy, the right to exist and be left alone by the dominant society, but not to be included within it. Maroon communities represent this flux between ideal and material, this utopian move beyond state recognition alongside the material reality of needing the colonial state to recognize their autonomy in order to prevent further attack and invasion.

Marronage at a society-wide level is sovereign marronage. The Haitian Revolution is a key example of this form. Roberts (2015) defined sovereign marronage as "non-fleeting mass flight from slavery on a scale much larger than grand marronage. Its goal is emancipation, its scope is social-structural, its spatialization is polity-wide, its metaphysics includes the individual and community, and its medium is the lawgiver" (p. 103). Although the Haitian Revolution achieved sovereignty and autonomy, Haiti nonetheless remained embedded within a larger world order that continued to threaten its capacity to survive, that saw an independent Black nation as a threat to the white-natured order. It would seem that the achievement of sovereign marronage is historic: however, the Haitian Revolution is not normally understood through marronage. Instead, the Haitian Revolution becomes placed under the terms of European Enlightenment and the French Revolution (Dozono, 2016). Studying marronage as a geopolitical entity enables a different way of understanding global geographic actors.

Addressing marronage in the history classroom moves questions of sovereignty beyond narratives of nation-states and international relations, to how sovereignty over bodies and minds become contested within classroom spaces of racialized power dynamics. "The geographic relationship between the past and the present and racial geographies is crucial here, as it works to examine the ways in which understanding blackness has been twinned by the practice of placing blackness and rendering body-space integral to the production of space" (McKittrick, 2006, p. xxvii). McKittrick's framing of Black geography allow teachers and students to read the classroom as a contested space for bodies and minds. The battles over what the state wants young Black people to know and be is juxtaposed against the history of marronage in its multiple forms.

Through marronage, geographic spaces of the abject become spaces of refuge. Daniel Sayers's book *A Desolate Place for a Defiant People* (2014) emphasized the negative connotations of the terrain that maroon communities inhabited. The Great Dismal Swamp in Virginia and North Carolina had great utility because of its undesirability and disregard. This work in maroon studies reflects Afropessimist and queer embraces of the abject position, of engaging the space of negation as an opening of possibility.

The exile's sense of being-in-the-world consistently exists in a dialectical relation with the former, present, and future homeland that originates from the original physical rupturing of her existence within an original homeland. Thus, we might expect those living in exilic conditions, such as captive enslaved African diasporans or Indigenous American diasporans, to act in the world with a sense of belonging to another place while also engaging the alien secondary homeland in ways that might reflect this ambiguous positionality that they have. (Sayers, 2014, p. 75)

This exiled position allows one to consider a stance against Western epistemologies and histories that acknowledges the past, present, and remains oriented to an open future. Marronage as geography enables inquiry in the classroom through spatial exile and displacement.

In the act of taking attendance, teachers mark certain bodies as absent or present, condoning the devaluation of absent and truant bodies. When teachers apply marronage as Black geography to how they survey their own classroom, they must reckon with their role in reinforcing a value system of exile. "If who we see is tied up with where we see through truthful, commonsensical narratives, then the placement of subaltern bodies deceptively hardens spatial binaries, in turn suggesting that some bodies belong, some bodies do not belong, and some bodies are out of place" (McKittrick, 2006, p. xv). Marronage disrupts teachers' reliance on these bifurcating lines used to evaluate Black and Brown bodies within the classroom as white supremacist governmental space. How might teachers attend to absence with as much energy as they attend to presence in the room?

Applying marronage as geographic lens, we learn to read physical absence and negative space differently. Marronage offers the geographic concept of the abyss, as a zone of nonbeing that is simultaneously a source of world-building. In the oceanic abyss, life as we terrestrially know it cannot survive, yet otherworldly creatures thrive in such spaces. Roberts applied the abyss as a useful concept in understanding marronage as negative dialectics, as a photographic negative emphasizing a perceptual reversal to our normal reading practice of light over dark. Roberts (2015) asserted:

The abyss is a realm of the unknown and zone of nonbeing that paradoxically is a source of knowledge and world-building. Representations of the abyss at the point of entanglement in slavery are the womb abyss on the belly of the slave ship, the abyss in the depths of the sea, and a reverse image of all that an enslaved agent leaves behind in the savannas of the imagination. (p. 167)

Roberts offered historical examples from the African diaspora where the zone of nonbeing becomes a portal of inquiry. The abyss allows an inquiry into dark crevasses in the historical narrative for their otherworldly potential beyond our imagination. The abyss as absence reinterprets those spatial absences in the classroom as well, those empty seats, named on a seating chart mapping the room, yet lacking a present body and mind. Marronage as Black geography enables new readings of those negative spaces in the history classroom (marginalized off the classroom and curricular map) that go unattended, deemed insignificant for their absence.

## MARRONAGE AS HISTORY/GENEALOGY

Part of my larger academic project is to invert the relationship between historical content from the margins and disciplinary skills (Dozono, 2021). My aim is not to consider how we apply historical thinking skills to the study of marginalized peoples, but rather, how does the study of marginalized peoples challenge historical thinking and the history discipline? What questions does marronage raise that disrupt the discipline? The study of marronage in history must move beyond multicultural celebration, forcing us to reconsider what we study in the history classroom, why we study it, and how. Marronage brings to bare questions of historiography regarding historical significance, narrativization, and close readings of the past.

Studying marronage in K–12 classrooms challenges how we determine and measure what is worthy of historical study. Teachers are pressured to teach large amounts of content, so why would something like maroon communities be worthy of replacing content long upheld as significant? Within a teleological narrative of progress, marronage might appear to represent failed events without lasting effects. Abolitionist movements among white Europeans provide a more legible curricular thread to teach, as they maintain a progressive narrative of Enlightenment thought. However, historic cases of maroon communities represent fleeting moments of failed rebellion within this narrative construction.

The illegibility of maroon societies in history should not necessarily be seen as a detriment. Rather, illegibility and invisibility were strengths and strategies of value. Stefano Harney and Fred Moten (2013) turned to this power of maroons to frame a fugitive dynamic of the undercommons, stating, "The undercommons, its maroons, are always at war, always in hiding" (p. 30). Marronage embraces the hidden realm, away from legibility. This challenges history's disciplinary value system, that one becomes historical through legibility. Conceptually, marronage asserts its historical importance through that very illegibility, as a strategy of resistance and survival. The aim for maroon societies was to be hidden, illegible, and they enacted a certain success through their fleeting sparks of existence across the African diaspora in the Americas.

Studying marronage pushes the discipline toward genealogical methods, pointing to the limitations of the disciplinary focus on cause-effect linear narratives of progress, and notions of historic success and failure. Genealogy, Foucault (1977) explained, opens space for the historical study of dead ends in history, valuing the ephemeral over the eternal . Marronage requires a recalibration of history's disciplinary value system, beyond the dichotomy of success/failure to comprehend maroon communities' historical significance.

Defining the historical significance of marronage additionally involves questioning a Western value of permanence, and success for whom. Many rebellions come to be understood as historically insignificant because they "weren't successful," but those fleeting moments of sovereignty by the oppressed blast through the status quo's impenetrable grasp on permanence and dominance. For the oppressed, sparks of hope and disequilibrium offer openings into other realms of possibility. Joy James (2013) pointed to the continued significance for marginalized groups today:

> Maroon resistance failed to convince the tyrannical majority of the soundness of its reasoning, and the legitimacy of its definitions. Still the diaspora's fugitives fought, fled, and bargained with enslaving armies, and their authorized reformers who followed in their wake. Their ancestral resistance is embodied in contemporary rebels, revolutionaries, and political prisoners and exiles that self-identify as realists rather than idealists. (p. 127)

Maroon societies challenged the colonial state in their own time, and their curricular importance today challenges how state curricular frameworks and narratives limit and negate vast historical possibilities.

Challenging marronage's historical significance is intertwined with its emplotment within larger historical narratives (White, 1978) and how historians construct secondary retellings of marronage. The emphasis on primary-source pedagogy has taken precedence over the skills required to critique a historian's narrativization, underlying ideology, and positionality. Although maroon communities rarely surface in U.S. state-sanctioned curriculum, maroon communities and leaders have played an important role within national heritage in Haiti and Jamaica, and larger African diaspora narratives. But historical figures of marronage have also been vilified through narratives as violent against the white supremacist order (Buck-Morss, 2000). Teachers might ask students to compare how several secondary sources place maroon communities within narrative frameworks.

In the classroom, the study of marronage brings forth questions of how we conduct historical study, how to best attend to all of marronage's complexities and contradictions. This work pairs negative dialectics with the historical thinking skills of close reading and contextualization. Practicing contextualization is not just about understanding the past moment differently, but more importantly, understanding our present condition differently than we currently do. The utility of historical documentation is not that it affirms what we think we know about the past, but its capacity to explode us out of our present condition. Walter Benjamin's (1982/1999) conception of the dialectical image juxtaposed historical moments that refract rather than directly reflect our own present condition. Whereas reflection mirrors what we understand reality to be, refraction shifts the path of light. Benjamin's dialectical image was set in contradiction to historical narrative, to allow the past to put our present condition into question. Historical cases of marronage provide students with dialectical images (Benjamin, 1982/1999), with the possibility to blast open the status quo narrative and shift the path of inquiry. From a position of marginalization, historical cases of marronage might be understood as flashes of light and liberation, these singularities as stars exploding brilliantly in the vast space of whiteness, the dots some of us need to connect to, painting a constellation of possibility beyond our present condition.

We must be careful to not expect marronage to say what we want it to say, to be a solution to problems we confront. The study of marronage requires lessons in close reading, to resist temptations to easily translate past moments into solutions to current problems (Freeman, 2010, p. 16). Close reading means confronting contradictions and negotiations beyond the ideal we might want it to be, embracing the complexities of material lived realities. We are haunted by the legacies of related problems, but we also live in a very different time and place, despite those lineages. Historical cases of marronage cannot be reified into the identities we want them to be, bound under our contemporary categorizations.

Historical study of marronage requires contextualizing these rebellions amidst their complex negotiations with the surrounding dominant society. The realities of these negotiations draw us back from idealizing maroon societies as idyllic utopias. Alvin Thompson's (2006) historical study of marronage presented the complexities of marronage beyond an idealized image of marooners as heroes or villains, as an ideal image of freedom, moving to confront these communities' complex relationships with violence: "Much of what has survived in contemporary written records is enmeshed in myths, legends and biased contemporary views. . . . I have tried to provide new insights into the despotism of Maroon leaders, the large-scale abduction of women from the plantations, and Maroon enslavement of others in their communities" (Thompson, 2006, p. 8). By confronting these contradictions in reality, these cases of marronage traverse the dichotomous membranes of success/failure, permanent/fleeting, freedom/slavery, ideal/material, and legible/hidden. Cases of marronage are less models instructing us how to be, and more aids in breaking through the restrictions of our contemporary problem-space. Marronage points to the possibilities of something else, not directing us to what that something else ought to be.

## CONCLUSION

Through epistemology, Black geography, and historical case studies, marronage opens new lines of inquiry in the history classroom. Marronage presents an engagement through negation, encouraging teachers to broaden their approaches to some of their most marginalized students. Marronage as epistemology enables inquiry through experiences of negation. Marronage as Black geography challenges our normative readings of terrestrial value and provides a vocabulary for new readings of the classroom as contested space of power over bodies and minds. Marronage as historical case study encourages deeper historiographic inquiry by questioning the dominant narrative and historical thinking practices.

I do not mean this to imply that all students who refuse to learn do so because they identify with these ideas. Students refuse to learn for a wide range of reasons. I write this as an educator of color dedicated to meeting the needs and cherishing the complexities and capacities of marginalized communities. There is a deep caution in how marronage can be taken up, the caution of turning this work back into teleological narratives that predetermine students' paths. This is also not meant to be an instructive path for all students who feel alienated from the education system. I reiterate Foucault's (1977) emphasis on genealogy over historicism here. Students and historical examples of marronage must not be reified into the identities we want or assume them to be. Such examples can serve as sparks of inquiry for both teachers and students, to move study beyond assumed identities and exclusionary value systems, to consider the realms opened through experiences of negation beyond the status quo.

How do these cases of marronage spark new questions we might ask of the present condition? How might the study of marronage reveal hidden power dynamics in the classroom for students who refuse to participate? This chapter calls for further work in developing and incorporating new disciplinary spaces, such as rebellion studies and marronage studies, that offer theories and methods to meet the needs of the most marginalized publics in our communities.

## REFERENCES

Adorno, T. W. (2007). *Negative dialectics* (E. B. Ashton, Trans.). Continuum. (Original work published 1966)

Alexander, M. (2012). *The new Jim Crow: Mass incarceration in the age of colorblindness*. The New Press.

Althusser, L. (1971). *Lenin and philosophy* (B. Brewster, Trans.). Monthly Review Press.

Benjamin, W. (1999). *The arcades project* (H. Eiland & K. McLaughlin, Trans.). Belknap Press of Harvard University Press. (Original work published 1982)

Bledsoe, A. (2017). Marronage as a past and present geography in the Americas. *Southeastern Geographer, 57*(1), 30–50.

Bowles, S., & Gintis, H. (2011). *Schooling in capitalist America: Educational reform and the contradictions of economic life*. Haymarket Books. (Original work published 1976)

Brantlinger, E. (2006). Winners need losers: The basis for school competition and hierarchies. In E. Brantlinger (Ed.), *Who benefits from special education?: Remediating (fixing) other people's children* (pp. 197–231). Lawrence Erlbaum.

Buck-Morss, S. (2000). Hegel and Haiti. *Critical Inquiry, 26*(4), 821–865.

Dozono, T. (2016). Historical experience and the Haitian Revolution in the history classroom. *The Social Studies, 107*(1), 38–46.

Dozono, T. (2021). Race and the evidence of experience: Accounting for race in historical thinking pedagogy. *Critical Studies in Education*.

Epstein, T. & Gist, C. (2015). Teaching racial literacy in secondary humanities classrooms: Challenging adolescents' of color concepts of race and racism. *Race Ethnicity and Education, 18*(1), 40–60.

Foucault, M. (1977). Nietzsche, genealogy, history. In D. F. Bouchard (Ed.),. *Language, counter-memory, practice: Selected essays and interviews* (pp. 139–164). Cornell University Press.

Freeman, E. (2010). *Time binds: Queer temporalities, queer histories*. Duke University Press.

Freire, P., & Macedo, D. (1987). *Literacy: Reading the word and the world*. Bergin and Garvey.

Gramsci, A. (1971). *Selections from prison notebooks* (Q. Hoare & G. N. Smith, Trans.). International Publishers.

Harney, S. & Moten, F. (2013). *The undercommons: Fugitive planning and Black study*. Autonomedia.

Hegel, H. G. W. (2004). *Phenomenology of the spirit*. Oxford University Press. (Original work published 1807)

Hereth, J., Kaba, M., Meiners, E., & Wallace, L. (2017). Restorative justice is not enough: School-based interventions in the carceral state. In S. Bahena, N. Cooc, R. Currie-Rubin, P. Kuttner, & M. Ng (Eds), *Disrupting the school-to-prison pipeline* (pp. 240–264). Harvard Education Press.

James, J. (2013). Afrarealism and the Black Matrix: Maroon philosophy at democracy's border. *The Black Scholar, 43*(4), 124–131.

King, L. (2016). Teaching Black history as a racial literacy project. *Race Ethnicity and Education, 19*(6), 1303–1318.

Love, B. (2019). *We want to do more than survive: Abolitionist teaching and the pursuit of educational freedom*. Beacon Press.

McKittrick, K. (2006). *Demonic grounds: Black women and the cartographies of struggle*. University of Minnesota Press.

McLaren, P. (1988). On ideology and education: Critical pedagogy and the politics of empowerment. *Social Text, 19/20*, 153–185.

Moten, F. (2013). Blackness and nothingness (Mysticism in the flesh). *South Atlantic Quarterly, 112*(4), 737–780.

Rios, V. M. (2011). *Punished: Policing the lives of Black and Latino boys*. New York University Press.

Roberts, N. (2015). *Freedom as marronage*. University of Chicago Press.

Sayers, D. (2014). *A desolate place for a defiant people: The archaeology of Maroons, Indigenous Americans, and enslaved laborers in the Great Dismal Swamp*. University Press of Florida.

Scott, D. (2010). *Extravagant abjection: Blackness, power, and sexuality in the African American literary imagination*. NYU Press.

Thompson, A. O. (2006). *Flight to freedom: African runaways and Maroons in the Americas*. University of the West Indies Press.

White, H. (1978). *The tropics of discourse: Essays in cultural criticism*. Johns Hopkins University Press.

Willis, P. (1977). *Learning to labor*. Columbia University Press.

## CHAPTER 8

# Racial Literacy and Historic Plantation Sites

## A Tale of Two Plantations

*Kristen E. Duncan*

### INTRODUCTION

While hearing the word "plantation" conjures up images of the 19th-century South, a quick Google search shows that there are still dozens, if not hundreds, of plantations open and available for tours and other events over a century and a half after the end of the Civil War. In South Carolina, the first state to secede from the United States as the Civil War began, well over 50 plantation sites are available for tourists and wedding guests to peruse. One afternoon, as I engaged my students, preservice social studies teachers, in a discussion about teaching difficult history, I thought to ask them if any of them had visited a plantation during their K–12 schooling. I was honestly astonished, as every student in the room had a hand in the air. I followed up by asking if they remembered what happened on these tours. One student remembered picking the seeds out of cotton, but for the most part my students remembered very little about their visits to plantation sites. As we sat in our classroom on a campus whose land once served as a plantation, my mind began to generate numerous questions about plantation site visits: What led people to visit these sites? What experiences did they have when visiting plantations? What do visitors learn about the institution of enslavement during these visits?

The teaching of the institution of slavery has always been a nebulous topic in K–12 classrooms in the United States. A quick social media scroll displays news stories of students subjected to reenacting the experiences of the enslaved on slave ships (CBSLA, 2017), simulating slave auctions in which white students bid on their Black peers (Griffith, 2019), and playing games in which they pretend to be runaway enslaved persons (Gonzalez, 2019). Combine these news stories with the Southern Poverty Law Center's (2018) study on the teaching of enslavement in U.S. schools, and it seems that American students learn very little substantive information about the institution of enslavement, the role it played in the colonies and later the United States, and the connection between enslavement and contemporary race relations in the United States.

For the preservice teachers in my classes, it seems that plantation tours were a part of their U.S. history curriculum as K–12 students. The fact that students are engaging with history at these historical sites makes them worthy of study by social studies education researchers. We have a responsibility to make sure that not only are students learning an accurate history, but also that the history learned at these sites is connected to contemporary realities. In this chapter, I will analyze the tours offered at two different plantation sites in an effort to determine if and/or how these sites help visitors gain a sense of racial literacy. As plantations played an instrumental role in developing the racial hierarchy that has existed in the United States for centuries, it seems that visiting a plantation may be an appropriate place to begin to understand that hierarchy. In this chapter, I will analyze the tours offered at Magnolia Plantation and Gardens (South Carolina) and the Whitney Plantation (Louisiana).

## WHAT DO WE KNOW ABOUT THE TEACHING AND LEARNING OF ENSLAVEMENT IN K-12 SCHOOLS?

There is a small but growing body of research about the teaching and learning of enslavement in U.S. K–12 schools. Most of this research exposes the problematic ways in which this historical topic is approached in classrooms. King and Woodson (2017) analyzed several news stories like those previously mentioned involving the teaching of slavery in U.S. K–12 classrooms. They illuminated the notion that using such superficial or reductive instructional methods to teach about enslavement inflicts educative-psychic violence on students. Bery (2014) studied a school play that purported to celebrate Black history, where white students took on the roles of enslaved Africans and abolitionists while Asian American and Latinx students played enslavers. The Black students and parents at this school boycotted the play altogether. Bery (2014) found that by allowing white students to believe they had experienced the horrors of slavery, while not having to account for the privileges that enslavement afforded them contemporarily, ultimately affirmed white supremacy instead of celebrating Black history. These problematic teaching methods are perhaps related to a curriculum that is anemic regarding its emphasis on slavery, as Anderson and Metzger (2011) found that state standards "depersonalize the institution of slavery and frame its consequences as a lamentable but temporary roadblock" in the evolution of the United States (pp. 401–402). All of this research supports the findings of the Southern Poverty Law Center's (2018) study on the teaching and learning of slavery in U.S. schools. In surveying high school students and teachers, reviewing state standards, and reviewing popular U.S. history textbooks, SPLC (2018) found that U.S. high school students knew alarmingly little about enslavement in the United

States, as only 8% of students correctly identified slavery as the cause of the Civil War. This study also found that while the overwhelming majority of teachers understand the importance of teaching about enslavement in U.S. history, teachers find little support in the textbooks they are provided or other resources provided by the state.

## WHAT DO WE KNOW ABOUT PLANTATION SITES?

While there is little research in K–12 history education about historical plantation sites, researchers in other fields have begun to study the narratives presented and other aspects of these sites. These researchers have found that the narratives presented at historic plantation sites marginalize the historical presence of the enslaved Africans who were held captive at these sites, despite calls to bring their histories to the forefront (Modlin, 2008; Shields, 2017). Modlin and colleagues (2011) refer to the disparity between the emotionally evocative narratives that visitors hear about the planter class family and the lack thereof regarding the enslaved people who toiled and lived at these sites as "affective inequality" (p. 5). Butler (2001) studied the brochures that historical plantation sites use to advertise their tours, finding that key words that referred to enslavement, such as "slaves" or "slave cabins," appeared in these texts less than half as much as references to "owners." Butler also found that federally owned historic plantation sites had considerably more information about enslavement available than those owned by other entities, and enslavement was rarely mentioned or outright ignored in the information made available by private owners or foundations. Shields (2017) compares plantation sites to a palimpsest, which is a document that has been written, erased, and rewritten, with previous portions of the document becoming visible at unexpected moments. In this comparison, she refers to the ways that plantation tour operators have attempted to erase or revise the narrative of enslavement at these sites, although vestiges of the institution and the African and African-descended people held captive at these sites continuously reappear. Carter (2016) notes that historic plantation sites lie at the center of the divide between "tourism as amusement" and "tourism as memorial" (p. 245), as tourists approach these sites with varying expectations. Recent news stories, however, indicate that many plantation visitors take offense to the mere mention of enslavement, as one tour guide reported that a visitor exclaimed that "dragging all this slavery stuff up again is bringing down America" (Biser, 2017), and some visitors leave scathing viral reviews about tours that center the lives and experiences of the enslaved (Avery, 2019). Despite these antagonistic views toward the mere mention of slavery and enslaved people, some historical plantation sites are beginning to alter the narratives presented on their tours to center the enslaved people who lived and worked on these lands (Graves, 2017).

## WHAT IS RACIAL LITERACY?

Conceptualized by critical race theorist Lani Guinier (2004), racial literacy is "the capacity to decipher the durable racial grammar that structures racialized hierarchies and frames the narrative of our republic" (p. 100). Reading race in its psychological, interpersonal, and structural dimensions, racial literacy focuses on the connection between race and power. While it acknowledges the significance of individual agency, racial literacy does not remove its focus from the institutional and structural forces within which that agency exists. What this means is that while racially literate people understand the significance of individual acts of racism as well as the ways racism impacts individual people, a racial literacy analysis focuses largely on the structures that maintain racial hierarchy. As Guinier explains, "racism normalizes these racialized hierarchies; it diverts attention from the unequal distribution of resources and power they perpetuate" (p. 114). Additionally, racial literacy reads race as epiphenomenal, as people in power have traditionally influenced and deployed race to benefit themselves socially, economically, and politically. Finally, racial literacy does not lose sight of race, but it does not focus exclusively on race. Racial literacy notes that racial hierarchies mirror the distribution of power and resources and that many of the problems that Black Americans experience on the bottom of the racial hierarchy are attributable to large societal dysfunction (Guinier, 2004).

Racial literacy poses a stark contrast to the paradigm through which issues of race and racism are commonly analyzed, which is racial liberalism. A racial liberalism approach to racism focuses on individual prejudices and individual racial tolerance, as opposed to racial literacy's focus on the relationship between power and racial hierarchy. The architects behind the *Brown v. Board of Education* (1954) U.S. Supreme Court case used racial liberalism to stress the destructive effect that individual prejudice had on Black children and the importance of interracial contact to promote tolerance. Guinier (2004) notes that this attempt to gain sympathy from the justices did not help Black Americans gain any semblance of equality despite the decision that school segregation was unconstitutional, as "the ideals of racial liberalism produced a legal icon but did little to disrupt the historic pattern in which race was used to manufacture dissensus" (Guinier, 2004, p. 113). While on its surface racial liberalism may appear to be a necessary approach to resolving issues of race and racism, it undermines goals of racial equity by shifting from a structural and systemic focus of racism and the allocation of resources to focusing on race through an individual lens. If we understand racism to be the "maintenance of, and acquiescence in, racialized hierarchies governing resource distribution" (p. 98), a racial liberalism approach to addressing structural and institutional issues of race is tantamount to using tape to cover up a hole in a dam.

While most of the research involving racial literacy in education exists within the fields of English education and literacy education (e.g., Rogers &

Mosely, 2006; Sealey-Ruiz, 2013; Skerrett, 2011), there is an emerging body of research in which history education researchers are using racial literacy to study the teaching and learning of history. King (2016) used racial literacy to study how preservice teachers used Black history to discuss race in secondary U.S. history classrooms, while Epstein and Gist (2015) used racial literacy as part of their framework in examining how culturally relevant history teachers challenged their students' conceptions of race and racism. Additionally, Smith (2014) wrote about the importance of using a racial literacy framework to teach about the election and presidency of Barack Obama, as well as the dangers of using an approach of racial liberalism that focuses solely on his "firstness" (p. 65). Given racial literacy's focus on the relationship between race and power and understanding the structures that created and maintain racial hierarchy, what better place could there be to gain a sense of racial literacy other than the place where the connection between race and power began—a plantation?

## WHAT IS MY RELATIONSHIP TO THIS TOPIC?

As a Black woman from the metropolitan Atlanta area, the idea of visiting a plantation was never something that I, nor my family, had ever considered. As General Sherman and Union soldiers destroyed most of the plantations within an hour's drive of where I grew up, I had reached adulthood before learning that visiting plantations was even something that people did. The first question that came to my mind after learning this was: Why would anyone want to visit a place where my ancestors were treated as subhuman? While for some plantations conjure up images of a genteel South that includes hoop-skirts and mint juleps, for me plantations are primarily associated with the brutality that my ancestors endured as they toiled from sunrise to sunset each day.

I also approach this topic as a researcher who knows the impact that historic sites of racialized trauma can have on visitors (Dillard et al., 2017). More than once, I have visited the Cape Coast Castle in Ghana, which is the last place many enslaved Africans were held on the continent before boarding the ships of the Middle Passage as part of the transatlantic slave trade. Each time I visited the castle, I learned about the different imperial European powers that owned this castle. I was also presented with the stark contrast of the well-lit upstairs offices, chapel, and rooms where the lords and governors worked and lived, and the cold, dark dungeons where enslaved Africans were held captive while tightly packed into cells to live in one another's excrement. The tour guides at this historic site curated an experience that juxtaposed the nobility of the Europeans who participated in the slave trade with the brutality and subhuman conditions in which they forced Africans to exist. The curators of this site also helped visitors make clear connections between Africans on the continent and those of the diaspora. It is these sentiments that brought me to this work and guided me through my analysis of racial literacy at historic plantation sites.

## WHAT PLANTATION SITES ARE WE DISCUSSING?

### Magnolia Plantation & Gardens

Located a few miles outside of Charleston, South Carolina, Magnolia Plantation and Gardens claims to be the most visited plantation in the Charleston area (Magnolia Plantation & Gardens, n.d.). This is quite a feat when one considers that there are well over a dozen plantations available for touring in this area. This former rice plantation was and is still owned by the Drayton family. There are numerous tours available for visitors to take at Magnolia Plantation and Gardens, including a nature tram tour in which visitors tour the plantation's wetlands, forests, lakes, and marshes; a tour of the plantation house; and a rice field boat tour where tourists are encouraged to "slip back in time" as they "cool [their] heels and enjoy the breeze of the Ashley River" (Magnolia Plantation & Gardens, n.d.). There is also a tour of the cabins in which enslaved people lived titled "From Slavery to Freedom." According to each of the employees I spoke with on my visit, the plantation house tour and the nature tram are by far the most popular tours at this historic plantation site.

### Whitney Plantation

The Whitney Plantation is located in Wallace, Louisiana, less than one hour's drive from New Orleans, and it bills itself as the only plantation museum in the area to focus exclusively on the lives of the people who were enslaved on this land. During the time of enslavement and for decades after, this plantation was owned by the Haydel family. There is only one guided tour available at this historic plantation site, and on this tour visitors learn about the 350 people who were enslaved from 1752 to 1865 at this former sugar, rice, and indigo plantation. Additionally, the visitors center has two exhibits through which visitors can take self-guided tours. The Whitney Plantation includes numerous buildings, including an original kitchen building, a church, slave quarters, and the big house. This historic plantation museum also contains numerous memorials dedicated to those who were enslaved at the Whitney Plantation.

## WHAT HAPPENS ON PLANTATION TOURS?

### Magnolia Plantation

While there are several tours offered at Magnolia Plantation and Gardens, here I'll only be discussing two tours: the Plantation House Tour and From

Slavery to Freedom. I have chosen to focus on these tours because they are the two tours where visitors are most likely to learn about the relationship between race and power on this plantation. The Plantation House tour is one of the most popular tours offered at Magnolia Plantation, along with the Nature Tram tour. On the Plantation House tour, visitors tour the home of the Drayton family, who owned the entire plantation. Before the tour begins, visitors are told that they are not to take photos inside the home. Once inside the home, visitors listen to tour guides discuss the history of the edifice in the passive voice, referring to when the home "was built" without acknowledging the enslaved Africans who mostly likely built the home. As docents guide groups of visitors through the home, they tell visitors delightful stories of parties thrown by the Drayton family and include detailed narratives about each family member who lived in the house, while simultaneously excluding the existence of the enslaved Black people who worked in this house and on the land surrounding it.

The tour titled "From Slavery to Freedom" begins with visitors taking a tram from the ticket booth to the area where the slave cabins are located. After deboarding the tram, visitors are escorted to a set of covered tables where historical documents like runaway slave notices hang from makeshift walls. As visitors sit in this covered area, the tour guide discusses the Drayton family's journey to South Carolina from Barbados and the process of harvesting rice. He also tells visitors about the need to build cabins for enslaved Africans to live in, after the slave trade legally ended in 1808, revealing that prior to the legal end of the slave trade in 1808, slaveowners would force enslaved Africans to work until they died, and simply import more enslaved Africans to replace them. After this 15-minute history lesson, which focuses on the Draytons and makes shallow connections between slavery and political and economic power, visitors guide themselves through three cabins in which enslaved people lived. Because people actually lived in these cabins until the 1990s, the three cabins were restored to appear as they had in the years 1850, 1930, and 1969. Inside the cabins sit furniture, tools, and other household trinkets that one would need to survive during each time period. Absent from these cabins are any information about the enslaved people who toiled in the marsh during the day and slept in these cabins at night.

## Whitney Plantation

Whereas the Plantation House tour at Magnolia Plantation completely ignores the institution of slavery and how it sat at the foundation of all that happened on that property, the tour at the Whitney Plantation focuses exclusively on the institution of slavery and the lives of the enslaved people held captive at this site. While visitors learn the name of the Haydel family, who owned this land for centuries, they exist peripherally to the enslaved people whose stories are centered here. Additionally, the Haydel family is explicitly referred to as slaveowners, whereas the Drayton family's slaveowning status was not mentioned at all on the Plantation House tour. At Whitney Plantation, visitors stop at a memorial that holds the names of 107,000 people who were enslaved in the state of Louisiana. Here, tour guides tell visitors how enslavers stripped enslaved Africans of any knowledge of their homelands, as they removed the names of the enslaved and created situations where they were also forced to lose their native languages. Visitors also stop at other monuments, including the Field of Homage, which features a Black woman angel holding a baby. This memorial pays homage to the 2,200 enslaved children who died before age 3 in St. John the Baptist Parish, Louisiana. Visitors also have the opportunity to see, touch, and enter a slave jail. This jail would not have been located on the plantation, but it would have been packed full of the enslaved at markets where enslaved Black people were purchased and sold. In this sense, the tour at Whitney Plantation also helps visitors learn about the lives of the enslaved before they came to the plantation and after they were sold to another slaveowner.

When visitors at Whitney Plantation finally make it to the big house where the plantation owners lived, tour guides do not provide humorous tales of the Haydel family or stories about elaborate parties that the Haydel family threw. In the house, visitors learn about the role that the enslaved played in this house and keeping the Haydel family's business going, as well as how many of the practices of enslavement continued well after the ratification of the 13th amendment, as sharecropping continued on this plantation until the 1970s.

## DISCUSSION

At Magnolia Plantation and Gardens, visitors learn about the life of the family who owns the property, and visitors only learn about slavery at this historic plantation site on the tour titled "From Slavery to Freedom." In relegating even the mere mention of slavery to a single tour and keeping the institution of slavery completely separate from the narrative of the Drayton family, on a plantation that was built and sustained by enslaved Africans, the Drayton family (who still own the property) is essentially reifying the racial hierarchy that began with slavery in the United States, placing wealthy white Americans at the top and Black people at the very bottom. The ways that slavery is approached (and avoided) at Magnolia Plantation implicitly tell visitors who belongs where and whose stories deserve to be told, all of which is antithetical to racial literacy. As Guinier (2004) explains, "racism normalizes these racialized hierarchies" (p. 114). Because slavery is rendered largely invisible at this plantation, visitors do not have the opportunity to understand the connection between race, capitalism, and political power or to "rethink race as an instrument of social, geographic, and economic control of both Blacks and Whites" (Guinier, 2004, p. 114), which leaves space for them to leave this historic site believing any number of dangerous fallacies about slavery, from its brutality to its role in the foundation of our nation.

The Whitney Plantation, on the other hand, makes a concerted effort to help visitors understand slavery to be the bedrock of our nation's racialized hierarchy. In centering the narratives of the enslaved people who worked and were held captive on this property, and helping visitors make connections between enslavement and contemporary racial issues, tour guides at the Whitney Plantation help visitors begin to understand the connection between race and power and that "racialized hierarchies mirror the distribution of power and resources in society more generally" (Guinier, 2004, p. 115). Whereas Magnolia Plantation and Gardens follows the playbook of racism, in which it "diverts attention from the unequal distribution of resources and power" (Guinier, 2004, p. 115), the Whitney Plantation uses this maldistribution as the focal point of the museum, helping visitors understand the social, political, and economic effects of slavery while humanizing the enslaved people on whose backs this nation was built. While no one tour can provide visitors with the totality of what slavery entailed and the role it played in the nation's social, political, and economic spheres, the tour offered at the Whitney Plantation certainly provides visitors with enough information to begin to make those connections.

## CONCLUSION

Although I came into this work expecting plantation sites to present narratives that suppressed the horrors of slavery and placed enslavers in a glowing light, the Whitney Plantation is proof that not all plantations do attempt to revise history in this way. While Magnolia Plantation and Gardens attempts to hold onto traditional narratives that marginalize and sometimes outright erase the enslaved people who were once held captive on that land, the Whitney Plantation centers the lives of the enslaved and the ways slavery was embedded in the nation's social, political, and economic foundation. Whereas Magnolia Plantation allows visitors to leave believing dangerous fallacies about slavery, the Whitney Plantation pushes its visitors to make pivotal steps toward racial literacy.

If teachers are going to take students on field trips to historic plantation sites, just as my students' K–12 teachers had, they first need to firmly understand what it is that they want students to take away from the experience. If teachers want students to gain an understanding of how slavery laid the foundation for our nation's lasting racial hierarchy, a trip to a plantation site where enslaved Black people are nearly erased will certainly not help achieve this goal. In cases where this is not the goal, teachers would still be wise to consider the harmful effects that such a trip could have on students, particularly Black students, as a visit to a historical plantation site that focuses largely on the owners and does not humanize the enslaved could lead to the spirit murdering (Williams, 1987) of Black students. Not only do field trips to sites like Magnolia Plantation and Gardens allow students and other visitors to leave without gaining a sense of racial literacy in the least, but it could actually make them confident in their racial illiteracy as they position themselves as experts who have had direct contact with a historic plantation site. In an effort to avoid this, teachers should do as much research as possible regarding the narratives presented at these historic sites, and perhaps visit themselves before taking students. School districts could also help by providing professional development for teachers at these sites. Returning to my original questions, is the Whitney Plantation a site that can help students gain a sense of racial literacy? Absolutely. Magnolia Plantation and Gardens? Not so much.

## REFERENCES

Anderson, C., & Metzger, S. (2011). Slavery, the Civil War era, and African American representation in U.S. history: An analysis of four states' academic standards. *Theory & Research in Social Education, 39*(3), 393–415. https://doi.org/10.1080/00933104.2011.10473460

Avery, D. (2019, August 27). A visitor didn't want to hear about slavery on her plantation tour. This historical interpreter has something to say about that. *Newsweek.* https://www.newsweek.com/yelp-plantation-michael-twitty-1455983

Bery, S. (2014). Multiculturalism, teaching slavery, and white supremacy. *Equity & Excellence in Education, 47*(3), 334–352. https://doi.org/10.1080/10665684.2014.933072

Biser, M. (2017, August 28). I used to lead tours at a plantation. You won't believe the questions I got about slavery. *Vox.* https://www.vox.com/2015/6/29/8847385/what-i-learned-from-leading-tours-about-slavery-at-a-plantation?fbclid=IwAR0XJjgLC2WrVPBlotozwoUmzsOk5Qm_Efh0JH4AZzb6SUZvOMye7hR_lOU

*Brown v. Board of Education,* 347 U.S. 483 (1954).

Butler, D. (2001). Whitewashing plantations: The commodification of a slave-free antebellum South. *International Journal of Hospitality & Tourism Administration, 2*(3–4), 163–175. https://doi.org/10.1300/J149v02n03_07

Carter, P. (2016). Where are the enslaved?: TripAdvisor and the narrative landscapes of southern plantation museums. *Journal of Heritage Tourism: Memory, Slavery and Plantation Museums: The River Road Project, 11*(3), 235–249. https://doi.org/10.1080/1743873X.2015.1100625

CBSLA. (2017 September 18). *High school under fire for project reenacting slavery.* CBS Los Angeles. https://losangeles.cbslocal.com/2017/09/18/high-school-under-fire-for-project-reenacting-slavery/

Dillard, C., Duncan, K., & Johnson, L. (2017). Black history full circle: Lessons learned from a Ghana study abroad in education program. *Social Education, 81*(1), 50–53.

Epstein, T., & Gist, C. (2015). Teaching racial literacy in secondary humanities classrooms: Challenging adolescents' of color concepts of race and racism. *Race Ethnicity and Education, 18*(1), 40–60. https://doi.org/10.1080/13613324.2013.792800

Gonzalez, J. (2019, February 22). *Virginia students instructed to play "runaway slave game" in P.E. class.* WJLA. https://wjla.com/news/local/ashburn-elementary-students-instructed-to-play-slave-game-during-pe-class

Graves, B. (2017). Return and get it: Developing McLeod Plantation as a shared space of historical memory. *Southern Cultures, 23*(2), 75–96. https://doi.org/10.1353/scu.2017.0015

Griffith, J. (2019, May 29). *Black students were cast as slaves in New York teacher's mock "auctions," state finds.* NBC News https://www.nbcnews.com/news/nbcblk/black-students-were-cast-slaves-new-york-teacher-s-mock-n1011361?cid=sm_npd_ms_fb_ma&fbclid=IwAR1ECDvzn-Menaiz2DOgmvYAjvI-pnJaJzCeMwo UUI2EhKhPZADO0geFGLc&fbclid=IwAR31Hg8Z66wSGXYLHQlWSWya6df wL9CVnNYJ6cXTcLaCO9IxXR_lZcaOVm4

Guinier, L. (2004). From racial liberalism to racial literacy: *Brown v. Board of Education* and the interest-divergence dilemma. *The Journal of American History 91*(1), 92–118. https://doi: 10.2307/3659616

King, L. (2016). Teaching Black history as a racial literacy project. *Race Ethnicity and Education, 19*(6), 1303–1318. https://doi.org/10.1080/13613324.2016.1150822

Magnolia Plantation & Gardens. (n.d.). Retrieved from https://www.magnoliaplantation.com

Modlin, E. (2008). Tales told on the tour: Mythic representations of slavery by docents at North Carolina plantation museums. *Southeastern Geographer, 48*(3), 265–287. https://doi.org/10.1353/sgo.0.0025

Modlin, E., Alderman, D., & Gentry, G. (2011). Tour guides as creators of empathy: The role of affective inequality in marginalizing the enslaved at plantation house museums. *Tourist Studies, 11*(1), 3–19. https://doi.org/10.1177/1468797611412007

Rogers, R., & Mosely, M. (2006). Racial literacy in a second grade classroom: Critical race theory, whiteness studies, and literacy research. *Reading Research Quarterly, 41*(4), 462–495. https://doi.org/10.1598/RRQ.41.4.3

Sealey-Ruiz, Y. (2013). Building racial literacy in first year composition. *Teaching English in the Two-Year College, 40*(4), 384–398.

Shields, T. (2017). Magnolia longing: The plantation tour as palimpsest. *Souls: A Critical Journal of Black Politics, Culture, and Society, 19*(1), 6–23. https://doi.org/10.1080/10999949.2017.1268517

Skerrett, A. (2011). English teachers' racial literacy knowledge and practice. *Race Ethnicity and Education, 14*(3), 313–330. https://doi.org/10.1080/13613324.2010.543391

Southern Poverty Law Center. (2018). *Teaching hard history: American slavery.* https://www.splcenter.org/sites/default/files/tt_hard_history_american_slavery.pdf

Smith, W. (2014). Not stopping at first: Racial literacy and the teaching of Barack Obama. *Multicultural Perspectives, 16*(2), 65–71. https://doi.org/10.1080/15210960.2014.889567

Williams, P. (1987). Spirit-murdering the messenger: The discourse of fingerpointing as the law's response to racism. *University of Miami Law Review, 42*(1), 127–158.

## CHAPTER 9

# Beyond Curricular Acknowledgment

## Islam in the Classroom

*Natasha Hakimali Merchant*

### RACIAL LITERACY AND ISLAM: A PROLOGUE

Before delving into this chapter, it is necessary to address how this chapter fits into a volume addressing racial literacy in social studies. After all, Muslims are not a race, though they are racialized. While racial literacy must be intersectional if it is to honor the complexity of the fluid and varied realities of race, I admit a feeling of anxiety in broadening racial literacy to an extent where race talk risks becoming a tactic in avoiding the acute and intentional cruelty inflicted upon Indigenous and Black people, a common reflex of the guilt-ridden in the United States. Yet I am reminded that studying "race" by exclusively focusing on those racialized can reinforce racist logic. After all, race as a distinct categorization schema meant to classify and subjugate is the creation of white supremacy. Therefore, the study of race (and racial literacy) must include the precepts and functions of white supremacist knowledge systems and cultures so that they are exposed, examined, and dismantled.

The project of white supremacy, particularly through colonization, intersects in a variety of ways with Muslim histories. The fact that Muslims are racialized today in the United States is deeply connected to the story of the origins of racial oppression on this land. Critical histories connect the conquest of Al-Andalus in the late 15th century directly with the following colonization of the Americas, not only because the first provided power and funding for the latter, but also because the technologies of "epistemicide" and "spiritualicide" were practiced in the first and intensified with a racial logic in the second (Grosfoguel, 2013). In turn, the racial logic utilized and refined in the Americas traveled back to Spain and resulted in a "new"(racial) justification for oppressing the "Moriscos" (converted Muslims) and "Marranos" (converted Jews) under Spanish rule, demonstrating the global power of racial hierarchies (Grosfoguel, 2013). What remains as a result of white supremacy even today is not simply the racialization of Muslims in the United States, Canada, Europe, and other parts of the "Western" world, but also the knowledge that has been systematically eradicated as part of the colonial project.

In this chapter, racial literacy enters as a politics of asserting for complex and nuanced knowledge about Islam and Muslims in the social studies classroom.

## PERSONAL FOUNDATIONS IN COMPLEXITY

Singing, dancing, and chanting were the primary devotional expressions of my faith practice throughout childhood. I recall being encouraged to keep these practices contained within the walls of our communal spaces. As I grew, I became acutely aware of the paradox of subduing those expressions that are the most vibrant and spirited. When I inquired as to the reason for this paradox, I was told that these practices aren't considered "Muslim enough." When I inquired as to the reason for our seemingly un-Islamic practices, I was directed to a common communal narrative within the Ismāʿili Khoja segments of the Shi'a Nizari Ismāʿili Muslim community, to which I belong. The narrative stated that our ancestors were Hindu and belonged to a lower caste, and due to the misfortune of our social class, we were persuaded to convert from Hinduism to Islam. The narrative follows that the methodology used to convert from Hinduism to Islam employed practices like singing, dancing, and chanting. Thus, those "Hindu" practices remain today. This seemingly coherent historical explanation was one I internalized and propagated for many years until I came across the work of Ali Asani (2011a).

Asani (2011a) explained that the multivalent (seemingly contradictory) practices of my ancestral community—read today as both "Hindu" and "Muslim," "Shi'a" and "Sunni"—were commonplace in precolonial South Asia. Religious practice was conducted through local expressions and guided by wise sages, many of whom did not affiliate strongly with a categorized religious social identity. It was the colonial encounter,

> in which notions of religious identity and the categories "Hindu" and "Muslim" were contested and also rigidly and narrowly demarcated. The Khojas, like many other Indian communities, were pressured to reshape their identity to better conform to externally defined norms. (Asani, 2011a, p. 97)

After learning this, it struck me how significant external categories have been in codifying what seems to be the basis of one's identity.

This liberating knowledge demonstrated that the singing, dancing, and chanting were entirely consistent with the history of my community. Fluidity in expression has been a mainstay in its legacy (Asani, 2011a). I came to learn that multivalent expressions of faith, including musical and artistic articulations of religion, have been widespread within Muslim traditions. In fact, understanding Islam through a rigid set of beliefs and practices is a relatively new phenomenon in the history of Muslim civilizations (Ahmed, 2015). Today, dominant understandings of Islam as a canonized and narrow set of beliefs and practices permeate, not only through general discourses about Islam, but within many Muslim communities (Ahmed, 2015). Given this reality, how should educators approach Islam in the classroom? More specifically, this chapter explores the extent to which underrepresented interpretations and approaches to religion and culture (in this case, Islam), should be covered. To investigate this question, I pull from experiences reported by Muslim girls (13 to 18 years old) who belong to what I am calling *minority communities of interpretation*. As a point of clarification here, I am intentionally resisting the commonly used term "sect," as the term is associated with violence and a sense of political divide. Utilizing the term "communities of interpretation," which I first read in the work of Farhad Daftary (2004), offers the opportunity for a label that acknowledges the diversity and range in interpretation (philosophy and practice), not only at an individual Muslim level, but at the level of longstanding traditions. The shift in frame from political-fractious to dynamic and varied offers Muslims a respite from the one-dimensional, Orientalist tropes that continue today. I have used the term "minority," because the students I have learned from come from Muslim communities that have experienced minoritization in a variety of ways within specific Muslim contexts. Their knowledge is also minoritized, as it is seldom acknowledged within curriculum.

## QUESTIONS OF CURRICULAR ACKNOWLEDGMENT

Despite the inclusion of student experiences in empirical research on curriculum studies, students are often seen as passive recipients of curriculum (He et al., 2008). While scholarship on students' curriculum experiences has increased in the last three decades, more research is needed in order to shed light on the students' experiences with curriculum and contributions to co-constructing curriculum as a live process. Prominent scholars of social studies urge a better understanding of the role students' identities and affiliations play in the way they make sense of curriculum (Barton & McCully, 2010; Epstein, 1998, 2001; Mosborg, 2002). These scholars have established that students' identities mediate the ways in which they interpret the curriculum. Additionally, scholars of culturally responsive teaching (Ladson-Billings & Tate, 1995), including researchers of students' funds of knowledge (Moll et al., 1992), have shown how students' already existing (pre-instructional) sets of knowledge can serve as tools to further curricular goals. In addition, curricular acknowledgment of student subjects is recognized as essential to positive student identity development (Busey & Russell, 2016), particularly in early adolescence.

A microcosm of the outside world, classroom curricula reflect the dominant epistemologies in which students are already well versed. What was once an imperialist agenda is now a closely related, neoliberal one, disciplining bodies and knowledge. Therefore, the students in our classrooms (along with the teachers, the curriculum, and just about everything else) have already been socialized by commonsense frames (Gramsci, 1971). Students who embody histories and cultures outside of the dominant "enter a social studies classroom with many experiences and insights that will inform their understanding of global systems because they already have a tacit understanding of how people in power use their culture to justify inequity and injustice" (Merryfield & Subedi, 2006, p. 286). While many minoritized students are disturbed by the undervaluing of their inherent epistemologies, others are resigned to the notion that their tradition's ways of knowing and being will ever be acknowledged. As Laila, a high school student belonging to the Ahmadiyya Muslim community, explained:

> They [the teacher] taught stuff that I didn't know really about. They only teach about two sects . . . and that's all they teach from that view . . . There's so many sects that they can't teach all of them. That's why they only teach the main ones, the majority. (Merchant, 2016, p. 192)

The question of acknowledgment and representation is ripe for a student like Laila, who finds herself as the subject of curriculum but does not recognize what she learns about herself. On the one hand, the world's population of Ahmadiyya Muslims is estimated at roughly 12 million (Valentine, 2014), making them numerically a small minority within the various Muslim communities of interpretation. However, Ahmadiyya Muslims are arguably one of the most fiercely persecuted communities of Muslims today, as several Muslim scholars and clerics have decreed charges of heresy against many adherents for their beliefs (Valentine, 2014). Laila's resignation to not expecting a responsive curriculum highlights the commonplace experience of being invisible and marginal. One lesson educators might glean from Laila's curricular experience is the importance of investigating more representative or responsive curricular approaches. However, with the dynamic nature of social realities, identity representation (on its own) is not only incomplete, but also perpetuates static notions of "the other." Instead, a culturally sustaining pedagogical approach, as discussed in the following section, would better respond to a more complex understanding of Islam and Muslims.

## CULTURALLY SUSTAINING PEDAGOGY AND ISLAM

Culturally Sustaining Pedagogy (CSP) posits that students who "maintain their multiple ways of speaking and being" (Paris & Alim, 2014, p. 89), alongside dominant skills and knowledges, have greater access to power. Applying a CSP framework to Laila's case would suggest that beyond simply acknowledging her heritage for the sake of "honoring and valuing community" (Paris & Alim, 2014, p. 89), attending to multiple ways of being and knowing is a pedagogy necessary for greater access to power. While noble in intention, mere inclusion and acknowledgment within the curriculum can lend itself to reifying essentialist and static notions of marginalized identities (Merchant, 2018, p. 184) rather than allowing for the dynamism of heritage and community practices (Paris, 2012). The focus on culture as evolving, localized, and specific also recognizes and invites student agency in shifting the interpretation and performance of their identities. In Laila's case, a CSP approach to Islam might have opened up space for her lived experience of Islam as valid and worthy of curricular attention.

Using a CSP approach to teach about religion does not make sense if one's perception of religion depends upon a singular narrative (often sedimented in conceptions of otherness). In reality, community of interpretation, ethnicity, class structure, and a variety of other factors mediate the understanding and practice of Islam (Ahmed, 2015). Yet static beliefs and practices permeate what is taught about Islam. Dunn (2008) argued that although the study of anthropology has contradicted this assumption, K–12 world history curriculum largely operates on the premise that each "civilization possesses distinctive, indeed inherent traditions that emerged largely out of the operation of mechanism internal to the particular unit" (p. 187). He further explains that anthropomorphizing an entire culture or civilization assumes "historical agency" (p. 259).

One particular difficulty in teaching about religion (as opposed to other social identity categories) as varied and local is in how the concept of religion is seen as offering truth claims rather than a conceptualization of religion as a human phenomenon. In the context of widespread Islamophobia, many well-intentioned teachers strive to paint a positive picture of Islam, but actually reinforce the conceptualization of Islam as one defined by a unifying set of beliefs and practices. They do this by focusing on the commonalities with beliefs and practices of Christianity and Judaism (Merchant, 2018). This often takes the shape of teachers countering Islamophobic notions by presenting Islam as peaceful and familiar. While this is a noble pursuit, it continues to codify Islam as something existing on its own, independent of the believer (Merchant, 2018).

The complexity in exploring the question of how to approach studying Islam moves far beyond the K–12 context into common understandings of Islam today. As Ahmed (2016) summarizes,

> That this challenge has, unfortunately, not yet been met successfully—which is to say that the existing conceptualizations and uses of "Islam/Islamic" do *not* express a coherent object of meaning (or an object of coherent meaning)—is readily reflected in the fact that analysts, be they historians, anthropologists, sociologists, or scholars of art or religion, are often frankly unsure of what they mean when they use the terms "Islam/Islamic"—or whether, indeed, they should use the terms at all. (p. 9)

Research and scholarship contestations are robust and ongoing around the definition of religion (Murphy, 2006) and specifically Islam (Ahmed, 2015).

However, in K–12 curricula, religion is presented as a static package that adherents uniformly believe or practice. In what follows, I present data from Muslim students who face moments in the classroom where they disrupt dominant narratives about Islam/Muslims. Drawing on CSP, I describe these students as well positioned to reveal how to move toward a more rigorous teaching about Islam and Muslims.

## METHODS

This chapter pulls data from a 2014/2015 study conducted with Muslim girls from minority communities of interpretation. I engaged in the phenomenological case study to understand the conscious experiences of these students as they reflected on their curricular experiences with Islam (Merriam, 2009). Interviews and questionnaires were conducted with each study participant and analyzed by isolating each individual case and conducting a single-case analysis through pattern matching. The patterns that emerged from the single-case analysis were then compared across each case, determining commonalities and exploring conditions that may have caused differences (Yin, 2009).

The subject sample was bound in two ways. First, this study was bound by the focal religious identities: Ithnā ʿAsharīyah, Ismāʿili, and Ahmadiyya. This means that the students within each of these focal identities comprise a single case, making three separate cases. While religious identity categories provided a boundary in which subjects were analyzed, each student within the sample was also considered a distinct case, resulting in six individual case subjects.

I utilized my personal networks in the Ithnā ʿAsharīyah, Ismāʿili, and Ahmadiyya communities to conduct a purposeful sampling (Merriam, 2009). Since Muslim female gender is an identity of extreme focus in the American imagination (Mir, 2009), this study concentrated particularly on Muslim girls. Women's bodies have, in many ways, become a significant site where Muslims are determined as either "safe" or a potential "threat" to Western sensibilities. Similarly, gender performance and gendered behaviors have also been regulated by cultural gatekeepers from within the Muslim community, often landing Muslim women in the awkward position of being "safely suspended between mainstream normal" and "Muslim normal" (Mir, 2009, p. 250). For this reason, the study focused particularly on how girls experienced the curriculum against the backdrop of extreme gendered expectations and stereotypes.

To a certain degree, all students in the study identified with the immigrant experience, although most students were born in the United States to at least one foreign-born parent. All of the student-participants, to some degree, traced their origins back to India, Pakistan, and Iraq (see Table 9.1). Students in the sample identified themselves as actively connected to religious spaces. They regularly attended prayer services and participated in community activities such as religious education classes and/or service activities organized by their

**Table 9.1. Student Cases**

| Name | Community | Country of Origin | Grade | Description of School |
|---|---|---|---|---|
| Zehra | Ithnā ʿAšharīyah | Iraq & the U.S. | 12 | Homeschool With Co-op Classes |
| Zaynab | Ithnā ʿAšharīyah | India | 7 | Public Suburban Middle School |
| Laila | Ahmadiyya | Pakistan | 10 | Public Urban High School |
| Aiza | Ahmadiyya | Pakistan | 9 | Public Urban High School |
| Aaima | Ismāʿili | India | 10 | Public IB School |
| Tara | Ismāʿili | Pakistan | 10 | Public Suburban High School |

religious institution. Table 9.1 represents each focal student's pseudonym, country of origin, sectarian community, grade, and school type.

## STUDENT INTERVENTIONS: DISRUPTING CONFINING NOTIONS OF ISLAM/MUSLIM

One of the foundational findings of this study was that the Muslim girls from minority communities of interpretation (MCoIs) constantly found their own experiences of being Muslim or practicing Islam minimized and essentialized in the classroom context. In response to this, the data highlight moments when students disrupted the narrative to provide counterexamples.

There were several instances where South Asian origin subjects noted they were often correcting misperceptions of their non-Muslim peers about the geographic spread of Islam. Although misperceptions related to Muslim stereotypes were present, there were also misperceptions regarding who constituted a Muslim and who did not. For example, Zaynab, who wore hijab and was therefore easily identified as Muslim, was asked the infamous "What are you?" question by a peer. The following excerpt recounts that event:

> Sometimes they ask me where I'm from because there's a lot of Indian kids (in my school). I'm actually Indian, I'm pure Indian, I'm from Gujarat. They're just like, "Oh, are you Arab, are you Pakistani? Are you like Iraqi or Iranian?" I'm like, "No, I'm Indian." They're like, "What? No! Indians have to be Hindu and stuff."

Social research has documented many instances where brown communities are lumped together as "Muslim." Perhaps best-known are the incidents of hate crimes against the Sikh community, who are commonly mistaken as Muslims (Kaleem, 2013). In this case, we see that Zaynab's peers had a strong sense of where Muslims did and did not come from. Ironically, Zaynab told her peers she was from India in order to minimize confusion about her family's actual migration journey. Her family was part of the South Asian diaspora population in East Africa. Knowing that her peers would take issue with her parents being from Africa without her being Black, she thought she was making the safer choice by claiming to be "pure Indian." Unfortunately, she had not oversimplified herself sufficiently to satisfy her questioning peers.

Aaima had a very similar experience to Zaynab's. It is worth noting here that Aaima was enrolled in an International Baccalaureate® program, which prides itself on globally focused, high-caliber education. Aaima recounted that she had been challenged on being Muslim because of where she was born—India.

She explained, "Because I think the assumption is that most Muslims are coming from Pakistan or coming from Iran and that area. When I say I'm from India, they're like, 'No, but only Hindus are in India.'"

She talked about having an argument with a classmate who stated, "No. That's not normal for Muslims to come from India."

She tried to explain that it was, in fact, normal: "I was like, it's very normal. I'm pretty sure."

She continued by explaining that although this conversation happened with a white friend, there were many instances in which her Hindu friends assumed she was Hindu because she was from India. Curious about why her Hindu friends would make this assumption, I asked Aaima whether her Hindu friends were Indian and, if so, had they been to India. She told me that they were each of Indian origin, and though none of them had been born in India, they had each visited India at least once before.

Essentializing Muslim identity was echoed in the official curriculum. The response of students who didn't resonate with what they were learning varied from silence to refusal. Despite being the youngest in the sample, Zaynab showed tremendous confidence in correcting not only peers but teachers when her understanding of Islam was not acknowledged. Zaynab noted that in a classroom discussion of the Five Pillars she was very confused because she had not learned about Islam within a Five-Pillar framework. She became confused because the Five-Pillar framework was being taught as the essential and unifying set of beliefs/practices across Muslims. Zaynab was enthusiastic to be positioned as the expert on Islam in her class, and her teacher had previously encouraged her to contribute to the curriculum on Islam. During this discussion on the Five Pillars, Zaynab took the opportunity to talk about what she had learned through her religious education: five roots and 10 branches. It is important to note that in Zaynab's classroom context, she was the only Muslim, and therefore her perspectives on Islam were easily accepted as *the* Muslim perspective. According to Zaynab, her teacher was welcoming of her contributions even when they contradicted the curriculum.

Having other Muslim peers in the classroom, as Zehra learned, presented an added level of complexity that made offering counterexamples and narratives more difficult. Zehra talked about being approached by non-Muslim classmates who had heard from another Muslim student that Muslims do not celebrate Halloween.

She explained, "They said, 'No, Muslims don't celebrate Halloween. It's *Haraam.*' . . . . [they] assume that all Muslims are the same."

Zehra decided to speak up and offer her perspective to her classmates, even if her perspective would not resonate with the other Muslim student's experience. Zehra decided that she would offer her perspective, while making it clear that her perspective was colored by her community's interpretation. She said,

> Sometimes I'll say things, but then I'll have to right away sense myself. Not only am I trying to relate to them [non-Muslim peers] in a way that they'll understand, but I'm also trying to figure out a way to explain it with like, "Okay, it's coming from my Shi'a beliefs," but then I'm like, "Well, but the Sunnis . . . they might not agree with this, so if you find a Muslim that disagrees, like, that's normal."

Zehra demonstrated her awareness of the danger that non-Muslim peers might universalize a statement, after hearing a statement about Muslims/Islam from a Muslim individual. This awareness prompted Zehra to tell her peers that "if you find a Muslim that disagrees, like, that's normal." As a result of her minority-in-minority status, Zehra had the opportunity/burden to teach her non-Muslim peers that different Muslims practice and believe differently.

## STUDENT EXPERIENCES AND THE LESSON FOR CURRICULUM

The experiences of these students raise questions about acknowledgment, representation, and pluralism within classroom curricula. While many of the students felt called upon to interrupt dominant narratives of Islam/Muslims, there are just as many examples of when students did not (Merchant, 2016). The experiences of these students reveal that beyond the simple misunderstandings of the ethnic diversity of Muslims, or the diverse set of practices of Muslims, stands a deficient understanding of the complexity inherent within various constellations of individuals and communities. This becomes an epistemological challenge where instead of the easy fix of including more information about Muslims and Islam, the real challenge is in inculcating a mode of thinking oriented toward criticality.

The fact that Zehra had the foresight to not only offer an alternative narrative about Muslims and Halloween but to leave the field open for another experience to contradict her own exemplified the necessity to teach beyond static notions. Zehra, likely due to her position as a minority within Islam, had to vocalize something that should be obvious: "if you find a Muslim that disagrees, like, that's normal." One can imagine how shifting knowledge of the Muslim-other from the stance of larger unifying categories to localized experiences of Muslims (past/present) may foster a learning environment where essentializing Muslims is minimized.

Even in the cases where students offered counternarratives, they still occupied a seat of representation for an entire group (i.e., Shi'a, Ismāʿili, Ahmadiyya, etc.). Therefore, the option to be dynamic within their cultural practices of Islam was narrowed. The problem here is not simply that the curriculum on Islam does not include more about MCoIs; the problem is that collective conceptions or frames about religion (specifically othered religions) are so narrow that one generalization is simply replaced by another. In teaching about Islam in the classroom, the questions of *whose Islam* or *what Islam* are questions that can still lead to generalizations if a robust understanding of the personal-uptake of religion and spirituality is not an essential understanding of the nature of religion itself. Said differently, the tendency is still to teach and learn about Islam versus Islam/s (Asani, 2011b, p.14). Until teachers adopt frameworks like CSP, they will continue reinforcing the notion of history and contemporary culture as static and monolithic, thereby stifling the realities and possibilities for students.

## REFERENCES

Ahmed, S. (2015). *What is Islam?: The importance of being Islamic.* Princeton University Press.

Asani, A. (2011a). From Satpanthi to Ismaili Muslim: The articulation of Ismaili Khoja identity in South Asia. In F. Daftary (Ed.), *A modern history of the Ismailis* (pp. 95–128). I.B. Tauris Publishers.

Asani, A. (2011b). Enhancing religious literacy in a liberal arts education through the study of Islam and Muslim societies. In J. M. Shephard, M. S. Kosslyn, & M. E. Hammonds (Eds.), *The Harvard sampler: Liberal education for the twenty-first century* (pp. 1–31). Harvard University Press.

Barton, K., & McCully, A. (2010). "You can form your own point of view": Internally persuasive discourse in Northern Ireland students' encounters with history. *Teachers College Record, 112*(1), 142–181.

Busey, C. L., & Russell III, W. B. (2016). "We want to learn": Middle school Latino/a students discuss social studies curriculum and pedagogy. *Research in Middle Level Education Online, 39*(4), 1–20.

Daftary, F. (2004). *Ismaili literature: A bibliography of sources and studies.* I.B. Tauris.

Dunn, R. E. (2008). The two world histories. *Social Education, 72*(5), 257–263.

Epstein, T. (1998). Deconstructing differences in African-American and European-American adolescents' perspectives on US history. *Curriculum Inquiry, 28*(4), 397–423.

Epstein, T. (2001). Racial identity and young people's perspectives on social education. *Theory into Practice, 40*(1), 42–47.

Gramsci, A. (1971). *Selections from prison notebooks* (Q. Hoare & G. N. Smith, Trans.). International Publishers.

Grosfoguel, R. (2013). The structure of knowledge in westernized universities: Epistemic racism/sexism and the four genocides/epistemicides of the long 16th century. *Human Architecture: Journal of the Sociology of Self-Knowledge, 11*(1), 72–90.

He, M. F., Phillion, J., Chan, E., & Xu, S. (2008). Immigrant students' experience of curriculum. In F. M. Connelly, M. F. He, & J. Phillion (Eds.), *The Sage handbook of curriculum and instruction* (pp. 176–197). Sage Publications.

Kaleem, J. (2013). FBI to start tracking hate crimes against Sikhs, Hindus and Arabs. *Huffington Post.* huffingtonpost.com

Ladson-Billings, G., & Tate IV, W. F. (1995). Towards a critical race theory of education. *Teachers College Record, 97*(1), 47–68.

Merchant, N. H. (2016). Responses to Islam in the classroom: A case of Muslim girls from minority communities of interpretation. *International Journal of Multicultural Education, 18*(1), 183–199.

Merchant, N. H. (2018). Critical considerations in teaching about the Muslim-other in social studies teacher education. In C. C. Martell (Ed.), *Social studies teacher education: Critical issues and current perspectives* (pp. 175–191). Information Age Publishing.

Merriam, S. B. (2009). *Qualitative research: A guide to design and implementation: Revised and expanded from qualitative research and case study applications in education.* Jossey-Bass.

Merryfield, M. M., & Subedi, B. (2006). Decolonizing the mind for world-centered global education. In W. E. Ross (Ed.), *The social studies curriculum: Purposes, problems, and possibilities* (pp. 283–295). State University of New York Press.

Mir, S. (2009). Not too "college-like," not too normal: American Muslim undergraduate women's gendered discourses. *Anthropology & Education Quarterly, 40*(3), 237–256.

Moll, L. C., Amanti, C., Neff, D., & Gonzalez, N. (1992). Funds of knowledge for teaching: Using a qualitative approach to connect homes and classrooms. *Theory Into Practice, 31*(2), 132–141.

Mosborg, S. (2002). Speaking of history: How adolescents use their knowledge of history in reading the daily news. *Cognition and Instruction, 20*(3), 323–358.

Murphy, T. (2006). Cultural understandings of "religion": The hermeneutical context of teaching religious studies in North America. *Method and Theory in the Study of Religion, 18*(3), 197–218.

Paris, D. (2012). Culturally sustaining pedagogy: A needed change in stance, terminology, and practice. *Educational Researcher, 41*(3), 93–97.

Paris, D., & Alim, H. S. (2014). What are we seeking to sustain through culturally sustaining pedagogy? A loving critique forward. *Harvard Educational Review, 84*(1), 85–100.

Valentine, S. R. (2014). Prophecy after the Prophet, albeit lesser prophets? The Ahmadiyya Jama'at in Pakistan. *Contemporary Islam, 8*(2), 99–113.

Yin, R. K. (2009). *Case study research: Design and methods* (4th ed.). Sage Publications.

# Part IV

# RACIAL LITERACY AND TEACHER LEARNING

## CHAPTER 10

# Developing Racial Literacy With White Social Studies Teachers

## Reflections From a Critical Teacher Educator

*Tommy Ender*

One of the most difficult topics to cover is race. The current political climate has put race on the front page. We're fighting, as educators, with problematic leaders and media sources growing more and more questionable by the day.

—Patrick

Recently, I have realized how important it is to talk with students about white supremacy culture. I had not thought about white supremacy as something I participated in.

—Laney

Patrick and Laney (pseudonyms) reflected on the influence of race and racism while teaching social studies in Baltimore, Maryland. As part of a cohort of preservice (PST) and inservice teachers (IST), they learned current theoretical and practical research in a graduate social studies methods course. All students in the cohort identified as white, yet in Baltimore, the students were majority youth of color. According to the United States Census Bureau (2019), nearly 70% of the city's population identifies as either African American or Hispanic/Latino. This educational and social contradiction mirrors other teacher education programs across the United States. As students become more racially, ethnically, and linguistically diverse, the K–12 teacher force remains overwhelmingly white. Moreover, no other discipline retains a significant majority of white teachers, such as the field of social studies (Busey & Waters, 2016).

Working with the realities of white individuals seeking to teach social studies in a setting such as Baltimore, I sought to challenge their views on race and racism through critical reflections. Based on the research I conducted, I argue that a consistent focus on race via critical reflection is strongly needed to develop and continually grow racial literacies in white PSTs and ISTs. I also argue that teacher educators must engage in critical reflections of their own in continually assessing their racial literacies. The practice of critical reflections, accounting for personal and professional experiences with race and racism, will encourage teacher educators to consider the roles of race and racism within social studies, education as a whole, and in our daily lives.

## CONCEPTUAL FRAMEWORK

The framework draws from racial literacy (Guinier, 2004; Twine, 2004) and critical reflection (Shandomo, 2010; Smyth, 1989). This pairing provides a thorough understanding of how social studies educators and teacher educators can develop their racial literacies within different educational settings, such as K–12 and higher education (Sealey-Ruiz & Greene, 2015).

Racial literacy examines and challenges racism within society. Racism controls society through racial identities, socioeconomic status, and topography (Guinier, 2004). These controls, structured as power hierarchies, privilege a particular group of individuals. White people are privileged while marginalizing non-white people (Guinier, 2004). Guinier (2004) argues that for individuals to challenge these hierarchies, cultivating a racial literacy is necessary and contingent on the following:

1. Racial literacy is contextual.
2. Race and power go hand in hand.
3. Race intersects with gender, class, geography, and other variables.

Twine (2004) examined the different paths multiracial families in the United Kingdom navigated. White parents recognized the prevalence of racism in the United Kingdom; they consistently provided home and community spaces for their multiracial children to contest racism and the legacies of colonialism (Twine, 2004). The white parents acknowledged the lack of positive African and Black art, books, and historical narratives in British school curricula (Twine, 2004). Within their domiciles, the parents established Afrocentric, anti-racist home aesthetics with readings centered on Black thought and expression (Twine, 2004). Other parents sent their children to community-run after-school and weekend educational programs rooted in Black thought and awareness (Twine, 2004). Even with their efforts, the parents expressed continued concerns on schools' role as societal arbiters, forcing their multiracial children to pick a side (Twine, 2004).

In the United States, research (Brown, 2017; Colomer, 2019; Ewing Flynn et al., 2018; Mosley & Rogers, 2011; Sealey-Ruiz & Greene, 2015) suggests that teacher education programs ignore race and racism. Within social studies, the continued dominance of white people desiring to become teachers perpetuates these silences (Busey & Waters, 2016). The notion of colorblindness allows many white PSTs and ISTs to ignore the complexities of race and racism (Sealey-Ruiz & Greene, 2015). For non-white people studying to become social studies teachers, color-blindness forces them to internalize microaggressions (Colomer, 2019). Continued disregard for bilingualism and non-U.S. cultural practices by white colleagues causes many Latinx educators to ignore race (Ewing Flynn et al., 2018). Many African American educators are hesitant to develop as anti-racist teachers (McIntosh Allen, 2019). While the call for more teachers of color has been amplified by the growing diversity of K–12 students in the United States, the reality is that white educators continue to snub conversations on race and racism, especially with other white educators (Mosley & Rogers, 2011).

Research also suggests that conversations about race and racism must start with white teacher educators (Colomer, 2019; DiAngelo, 2012; Ewing Flynn et al., 2018; McIntosh Allen, 2019; Sealey-Ruiz & Greene, 2015). They must challenge the concepts, practices, and structures that maintain racism through critical pedagogical and content development (DiAngelo, 2012). These challenges come with a stipulation: white teacher educators must be responsible for not normalizing whiteness (Ewing Flynn et al., 2018). White teacher educators must be willing to discuss and criticize their personal experiences with race and racism (Sealey-Ruiz & Greene, 2015). When future Latinx and Black educators are involved in the conversations, white teacher educators need to demonstrate compassion and care for their racialized experiences (Colomer, 2019; McIntosh Allen, 2019). The concept of care is essential, developing racial literacy is profoundly personal and will require critical reflection. This approach can be effective in helping white teachers address conversations about race and racism (Brown, 2017).

I draw from Smyth's (1989) four-step concept of critical reflection. Engaging in critical reflection in teacher education programs requires a systematic approach. First, individuals create personal narratives that describe their intended actions. The descriptions detail confusing experiences or paradoxes they encounter. Then they use their narratives to inform themselves and their colleagues. The narratives seek to demystify the teaching profession. Third, the narratives isolate the individuals and confront the institutional and social forces that perpetuate inequalities while establishing critical communities with others. Last, the narratives provide educators with concrete examples of self-governance and control. Teachers and teacher educators use the power of their words to reconstruct teacher development (Smyth, 1989) actively.

Critical reflection continuously challenges educators' societal norms and assumptions (Fook, 2003; Howard, 2003; Shandomo, 2010). Critical reflection has been used with educators, considering the biases and beliefs they bring into the classroom setting (Ossa Parra et al., 2015). Critical reflections have helped educators recognize the deficit views of students of color (Shandomo, 2010). All teachers are "products of cultural conditioning," and social and political conditions of education put teachers and students in "unequal and exploitative circumstances" (Ingram & Walters, 2007, p. 30).

Engaging in critical reflection prevents an educator from becoming complacent in their pedagogy, primarily when race and racism influence everyday actions such as lesson planning, classroom management, and assessment (Liu, 2015).

With the continued standardization of the teaching profession, the re-segregation of public schools, and changing demographics of K–12 student populations, critical reflection in all teacher education programs is necessary (Ingram & Walters, 2007). Teacher educators and prospective educators need to understand and challenge how race influences how students learn on a day-to-day basis (Howard, 2003). Considering that social studies is the field that addresses historical and contemporary aspects of race and racism, critical reflection in the social studies would benefit teacher educators, preservice teachers, and inservice teachers.

The social studies classroom is the prime setting for racial literacy (Epstein & Gist, 2013; McIntosh Allen, 2019; Smith & Crowley, 2018). As Brown (2017) succinctly wrote, racism occupies a permanent role in U.S. history and society. Thus, the complexities of developing racial literacy will not occur in "safe spaces" (King, 2015, p. x). Instead, teachers who implement anti-racist pedagogies directly challenge their students' interpretations of race and racism (Epstein & Gist, 2015). In a study conducted by McIntosh Allen (2019), Marcus, a Black educator, used his racial literacy to help students understand how schools were historically structured to fail students of color. Teachers using famous speeches, such as President Barack Obama's "A More Perfect Union" speech, address the racial influences of housing policies, student tracking in education, and school funding, topics not commonly found in social studies curricula (Smith & Crowley, 2018). Busey (2016) argues that a collaboration of students and teachers learning about U.S. presidential elections must set race as a fundamental influencer in how presidential candidates are chosen and elected. Ignoring race upholds white supremacy in classrooms that reaffirm dominant historical narratives (Busey, 2016).

Using critical reflection in social studies teacher education courses is crucial. Due to the continued practice of lecturing as knowledge dissemination within higher education, social studies PSTs learn to mimic such actions. In turn, they replicate such practices once they enter the K–12 setting (Ross & Hannay, 1986). The social studies teacher's power dynamic instilling knowledge on the student reinforces the banking method of teaching, viewing the students as lacking knowledge and further stigmatizing social studies as irrelevant in their lives (Dinkleman, 1999; Freire, 1998). Ross and Hannay (1986) argue that reflection in association with critical theory pushes preservice teachers to consider different pedagogical practices that value critical discourse and personal examinations. Baber (2003) used reflection to deconstruct her decades-long journey as a social studies educator. Baber (2003) learned that race influenced her growth as an educator, her "unlearning" that occurred in mid-career, and her desire to resolve race within the social studies field. The potential to restructure social studies through a reflective examination of race also serves as motivation for political change (Baber, 2003). Using critical reflections in a social studies methods course with white educators is an example of this potential.

## BACKGROUND DETAILS

The critical reflection originates from a more extensive qualitative study of PSTs and ISTs in different social studies methods courses during the 2018–2019 academic year. The following research question guided the study: How do preservice and inservice educators teach social studies in an urban setting? I studied elementary and secondary students in two different social studies methods courses. Relying on Saldaña and Omasta (2018, p. 63), I chose to focus on the "material culture" developed by the students, such as final papers and projects. In assessing their initial work, I noticed constant references to race in three students' artifacts in our course: Patrick, Laney, and James. After sharing my initial findings with them, I asked if they wanted to participate in a second study (Saldaña & Omasta, 2018). Once they approved, I then created a new research question: How do social studies teachers develop racial literacy as part of their teacher education program experience? The next section will provide details about the participants.

## PARTICIPANTS

The participants enrolled as graduate students in a secondary social studies methods course. Patrick taught different grade levels of history at a local private high school. He grew up in Maryland and attended an in-state public university. Laney taught different middle and high school grades at a public school, serving students with special needs. She grew up in Massachusetts and attended an in-state public university, subsequently moving to Maryland after graduation. Laney chose to become a secondary social studies teacher after a career in a different profession. James grew up in Illinois and taught history and English language arts at a private middle school. He attended universities in different states before enrolling at the study site for his graduate degree. All three participants self-identified as white.

## POSITIONALITY STATEMENT

A full disclosure of the filters, lenses, and reflections I engage with daily is necessary for ensuring a substantive and informative chronicle (Saldaña & Omasta, 2018). I am a white male with Latino, Indigenous, and European ancestries. I grew up in the New York City metropolitan area. Before becoming a teacher educator, I taught history/social studies for 10 years in various

K–12 settings. I was unfamiliar with racial literacy until I read an article by LaGarrett King (2016) in graduate school. Since reflection has been an ongoing practice since my first year of K–12 teaching (Freire, 1998), I realized two things: I learned how my own teacher education preparation ignored race. I did not recall once ever talking about or engaging in work relating to race in my courses. I also realized the realities of race in my teaching during my first year. Working in a Southern U.S. high school, I saw the divide between the white, African American, and Latinx students. While I slowly integrated race conversations into my teaching as my teaching career progressed, I recognized the need to do more. As a result, I view my racial literacy as continuous, especially in the power positions I hold as a teacher educator and researcher.

## DATA COLLECTION AND ANALYSIS

I concentrated on three areas of material culture: online forum posts, digital files of student presentations, and narrative work (Saldaña & Omasta, 2018). I collected forum postings created by the students before our class meetings, in-person presentations using PowerPoint and other visual mediums, philosophy of teaching statements, and final reflective papers. I respected the artifacts as symbols of values, attitudes, and beliefs (Saldaña & Omasta, 2018). I analyzed the materials for attention and identity through a step-by-step process (Saldaña & Omasta, 2018).

I first focused on the participants' rhetoric and their analysis of race and racism. I then wrote bulleted points on a separate sheet of paper. Finally, I reflected on the identities of the participants. Even though I have known the participants through our shared time together in class, their use of particular vocabulary and narrative styles had the potential to reveal much about their interpretations of identity (Saldaña & Omasta, 2018). Next, I identified connections to race and racism as process codes. The process codes provided insights into the participants' actions and reactions on race and racism (Saldaña & Omasta, 2018). For the final step, I reflected on my analyses. Overall, I understood racial literacy as an ever-evolving practice for Patrick, Laney, and James. The next section's reflections illustrate the different ways I established and enhanced the notion of racial literacy in my methods course.

## A NOTE ON THE NEXT SECTION

You will read a narrative based on the students' critical reflections and considerations from analyzing the collected data. The narrative attempts to put into perspective my actions as a teacher educator engaging with students in developing racial literacy. It also captures a moment in time when I sought to include racial literacy as a pedagogy in my courses.

Even as I write this chapter, working in a new higher educational setting and dealing with the COVID-19 pandemic, I still believe that racial literacy must be developed in all teacher education programs. In particular, with social studies, viewed by the National Council for the Social Studies (2020) as the one subject in K–12 education that can teach students to participate in a multicultural society actively, it is essential that *all* future educators engage in racial literacy.

## REFLECTIONS FROM A CRITICAL TEACHER EDUCATOR

I spent the summer of 2017 restructuring the social studies methods courses in our teacher education program. Program leadership stressed a social justice approach in training future educators. In studying past syllabi, instructors relied on teacher-centered pedagogy that focused solely on lesson planning, assessments, and classroom management. No topics focusing on race or racism were found. It reaffirmed what Ross and Hannay (1986) argued: Previous iterations of the social studies methods courses focused on the procedural development of teachers. After one year of teaching these courses, I made adjustments based on in-class and end-of-semester student feedback. The changes encouraged me to formally study how a new cohort of students would respond to a consistent focus on race in social studies methods.

One week prior to the start of the fall semester, I sat outside on the stoop with my daughter. Living in Baltimore, this was a common social practice. We were speaking Spanish when a neighbor, a school counselor, came over. She always raved about her experiences at the university where I taught, saying that she loved how her colleagues supported all students at her high school. However, the conversations took a drastic turn when she issued a warning: Don't take the bus. Confused, I asked her why.

She said, "That bus line brings up those people from downtown."

My daughter immediately gave me a look of disbelief.

I challenged the neighbor by asking, "What do you mean, 'those people'?"

She said crime had risen in the area because the bus line had become a 24-hour route, and it originated from the bus depot in the heart of downtown Baltimore. Stunned by her response, I excused my daughter and me from the conversation and we went inside. I then wondered: "Why did this alum, who works as a high school counselor and interacts with different student groups, demean people of color in that way?"

That interaction influenced how I wanted to address race with the students. I sought to directly address race in social studies from the start. The cover page of the syllabus showed an image of a diverse group of individuals sitting in a circle, engaging in conversation. I included the following words in describing the pedagogy of the course:

Teaching social studies in today's educational environments, especially urban education contexts, requires a variety of techniques that allow both the teacher and students to learn about the world, each other, and themselves. As a result, this methods course will not teach you "how to teach social studies." We will engage such topics as race, gender, politics, and the standardization of the curriculum.

When I distributed the syllabus to the students via email, I also encouraged them to post their first response in an online forum. The forum resembled a social media platform: I posted a question, statement, or image, and my students would respond to it. I needed to create an experiential space where students could start their engagements with race and tap into the students' digital nativeness (Prensky, 2001; Shandomo, 2010). The first question of the semester asked them to create a narrative of themselves as educators of change, challenging racism and other injustices. The students responded with long narratives, complemented with images and songs. The forum established the practice of critical reflective assignments that elevated awareness of inequitable educational practices while promoting transformative learning (Ossa Parra et al., 2015; Shandomo, 2010).

I posted the following question in the forum: "Thinking about our urban educational contexts, how would you address the topic of race in social studies?" The students were already aware that race was going to be the discussion topic for the third week of the course. I included scholarship that complicated race in social studies, such as Busey and Waters (2016), Castro et al., (2015), and Woodson (2015). I also included an image of Baltimore from the 1940s, illustrating redlining practices that established demarcation lines between white and African American residents.

The responses suggested how prominent race was in the minds of Patrick, James, and Laney. James wrote, "When teaching race in the classroom, we must also take into consideration our own professional growth. Are we attending lectures and training led by diverse instructors that challenge our own preconceptions and beliefs?"

Patrick challenged his fellow colleagues regarding the lack of in-class discussions on race. He wrote, "Race within social studies is something that needs to be addressed more often. We, as teachers, can't be afraid to talk about such an important issue."

Laney addressed the relationship between social studies and race:

If we don't address race in social studies, where else are we supposed to address it? Social studies is the perfect arena for discussing the construction and meaning of socially constructed identities, where those ideas came from, and how the dichotomies created by our constructions perpetuate (and are used to justify) inequality and injustice.

As the semester progressed, posts by Laney, Patrick, and James suggested an intersectional view within their racial literacies. For Laney, her racial literacy connected to gender, class, and culture. In her final reflection paper, she identified herself as a social justice educator.

She wrote, "Teaching for social justice means recognizing oppression in its multiple forms and then taking action in the classroom to interrupt the cycles of oppression." On race, Laney wrote, "Recently, I have realized how important it is to talk with students about 'white supremacy culture.'" Since she identifies as a social justice educator, she sees her classroom as a space to be "hard on systems, not people" and "place labels on systems, not humans." Extending to gender, she wrote,

> Traditional history curriculum represents a glorified depiction of hegemonic masculinity that discounts other marginalized expressions of manhood; males in history who were not White European Heterosexuals have been erased from history as though gay men and men of color did not exist until the mid-late 20th century—as though they were somehow not *real men* (original emphasis).

She closes out by writing that as educators, "if we do not talk about white supremacy and impacts of racial inequality, oppression of and violence against women, homophobia and hate crimes against members of the LGBTQ community, and all of the other social injustices across history and today, we are effectively saying that these experiences do not matter."

Patrick's posts referenced history and gender, but also current events. Patrick connected race with economics in one post. He wrote in one post, "I don't think there is a time in American history where money wasn't a motivating factor within issues of gender, race, and culture. There have always been tensions amongst classes." In a different post, he saw connections between recent historical events and race. He wrote, "When the Charlottesville events happened, I made it a point to talk about race, guns, assembly, etc. with my students."

Regarding the marginalization of social studies in favor of STEM programs within secondary schools, Patrick argued that race was one of the reasons. He wrote,

> Social studies is a touchy subject for some. The powers that be don't want to ruffle feathers, so contemporary moral issues, culture, race, gender, etc. are kept out of the classroom because no one wants to deal with an angry parent or a possible lawsuit. This is why we see names, dates, events, etc. and not legitimate discussion and analysis.

Last, Patrick contemplated the intersection of race and pedagogy. Patrick considered his identities as a white history teacher while recognizing a fundamental change in his department.

> At my school, after the one woman in our department left last year, the social studies teachers are now entirely white males. This has been a large motivating

factor in what I have done so far this year. I refuse to perpetuate the same story-lines within American and world history. Teaching in a school that is near 90% Black and growing, with an all white male social studies department, begs for a culturally relevant pedagogy.

James addressed race through his online posts and his presentation. In one post, he wrote, "Like race, class, and culture, we as teachers and the students bring in our identifications, and this influences our teaching and learning."

When addressing the influence of class in teaching social studies in a different post, James wrote, "Class must be present in our classrooms and must be discussed in unison with narratives on race, gender, and culture. Without it, students are left with an incomplete understanding of the problems of today."

When students were tasked with selecting a topic for a 45-minute presentation, James chose race. James had previously written that "discussions on race present the more complex historical picture, allowing our students to think more critically."

As a starting point for his presentation, James juxtaposed two images taken at different periods in U.S. history. The images were a picture of John Lewis and others being approached by police officers in Selma, Alabama, on a march during "Bloody Sunday" in 1965 and the 2016 Baton Rouge, Louisiana, Black Lives Matter protest and policing approaching Ieshia Evans to arrest her (Bachman, 2016; U.S. Department of the Interior, 2018). According to James, even though the pictures were taken decades apart, race still plays a major role in our society. James's presentation then questioned the avoidance of race in history/social studies textbooks. Using Woodson (2015) and Zinn (2005), James argued that only positive contributions to society, such as the Civil Rights Movement, were illustrated in textbooks. James also questioned why the causes of racism were not part of the learning. Through the inclusion of song lyrics from the dead prez song "They Schools," he accused other social studies teachers of avoiding race. He pointed to the high percentage of white female teachers in the profession and how teacher education programs pushed a transmission model of learning rather than an inquiry-based one.

This graduate course facilitated weekly discussions on race, helping develop racial literacy among the students. The structure of the forum began the process of understanding the different levels of racism in the United States (Brown, 2017). The students recognized how race is a prevailing yet volatile influence in the history of the United States, manifesting in complex ways within the social studies curriculum (Guinier, 2004; Nelson & Ooka Pang, 2014). As white teachers, they recognized the relevance of race and racism in their lives (Ewing Flynn et al., 2018).

In her final reflective paper, Laney asked the following question: How is a white, middle-class, female teacher who has never been discriminated against based on her skin color supposed to guide students in unpacking the construction of race and the disparaging impact of racial inequality on people of color? Laney visualized and problematized race and racism in her classroom (Epstein & Gist, 2013). These interpretations encouraged her students to develop a new, more critical sense of community: they openly, and consistently, discussed race (Epstein & Gist, 2013). Even though she did not share further data about these conversations, her paper chartered a future path of developing racial literacies within her and her K–12 students as they navigated daily experiences (Ewing Flynn et al., 2018). Laney also learned how to analyze race through her lessons (Howard, 2003). Laney's commentary urged me to reflect on my pedagogical practices during this time period.

As I pushed the students to develop their racial literacies during the semester, I saw a divide developing. At the start of the semester, it was common for students to create dynamic student groups, depending on the assignment or topic. A community had been established through the students' counter-articulations on the forum (Ender, 2019). However, the continual focus on racial literacy forced the class into two sections: one group, including James, Laney, and Patrick, sat on the left side of the classroom, willing to discuss their racial literacies openly. The second group, on the other side, remained quiet during most discussions. Even during breaks, when students could exit the classroom, the two groups stayed together. I needed to openly discuss my personal experiences with racial literacy in an effort to encourage more communication between the two groups (Brown, 2017).

I pointed out the shortcomings of my K–12 teaching experiences. I specifically acknowledged my silence on race and racism at the beginning of my teaching career, which I saw through personal reflections (Fook, 2003). I did this because I taught in a "right-to-work" state in the United States. In a right-to-work state, I could be dismissed from my teaching position by the school district without due process. I was afraid of losing my job for addressing race and racism in the classroom, something that had happened to a colleague during my first year of teaching. The turning point came during my third year. A student who self-identified as Mexican American complained that all narratives on Latino people in the textbooks were negative. It was the first time a student had articulated the effects of racialized narratives on them.

While that specific experience induced a philosophical shift, it did not happen overnight. I shared with the class that it was not until my fifth year of teaching that I sought to address the influence of racism in social studies on a daily basis (Guinier, 2004). It also helped that with union representation, I had more latitude in addressing race and racism. With the students, we inserted the topic of race into the curriculum, analyzing periods such as World War I and post–Civil Rights Movement America (Sealey-Ruiz & Greene, 2015). I employed the practice of freewriting at the end of every class. I encouraged the students to develop new narratives as examples of their critical thought; it was up to them to share out (Colomer, 2019). The social studies methods students saw freewriting as an important practice in processing their racial literacy development. For the remaining weeks of the semester, the PSTs and ISTs freewrote narratives at the end of every class session. While the students whom I expected to share out (Patrick, James, and Laney) shared particular stories about race in their practices, the other students kept those stories to themselves. I am hoping that those students scrutinized their identities and privileges in developing their racial literacies (Sealey-Ruiz & Greene, 2015).

## CONCLUSION?

I realize that I have barely scratched the surface. Hence, the question mark at the end of this section's title. I have argued that employing critical reflections in a social studies methods course helps white preservice and inservice teachers cultivate their racial literacies. Whether occurring at the start of the semester, before class meetings, during in-class presentations, amidst conversations, or in final papers, there are numerous opportunities to engage in critical reflection.

As Laney stated in her final paper, "We must also be brutally self-reflective to make sure that what we are teaching in the name of social justice is not, in fact, perpetuating bias and inequality." Ingram and Walters (2007) cautioned that if responsive teacher educators attempt to evoke numerous opportunities of critical reflection, it "may or may not move a person to engage in thoughtful introspection about self and the *shoes another may walk-in*" (p. 37). This chapter has shown that deliberate conversations about race were established at the start of the course and continued throughout the semester. As a result, shy students such as Laney, Patrick, and James have been open-minded and willing to share their thoughts and experiences. Future research should examine how social studies teacher educators develop racial literacy while engaging in anti-racist pedagogies.

Equally problematic are the students not mentioned in this chapter. While they responded to the Week 3 question on race, they did not fully address race in other assignments. Two of the students considered race and racism in education in their final reflective papers. However, they repeated what they wrote in their Week 3 posts. One student did not acknowledge race in their final assignment. Future research on racial literacy should examine the reluctance of white social studies preservice and inservice social studies teachers in developing racial literacy.

## REFERENCES

Baber, C. R. (2003). A reflection on my journey through the profession. In G. Ladson-Billings (Ed.), *Critical race theory: Perspectives on social studies* (pp. 45–70). Information Age Publishing.

Bachman, J. B. (2016). *Black Lives Matter Protester in Baton Rouge* [Photograph]. https://www.jonathanbachmanphotography.com/portfolio

Brown, K. D. (2017). Why we can't wait: Advancing racial literacy and a critical sociocultural knowledge of race for teaching and curriculum. *Race, Gender & Class,* 24(1–2), 81–96.

Busey, C. L. (2016). Teaching the election with purpose: Toward a framework of racial media literacy and [socio]political consciousness when discussing elections in the social studies classroom. *The Clearing House, 86*(6), 228–234.

Busey, C. L., & Waters, K. S. (2016). Who are we? The demographic and professional identity of social studies teacher educators. *Journal of Social Studies Research, 40*(1), 71–83. https://doi: 10.1016/j.jssr.2015.07.001

Castro, A. J., Hawkman, A. M., & Diaz, J. (2015). Teaching race in high school social studies: Lessons from the field. In P. Chandler (Ed.), *Doing race in social studies: Critical perspectives* (pp. 127–152). Information Age Publishing.

Colomer, S. E. (2019). Understanding racial literacy through acts of (un)masking: Latinx teachers in a new Latinx diaspora community. *Race Ethnicity and Education, 22*(2), 194–210. https://doi: 10.1080/13613324.2018.1468749

DiAngelo, R. (2012). *What does it mean to be white? Developing white racial literacy.* Peter Lang.

Dinkleman, T. (1999). Critical reflection in a social studies methods semester. *Theory & Research in Social Education, 27*(3), 329–357.

Ender, T. (2019). Counter-narratives as resistance: Creating critical social studies spaces with communities. *The Journal of Social Studies Research, 43*(2), 133–143. https://doi.org/10.1016/j.jssr.2018.11.002

Epstein, T., & Gist, G. (2018). Teaching racial literacy in secondary humanities classrooms: Challenging adolescents' of color concepts of race and racism. *Race Ethnicity and Education, 18*(1), 40–60. https://doi: 10.1080/13613324.2013.792800

Ewing Flynn, J., Worden, L. J., & Rolón-Dow, R. (2018). The responsibilities of white teacher candidates and teacher educators in developing racial literacy. *Multicultural Perspectives, 20*(4), 240–246. https://doi.org/10.1080/15210960.2018.1527156

Fook, J. (2003). Reflective practice and critical reflection. In J. Lishman (Ed.), *Handbook for practice learning in social work and social care* (pp. 440–454). Jessica Kingsley Publishers.

Freire, P. (1998). *Teachers as cultural workers: Letters to those who dare teach.* Westview Press.

Guinier, L. (2004). From racial liberalism to racial literacy: *Brown v. Board of Education* and the interest-divergence dilemma. *The Journal of American History, 9*(1), 92–118.

Howard, T. (2003). Culturally relevant pedagogy: Ingredients for critical teacher reflection. *Theory Into Practice, 42*(3), 195–202. https://doi: 10.1207/s15430421tip4203_5

Ingram, I. L., & Walters, T. S. (2007). A critical reflection model to teach diversity and social justice. *Journal of Praxis in Multicultural Education, 2*(1), Article 2.

King, L. J. (2015). Foreword. In P. T. Chandler (Ed.), *Doing race in social studies: Critical perspectives* (pp. ix–xii). Information Age Publishing.

King, L. J. (2016). Teaching black history as a racial literacy project. *Race, Ethnicity and Education, 19*(6), 1303–1318.

Liu, K. (2015). Critical reflection as a framework for transformative learning in teacher education. *Educational Review, 67*(2), 135–157.

McIntosh Allen, K. (2019). Transformative vision: Examining the racial literacy practices of a black male teacher with his black male students. *Journal for Multicultural Education, 13*(1), 82–93. https://doi.org/10.1108/JME-04-2017-0029

Mosley, M., & Rogers, R. (2011). Inhabiting the "tragic gap": Pre-service teachers practicing racial literacy. *Teaching Education, 22*(3), 303–324.

National Council for the Social Studies. (2020). About. https://www.socialstudies.org/about

Nelson, J. L., & Ooka Pang, V. (2014). Prejudice, racism, and the social studies curriculum. In E. W. Ross (Ed.), *The social studies curriculum, 4th edition* (pp. 203–226). State University of New York Press.

Ossa Parra, M., Gutiérrez, R., & Aldana, M. F. (2015). Engaging in critical reflective teaching: From theory to practice in pursuit of transformative learning. *Reflective Practice, 16*(1), 16–30. https://doi.org/10.1080/14623943.2014.944141

Prensky, M. (2001). Digital natives, digital immigrants part 1. *On the Horizon, 9*(5), 1–6. https://doi.org/10.1108/10748120110424816

Ross, E. W., & Hannay, L. M. (1986). Towards a critical theory of reflective inquiry. *Journal of Teacher Education, July-August 1986*, 9–15.

Saldaña, J., & Omasta, M. (2018). *Qualitative research: Analyzing life.* SAGE.

Sealey-Ruiz, Y., & Greene, P. (2015). Popular visual images and the (mis)reading of black male youth: A case for racial literacy in urban preservice teacher education. *Teaching Education, 26*(1), 55–76.

Shandomo, H. M. (2010). The role of critical reflections in teacher education. *School-University Partnerships, 4*(1), 101–113.

Smith, W. L., & Crowley, R. M. (2018). Barack Obama, racial literacy, and lessons from "A More Perfect Union." *The History Teacher, 51*(3), 445–476.

Smyth, J. (1989). Developing and sustaining critical reflection in teacher education. *Journal of Teacher Education, 40*(2), 7–19.

Twine, F. W. (2004). A white side of black Britain: The concept of racial literacy. *Ethnic and Racial Studies, 27*(6), 878–907.

United States Census Bureau. (2019). *QuickFacts: Baltimore city, Maryland; United States* [data file]. https://www.census.gov/quickfacts/fact/table/baltimorecitymaryland,US/PST045218

U.S. Department of the Interior. (2018.). *Bloody Sunday* [Photograph]. National Parks Service. https://www.nps.gov/semo/learn/historyculture/bloody-sunday.htm

Woodson, A. N. (2015). "What you supposed to know": Urban black students' perspectives on history textbooks. *Journal of Urban Learning Teaching and Research, 11*, 57–65.

Zinn, H. (2005). *A people's history of the United States.* Harper Perennial Modern Classics.

## CHAPTER 11

# "You and Your Racist Friend"

## Programmatic Considerations for Building Racial Literacy Through Anti-Racist Teacher Education

*Andrea M. Hawkman*

### INTRODUCTION

As the 45th president of the United States made clear in his attack on the Pulitzer Prize–winning *1619 Project* in September 2020, racism is a central part of the American experience. In his attempt to ban the use of the curricular project designed to retell the history of slavery in the United States, deriding it as "un-American," the 45th president inadvertently acknowledged that racism is, in fact, an American educational tradition (Liptak, 2020). The content, pedagogy, and policies of K–12 classrooms have long been defined by whiteness in an effort to protect the racial(ist) status quo. Instead of championing equality, education has served as a tool of white supremacy and racial injustice.[1] Race-evasive claims that the U.S. education system is a meritocracy have sought to shield the generations of intentional policies and decisions to protect white wealth, white knowledge, and white heritage. This is evident through nearly every avenue of education, including, but certainly not limited to, the persistence of racist opportunity gaps (Milner, 2012), the utilization of racist curriculum (King & Woodson, 2015), a reliance upon deficit ideologies (Delpit, 1995), and the enshrinement of discriminatory policies (Gillborn, 2005). Racism is normalized, maintained, and supported through the institutions and individuals that shape K–12 education.

Teacher educators must claim their responsibility for the perpetuation of racism detailed above. This recognition requires the examination and reimagining of the curriculum, practices, structures, and pedagogies that prepare future teachers. Just as the title and lyrics from They Might Be Giants (Flansburgh & Linnel, 1990) suggest, it is time for teacher education to recognize its relationship to the racist K–12 education system and work to disrupt it. It is time to stop listening to the old stories told about schooling—that it is the "great equalizer." Teacher education must adopt a new way forward that disrupts the structurations and machinations of whiteness, supports preservice teachers of color, centralizes non-white ways of knowing, challenges white preservice teachers to interrogate their relationship to/with whiteness, and promotes anti-racist aims through the development of racial literacy.

This work cannot be left to individual courses, content areas, or faculty. Rather, a programmatic, anti-racist approach to challenging the pervasiveness of white supremacy is necessary if teacher educators are serious about disrupting racism in education. In this chapter, I will detail the programmatic, structural, curricular, and political considerations for designing an anti-racist teacher education (ARTE) program.

## LIMITS OF MULTICULTURALISM FOR BUILDING RACIAL LITERACY

In recent years, multiculturalism has ascended to a position of prominence within the field of teacher education. Beginning with Gibson's (1976) foundational article on the components of multicultural education, followed by contributions from prominent scholars in the field of education (e.g., Banks, 2001, 2004; C. A. Banks & J. A. Banks, 1995; J. A. Banks & C. A. Banks, 2001; Sleeter, 1996; Sleeter & Grant, 1987), multiculturalism has retained a hearty presence in education circles. Although universal consensus has not been reached in defining multicultural education, generally this pedagogy features the following: content integration, attention to knowledge production, prejudice reduction, equity pedagogy, and an empowering school culture (Banks, 2004). While the multicultural narrative has substantially shifted the conversation to include issues of diversity and inclusion, many contend that multicultural education itself is not enough to directly challenge racism and white supremacy in the classroom (Bery, 2014; Castagno, 2013; McLaren, 1997).

Some suggest that the adoption of a critical multicultural education program achieves this goal (Bery, 2014; May & Sleeter, 2010; Sleeter, 2012). Notably, critical multiculturalism offers educators an approach to more directly engage in "structural analysis of unequal power relationships, analyzing the role of institutionalized inequities, including but not necessarily limited to racism that plagues schooling" (May & Sleeter, 2010, p. 10). However, despite the attention to structural and institutional oppression, critical multiculturalism often fails to insist upon attention to racism and white supremacy. Said in a different way, racism and white supremacy are included in the umbrella of multiculturalism—alongside class, sexuality, gender, ability, ethnicity—and may be intended to be featured in instruction, though educator and research interpretation may (un)intentionally remove the focus on racism and white supremacy, in service to "more polite" topics of conversation. Unfortunately, when implemented by white teachers in white spaces, multiculturalism tends to champion racial liberalism instead of racial literacy (Thompson, 1997).

Guinier (2004) suggested that building racial literacy necessitates a three-pronged approach. First, race/ism should be a central, although not singular, focus of concern. For multiculturalism, race/ism is one of many concerns, in no particular order. Second, education concerned with building preservice teachers' racial literacy should focus attention on the relationship between race/ism and power. Individuals should directly challenge the ways race/ism is used by those in power to justify the racial, social, political, and economic status quo (Guinier, 2004). Third, racial literacy requires the understanding of race/ism to be contextual, nuanced, and interactive. There is not a singular definition of race/ism, nor is there a singular solution. Racial justice requires deep and critical understanding of the ways that issues are connected and inform one another.

Therefore, while multiculturalism appears to advocate "the absence of discriminatory intentions," multicultural education does not inherently build racial literacy (Thompson, 1997, p. 14). To insist upon an activist-oriented approach to racism through the development of racial literacy, teacher education programs must consider overt anti-racist education as a framework. The point of anti-racism, Thompson (1997) contended,

> is to challenge naturalized presumptions of white privilege so that race relations can be problematized and reconstructed, anti-racist considerations apply wherever whiteness has been assumed as a standard or blackness treated as a foil—whether in moral relations, democratic relations, or standards of educational and intellectual achievement. (p. 15)

Thus, teacher education programs with a foundation of anti-racist instruction, pedagogy, and methodology will ensure direct attention to building racial literacy (King & Chandler, 2016; Picower, 2009; Thompson, 1997).

## ANTI-RACIST TEACHER EDUCATION (ARTE) FRAMEWORK

In this section, I will discuss the necessary features of an anti-racist teacher education (ARTE) program. The programmatic suggestions discussed here are not meant to be interpreted as a one-size-fits-all approach to building racial literacy. Rather, the suggestions necessitate contextualization and manipulation based on university enrollment and programmatic identities. What follows begins with large-scale considerations, followed by more nuanced particularities to be considered in preparation for systemic ARTE. It should also be noted that the experiences of students within this program will vary based on personal experiences and identities.

## A Note About Racial Identity

White faculty/students and faculty/students who are Black, Indigenous, Latinx, Asian, or otherwise identify as a person of color will not encounter the same emotionalities, experiences, or understandings as they progress through an ARTE program. Affordances and accommodations should exist to account for the unique and varied ways that race/ism influences individuals' prior knowledge and personal growth through the program. Throughout the discussion of the ARTE framework that follows, I will point to areas where these nuances should be accounted for. However, I recognize that my own positionalities as a white, queer woman influence my personal understandings of race/ism, anti-racism, and education. As such, while I set forth on this work with intention, it is possible that my own relationship to/with race/ism has shaped the suggestions I put forth. As you move forward in this chapter, I urge you to also consider the ways that your relationship to race/ism shapes your interactions with the text and your larger efforts toward enacting racially literate practices.

## Mission, Vision, and Values

To begin, we must first look at the mission, vision, and values articulated by teacher education programs. Often university mission statements are written from a perspective rooted in heteronormative whiteness (Iverson, 2007). Although many mission statements project the intent of promoting inclusion, they often include veiled language (i.e., social justice, multiculturalism, and cultural diversity) that does not overtly name anti-racism as an intended goal, but is intended to guide readers to the assumption that racism both is, and is not, addressed, depending on the audience. This investment in the discursive ideology of whiteness does little to implement the projected outcomes of the program (Fylkesnes, 2018). Lip service is not justice.

Rather, teacher education programs must be *overtly* anti-racist in both their words (stated mission) and their actions (enacted curriculum). Matias and colleagues (2014) noted that when students are aware of programmatic commitments to justice-centered goals, they are more likely to internalize the same expectations within their approach to teaching. The Center for Anti-Racist Education (2021) based their approach to this work on five principles that would be useful in ARTE programs: affirm humanity, embrace historical truths, develop a critical consciousness, recognize race and confront racism, and create just systems.

Teacher education programs should look toward the mission and position statements of other professional organizations for successful examples of how to ground these statements in anti-racist possibilities. A few recent examples could inform the mission, vision, and values statements of ARTE programs. First, in 2018, the National Council of Teachers of English (NCTE) released an updated position statement titled "Statement on Anti-Racism to Support Teaching and Learning," which was originally crafted by the Committee on Racism and Bias in the Teaching of English in 2007. This multifaceted statement acknowledges the racial realities of pre-K–12 classrooms, denounces racism, and affirms anti-racist teaching as integral to effective English teaching. In addition, the statement includes links to examples of how racism impacts students of color in the classroom as well as pedagogical support for teachers. Each of these components are essential to establishing stated and enacted commitments to anti-racism. ARTE programs could issue a similar guiding statement that could drive all coursework and decision-making within the program.

The University of North Carolina at Charlotte offers a graduate certificate, "Anti-Racism in Urban Education," that provides effective language for teacher education programs to consider. According to the program's website, the coursework associated with the certificate "all have the aim that students will uncover the underlying social, economic, psychological, and political conditions that disproportionately and inequitably channel advantages and opportunities to particular racialized groups while denying them to others" (UNC Charlotte, 2020). Going a step further, the certificate has two stated outcomes:

1. Candidates are able to use appropriate research and theory to identify and analyze anti-racist movements through a historical and cultural context.
2. Candidates are able to develop a plan of action to effectively address racism in local contexts. (UNC Charlotte, 2020)

Similarly, Wheaton College features a "Becoming an Anti-Racist Educator" initiative through their Center for Collaborative Teaching and Learning. The website draws upon anti-racist literature, such as Annelise Singh's *The Racial Healing Handbook* (2019) and Ibram X. Kendi's *How to Be an Anti-Racist* (2019), to provide an "action-oriented guide" that calls on educators to engage in personal reflection and educative action (Wheaton College, 2020). Across each of these example statements, programs centralize the necessity of personal reflection, understanding of racial histories and realities, and a necessity to pursue anti-racist educational aims.

## Faculty Considerations

Lee (1995) argued that in order for anti-racist pedagogy to be effective, it must be "the business of all teachers" (p. 9). ARTE is not to be left to a standalone diversity course offered by a single faculty member. I know when I taught social studies methods in an elementary teacher education program, my students reported that my class and their "diversity course" were the only instances in which anti-racism was discussed (Hawkman, 2019). For several students I was also the instructor of this single diversity course. A successful

ARTE program consists of a bevy of faculty members who represent varied backgrounds, identities, and positionalities that possess a shared commitment to anti-racist pedagogy. Programs must center the goals of anti-racism as they select individuals to join or to be retained within the faculty. More directly, historically and predominantly white institutions (HPWIs) will not be successful in challenging racism with a faculty population that is exclusively white. Preservice teachers must be surrounded by faculty from varying racial backgrounds. Yes, anti-racist white faculty members can successfully engage in preparing anti-racist teachers. The faculty population of an ARTE program must include anti-racist white people and BIPOC scholars committed to challenging white supremacy in education (Apple, 1998; Ladson-Billings, 2013; Leonardo, 2004, 2013; MacMullan, 2005).

The recruitment of BIPOC faculty requires two iterative steps. According to Greene (2018), recruitment should be intentional, insofar that search committee members examine and respond to their implicit biases when designing the job advertisement, reviewing application materials, conducting interviews, and hosting candidates for job talks. Intentionality also includes reevaluating the assessment of the "rigor," "quality," and "impact" of a candidate's contribution to the field. Additionally, Greene (2018) suggested recruitment of BIPOC faculty should be engaging. Search committees and administrators should connect with networks that support BIPOC scholars and graduate programs that have a track record of supporting BIPOC students. This engagement should continue through the hiring process in order to retain newly hired BIPOC faculty.

Once a diverse staff is in place, no guarantee exists that those individuals, regardless of their racial identity, are equipped to prepare preservice teachers to enact anti-racist praxis in their future classrooms. Therefore, teacher educators must also "grapple honestly with the reality of race, racism, and racial politics in the United States—and own their role in perpetuating systems of racial oppression" (Richert et al., 2008), p. 648). Faculty members, however well-intended they may be, are also products of the same educational system as their students, and therefore are often ill-prepared to engage in anti-racist dialogue themselves, let alone facilitate student learning around similar topics.

As such, when establishing an ARTE program, all faculty members should engage in anti-racist professional development in preparation for best serving the goals of the program and their future students (Lawrence & Tatum, 1997). Particularly important in preparing faculty for ARTE is the connection between ARTE and their respective content specialties. Some resistant faculty may insist angrily, *I teach about _____, not about racism. This stuff has nothing to do with me!* For an ARTE program to be successful, this misguided logic cannot be deemed acceptable or appropriate. Race/ism influences not only the creation, history, and consumption of every content area, but as humans we are all racialized beings under the influence of white supremacy. Educational systems within the United States have long failed to acknowledge the hegemonic influence of whiteness on education and have not obtained adequate results in combating racism. As a result, the work of the faculty within an ARTE program is to overtly position themselves, their work, and their classroom as a site of anti-racist praxis. ARTE programs should also establish a committee such as the Committee on Racism and Bias of NCTE. This committee, composed of faculty, staff, and administrators who identify as BIPOC and white, can coordinate this professional development and craft messaging associated with the goals of the ARTE program.

## Structure, Coursework, and Curriculum

In the enactment of an ARTE program, stakeholders should envision their journey through each of the levels detailed in Figure 11.1 as traveling up and down a spiral staircase. Tatum (1997) expressed a similar sentiment as she explained the process of racial identity development: "As you proceed up each level, you have a sense that you have passed this way before, but you are not exactly in the same spot" (p. 83). As evidenced in Figure 11.1, the four components of the ARTE framework often overlap and intertwine. Each segment informs the others and may necessitate repetition.

In addition to the interwoven framework, each of the four levels of the ARTE framework should be grounded in ongoing racial reflection. Borrowing and amending the work of several race scholars, Table 11.1 also includes scaffolded racial reflection questions that will help facilitate the goals of an ARTE program.

## Level I: (Re)Seeing Oneself: Looking in the Mirror

In this stage of ARTE, pedagogical decisions should focus on assisting preservice teachers in recognizing the impact of their racialization. For many white

**Figure 11.1. Anti-Racist Teacher Education Framework**

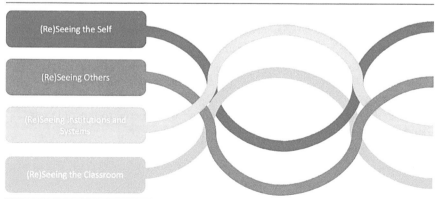

**Table 11.1. Questions for Engaging Faculty, Staff, and Students in Anti-Racist Teacher Education**

| Critical Questions |
| --- |

*Level I: (Re)Seeing the Self*

When did you first realize your racial identity?

What does your racial identity mean to you?

When did you first learn about racism?

Has anyone been influential in shaping your understanding of race/ism?

What privileges, if any, are associated with your racial identity?

In what ways has racism impacted your educational experiences?

How are people with your racial identity represented in media (e.g., books, television, film, social media), politics, education, and employment?

In what ways, if any, do you experience guilt or shame when it comes to race?

*Level II: (Re)Seeing Others*

How does your racial identity inform the way you see others?

What do you know about races other than your own?

What racial stereotypes have you heard about races different than your own?

Has anyone been influential in shaping your understanding of other racial identities?

Is it possible that two individuals from different backgrounds experience, or make meaning of, the same event in different ways?

How are people with different racial identities than your own represented in media (e.g., books, television, film, social media), politics, education, and employment?

*Level III: (Re)Seeing Systems and Institutions*

Which individuals, relationships, or programs helped you get to where you are today?

How do individual thoughts, beliefs, and suppositions inform law, media, education, and politics?

In what ways does education perpetuate racial inequity?

*Level IV: (Re)Seeing the Classroom*

How will your racial identity influence your work as a teacher with students with the same race as you? How will it influence your work with students with different racial identities?

How will your students' racial identities influence your work as a teacher?

What is the impact of your race on your beliefs as a teacher?

How do you situate yourself within the racial power structures that influence teaching and learning? How will you assist students in navigating the power structures successfully and safely?

To what degree are your experiences and knowledge superior to those of your students?

Are you willing to speak out against both overt and covert displays of racism in your classroom, regardless of the political climate of the space?

*Note:* Questions were compiled and amended from several sources (see Henze et al., 1998; Milner, 2003; Singleton & Linton, 2006; Tochluk, 2010).

teacher education students, this may be the first foray into racialized knowledge. As Ladson-Billings (2001) lamented, "Typically, White middle-class prospective teachers have little to no understanding of their own culture. Notions of Whiteness are taken for granted" (p. 81). At Level I, pedagogy should attempt to break this harmful assumption and position white preservice teachers in a place of reflexive inquisitiveness, in search of a racialized critical consciousness and the development of racial literacy (Picower, 2009). In addition, students of color should be given the opportunity to process the ways that whiteness and racism have impacted their personal and educative experiences. Foundationally, Level I seeks to build racial literacy by responding to two questions: (1) When did you realize your racial identity? (2) What does your racial identity mean to you? A good starting point in Level I would be to establish a shared set of understandings from which work can begin. If we ask students to reflect on the first time they realized their racial identities, it would be helpful if everyone shared a similar understanding of the construct of race. The National Museum of African American History and Culture (2021) provides a series of definitions about racial terminology (e.g., racism, oppression, privilege) that can be helpful in building a common vocabulary. Throughout an ARTE program, these foundational definitions should be revisited to maintain continuity and consistency throughout coursework.

Once students begin to take ownership of their racial knowledge, faculty can then assist students in interrogating the second question: What does this mean? Peggy McIntosh's (1992) article on white privilege is an especially eye-opening read for many white students. McIntosh's contribution serves as evidence of the property value inherent in whiteness (Harris, 1993). Likewise, ARTE programs should assist BIPOC students in processing the racial trauma and internalized oppression they have experienced. Singh (2019) suggested that it is necessary for people of color to reflect upon and acknowledge the ways that racism has influenced their experiences, self-perceptions, and perceptions of others. ARTE program faculty, thus, should have experience mitigating the white emotionalities that white students may perform and also an awareness of the complex ways that racism influences students of color.

Integral to the interrogation of one's own racial identity is the construction of a space where such work can take place. Too often, BIPOC students are subjected to the "awakening" of their white counterparts as they lift the veil of racialized ignorance. This labor is unnecessary for BIPOC students to endure, and therefore space should be constructed for white students and BIPOC students to process these steps independent of each other. One suggestion is to provide racial affinity spaces for preservice teachers with shared racial identities to process their racial knowledge and reflections (Blitz & Kohl, 2012; Michael & Conger, 2009). Racial affinity groups "are processes where people of the same racial group meet on a regular basis to discuss dynamics of institutional racism, oppression, and privilege" (Blitz & Kohl, 2012, p. 481). Essential to these spaces, Michael and Conger (2009) contended, is the willingness of participants to hold one another accountable for the influence of whiteness on group dynamics and exchanges. Racial affinity spaces should be imbedded within ARTE programs and facilitated by members of the faculty—as part of their scheduled teaching responsibilities—or graduate students whose work aligns with anti-racist aims. This facilitation should be seen as part of a faculty member's or student's workload and not as optional service to be completed outside of employment expectations.

### Level II: (Re)Seeing Others—Looking Through the Window

At Level II, racial literacy will be furthered through examining the influence of race/ism on others. Students should revisit racial stereotypes they have heard, internalized, or perpetuated against racial others and begin to develop a racially critical consciousness. For white students, this involves making the invisibility of whiteness more visible through articulating the presence of whiteness in society. For students of color, this necessitates recognizing the ways racial bigotry influences their perceptions of other people of color. ARTE instruction focuses on the question: How does your racialized self influence the way you view others?

Students should examine the cross-race relationships that they have. As a potential instructional activity, instructors could provide cross-race dialogue, relationship-building, or cultural explorations to assist students who have had racially isolated pasts to interact in positive situations with classmates. Again, burdens of racial teaching should not fall to the BIPOC students within ARTE programs through cross-race dialogue. These discussions should be facilitated by instructors knowledgeable with such processes.

Additionally, race-consciousness journaling would be an effective method for pre-services to consider their relationship to their racial peers and racial others (Allen, 2004; Hawkman, 2020; Matias & Mackey, 2016; Milner, 2003; Peller, 1990; Pewewardy, 2005). Building from the questions in Table 11.1, preservice teachers could interact with readings and content through written reflection. Their responses could be used to facilitate dialogue in and beyond their racial affinity groups. In a single social studies methods course, Hawkman (2020) embedded a series of race-consciousness journal activities that guided students through an introspective process of racial reflection. The pacing and questions suggested by Hawkman (2020) could easily be amended to fit within a larger ARTE program.

### Level III: (Re)Seeing Systems and Institutions: Putting the Pieces Together

At Level III, racial literacy will be furthered through attention to the structural forms of racism and ways that structural antiracist efforts can be effective. This stage of ARTE centers upon moving beyond individualized conceptions of racism and anti-racism toward the understanding of the structural versions.

Problematically, teacher education students often only engage in dialogue around white privilege as a summative experience in understanding racism. While privilege certainly remains a component of hegemonic whiteness, a singular focus on privilege does our students (and their future students) a severe disservice, and serves to perpetuate the terms of the racial contract (Leonardo, 2004). Moreover, a limited understanding of white privilege does little to advance racially literate teaching. White privilege discourses promote the assumption that if white people acknowledge the existence of racial privileges, and do their best to individually refute them in their daily lives, the battle to eradicate racism will finally end. Therefore, the central question of this level of ARTE is: How does racism influence systems, structures, and policy?

Leonardo's (2004) "The Color of Supremacy" is particularly useful in relation to Level III of the ARTE framework. Written in direct response to McIntosh's (1992) "Knapsack," this challenge to McIntosh's work problematizes the narrative of white privilege by providing a thorough list of structural and institutional applications of whiteness. If they have not done so already, white students will most likely demonstrate some discomfort as they engage with Leonardo's list, as it is generally easier for one to acknowledge individual acts of racism (i.e., privilege) than to bear witness to systems built exclusively with whiteness in mind. However, through discomfort comes revolutionary change, so ARTE educators should not give into the calls of students that "this stuff" is too tough to discuss.

At Level III, preservice teachers should also understand the ways that racism and white supremacy have shaped K–12 education and the world beyond the classroom. Content-area specialists can connect issues of race/ism and whiteness to the pedagogical trends and outcomes within their respective fields. In social studies teacher education courses, students can unlearn the traditional white social studies narratives that pervade the field (Chandler & Branscombe, 2016). Through engaging Black feminist (Vickery, 2017), AsianCrit (An, 2017), and anti-colonial (Sabzalian, 2019) scholarship, social studies teacher educators can aid preservice teachers in reshaping their racial pedagogical content knowledge guided by anti-racism. Literacy teacher educators might engage ARTE through critical race literacy pedagogy and the interrogation of children's or young adult literature (Mosely, 2010). As Vakil and Ayers (2019) suggested, there is a need to explore the racial politics of STEM education, and an ARTE program is just the site to take up this endeavor. For example, mathematics teacher educators can draw upon scholarship from Danny Martin (2019), whose work has long explored the ways that mathematics education has reified anti-Blackness. In science education, preservice teachers can investigate how whiteness and white ways of knowing have shaped scientific knowledge production (Samuel, 2009). Critical to Level III is the racialization of field-specific content so that preservice teachers reckon with the relationship between their area of study and the maintenance of white supremacy.

**Level IV: (Re)Seeing the Classroom**

At Level IV, racial literacy will be developed through specific attention to racially just racial pedagogical decision-making. Hawkman (2019) suggested that racial pedagogical decision-making refers to the ways that teachers make decisions about how to teach about race/ism and anti-racism. Existing on a continuum, racial pedagogical decision-making can range from racially literate to racially illiterate. Thus, racial pedagogical decision-making is influenced by teachers' sense of racial pedagogical content knowledge, their personal sense of racial literacy, and their investment in anti-racism. As students develop a sense of racial literacy in conjunction with the development of their teaching identities, instructors must begin to plant seeds of anti-racist pedagogy that will inform students' future practice. The essential question to be resolved in Level IV is: How will your understanding of race/ism inform your practice as a classroom teacher?

Assisting students in making connections between the racial lessons they learn through engaging in Levels I–III with their work as educators will help them to internalize and personalize a commitment toward anti-racist ends (Milner, 2003). ARTE faculty should support students in recognizing the impact of whiteness in education specifically. Historically, educators are taught to be apolitical upon entering classroom spaces. However, a teacher prepared in an ARTE program would assume the opposite stance, one of political commitment to directly challenging the official master narratives whiteness creates to perpetuate white supremacy through textbooks, content, curriculum, and policy.

At Level IV, preservice teachers should engage in work that turns their racial literacy into informed anti-racist pedagogical decision-making. Just because preservice teachers are exposed to anti-racist content does not mean they are prepared to enact anti-racism in their future classrooms (Hawkman, 2019).Therefore, preservice teachers should interact with materials that provide examples of anti-racist praxis. Selections from Rethinking Schools, such as *Teaching for Black Lives* (Watson et al., 2018) or *Rethinking Ethnic Studies* (Cuauhtin et al., 2019), provide concise examples and models for classroom practice grounded in anti-racism. Books from Mica Pollock—*Everyday Anti-racism* (2008) or *Schooltalk* (2017)—provide examples of teachers engaging in classroom-based anti-racism alongside students. It is also important for preservice teachers to build understanding of what it is like to confront racist practices, policies, and curriculum within schools. Duncan (2019) traced the efforts of Black teachers to interrupt the racist acts of their white colleagues within the classroom. Bettina Love's (2019) call for white teachers to serve as co-conspirators through abolitionist teaching can offer white preservice teachers a vision for the type of commitments needed to fully disrupt racism within their future schools. Based on these examples, students should then develop their own anti-racist lesson plans and action plans. After receiving feedback from peers and course instructors, these lesson plans can be deployed in real time with real students during clinical or student teaching experiences (Hawkman, 2020). Further, supervisors for these clinical experiences should hold preservice teachers accountable for embodying anti-racism in the classroom.

## ADDITIONAL CONSIDERATIONS AND CONCLUSIONS

The ARTE framework detailed above was designed with teacher education programs at HPWIs in mind. As the majority of teacher education programs exist in similar circumstances, this model can be amended to meet the needs of many institutions. Although HPWIs are filled mostly with white students, students of color are also strongly represented. If these institutions continue to center whiteness in their populations, curriculum, and pedagogy, efforts at anti-racism will be short-lived and ineffective. Hegemonic whiteness affects everyone, white folks and BIPOC folks, though often in markedly different ways. ARTE programs should be mindful of the experiences of students of color, as they are about challenging white students to adopt co-conspiracy. The attributes that lead white students to suggest a space is "safe" for them is often one that protects whiteness and white emotionalities. Often, "safe spaces" become places where white students avoid grappling with racism by evoking claims of feeling overwhelmed by the information shared by non-white students, thus leaving non-white students anxious for critical dialogue but lacking opportunity (Galman et al., 2010; Richert et al., 2008). This is a racially illiterate space that will enact harm on students of color. Additionally, Tochluk (2010) contended that some aspects of racial realizing should be conducted in single race spaces so as to not burden nonwhite students. In addition to white racial affinity groups, support should be provided to protect the mental health of BIPOC students and faculty. Racial battle fatigue can be overpowering to BIPOC students and faculty in teacher education programs at HWPIs (Smith, 2004).

An effective ARTE program is also one that interrogates and disrupts whiteness at all stages. Milner (2012) noted that for an authentic utilization of critical pedagogy, educators must provide time for authentic reflection, connect praxis to the lives of students, reflect on power structures, and encourage critical thinking and political action. If conversations regarding anti-racist pedagogy are left to a single course or are not implemented systematically, students will most likely come away from the program with shallow, even harmful understandings of anti-racist pedagogy (Matias et al., 2014). The ARTE framework presented here is intended to be layered throughout the 2 to 3 years of coursework associated with teacher education programs. Additionally, the four levels of the ARTE framework need not be traveled through in direct succession, as some questions and activities may be more challenging without having already attended to other concerns. For example, it may be difficult for a student to articulate how racialized power influences their practice in the classroom if they do not yet understand the hegemonic nature of whiteness.

Finally, efforts to build racial literacy will not be successful without directly accounting for the presence of whiteness in education (Apple, 1993; Ladson-Billings, 2013; Leonardo, 2009, 2013; MacMullan, 2005; Picower, 2009; Sleeter, 2012). The implementation of an ARTE framework necessitates individual and programmatic restructuring to intentionally disrupt the overwhelming presence of whiteness within educational systems. Consequently, throughout the enactment of the ARTE framework, the voices, perspectives, concerns, needs, and contributions of BIPOC scholars, educators, and students must be central. In this chapter, I've articulated some of the ways that the ARTE framework should centralize concern for students and faculty of color. This chapter is not meant to be a step-by-step checklist for teacher education programs, which after being completed will award them an anti-racist merit badge. No such badges exist. Rather, the ARTE framework presented here offers teacher educators a starting point for determining the specific strengths, needs, and challenges that are unique to their particular contexts, populations, and circumstances.

## REFERENCES

Allen, R. L. (2004). Whiteness and critical pedagogy. *Educational Philosophy and Theory, 36*(2), 121–136.

An, S. (2017). Teaching race through AsianCrit-informed counterstories of school segregation. *Social Studies Research and Practice, 12*(2), 210–231.

Apple, M. W. (1993). *Official knowledge: Democratic education in a conservative age.* Routledge.

Apple, M. W. (1998). Foreword. In J. L. Kincheloe, S. R. Steinberg, N. M. Rodríguez, & R. E. Chennault (Eds.), *White reign: Deploying whiteness in America*. St. Martin's Press.

Banks, C. A., & Banks, J. A. (1995). Equity pedagogy: An essential component of multicultural education. *Theory Into Practice, 34*(3), 152–58.

Banks, J. A. (2001). Multicultural education: Characteristics and goals. In J. A. Banks & C. A. Banks (Eds.), *Multicultural education: Issues and perspectives* (4th ed., pp. 2–23). Wiley.

Banks, J. A. (2004). Multicultural education: Historical developments, dimensions, and practice. In J. A. Banks & C. A. Banks (Eds.), *Handbook of research on multicultural education*. Jossey-Bass.

Banks, J. A., & Banks, C. A. (Eds.). (2001). *Multicultural education: Issues and perspectives* (4th ed.) Wiley.

Bery, S. (2014). Multiculturalism, teaching slavery, and white supremacy. *Equity & Excellence in Education, 47*(3), 334–352.

Blitz, L. V., & Kohl Jr., B. G. (2012). Addressing racism in the organization: The role of white racial affinity groups in creating change. *Administration in Social Work, 36*(5), 479–498. https://doi: 10.1080/03643107.2011.624261

Castagno, A. E. (2013). Multicultural education and the protection of whiteness. *American Journal of Education, 120*(1), 101–128.

Center for Anti-Racist Education. (2021*). CARE principles: Our vision for an antiracist future.* https://antiracistfuture.org/explore/tools/

Chandler, P. T., & Branscombe, A. (2015). White social studies: Protecting the white racial code. In P. T. Chandler (Ed.), *Doing race in social studies: Critical perspectives* (pp. 61–87). Information Age.

Cuauhtin, R. T., Zavala, M., Sleeter, C., & Au, W. (Eds). (2019). Rethinking ethnic studies. Rethinking Schools.

Delpit, L. (1995). *Other people's children: Cultural conflict in the classroom.* New York Press.

Duncan, K. E. (2019). "They hate on me!" Black teachers interrupting their white colleagues' racism. *Educational Studies, 55*(2), 197–213.

Flansburgh, J. & Linnel, J. (1990). Your racist friend. [Recorded by They Might Be Giants]. On *Flood.* Elektra Records.

Fylkesnes, S. (2018). Whiteness in teacher education research discourses: A review of the use and meaning making of the term cultural diversity. *Teaching and Teacher Education, 71*(1), 24–33.

Galman, S., Pica-Smith, C., & Rosenberger, C. (2010). Aggressive and tender navigations: Teacher educators confront whiteness in their practice. *Journal of Teacher Education, 61*(3), 225–246.

Gibson, M. A. (1976). Approaches to multicultural education in the United States: Some concepts and assumptions. *Anthropology & Education, 7*(4), 7–18.

Gillborn, D. (2005). Education policy as an act of white supremacy: Whiteness, critical race theory and education reform. *Journal of Education Policy, 20*(4), 485–505.

Greene, P. (2018). *Actively seeking diverse faculty.* Inside Higher Education. https://www.insidehighered.com/advice/2018/12/12/advice-attracting-and-retaining-diverse-faculty-members-opinion

Guinier, L. (2004). From racial liberalism to racial literacy: *Brown v. Board of Education* and the interest-divergence dilemma. *The Journal of American History, 91*(1), 92–118.

Harris, C. I. (1993). Whiteness as property. Harvard Law Review, 106(8), 1707–1791.

Hawkman, A. M. (2019). "Let's try and grapple all of this": A snapshot of racial identity development and racial pedagogical decision making in an elective social studies course. *The Journal of Social Studies Research 43*(3), 215–228.

Hawkman, A. M. (2020). Swimming in and through whiteness: Antiracism in social studies teacher education. *Theory & Research in Social Education, 48*(3), 403–430.

Henze, R., Lucas, T., & Scott, B. (1998). Dancing with the monster: Teachers discuss racism, power, and white privilege in education. *The Urban Review, 30*(3), 187–210.

Iverson, S. V. (2007). Camouflaging power and privilege: A critical race analysis of university of diversity policies. *Educational Administration Quarterly, 43*(5), 586–611.

Kendi, I. X. (2019). *How to be an anti-racist.* Penguin Random House.

King, L. J., & Chandler, P. T. (2016). From non-racism to antiracism in social studies teacher education: Social studies and racial pedagogical content knowledge. In A. R. Crowe & A. Cuenca (Eds.), *Rethinking social studies teacher education in the twenty-first century* (pp. pp. 3–22). Springer.

King, L. J., & Woodson, A. (2015*). Educative-psychic violence: Articulating and resisting the ramifications of slavery math problems* [Paper presentation]. Annual meeting of the College and University Faculty Assembly of the National Council for the Social Studies, New Orleans, LA.

Ladson-Billings, G. (2001). *Crossing over to Canaan: The journey of new teachers in diverse classrooms.* Jossey-Bass.

Ladson-Billings, G. (2013). Critical race theory—What it is not! In M. Lynn & A. D. Dixson (Eds.), *Handbook of critical race theory in education* (pp. 34–47). Routledge.

Lawrence, S. M., & Tatum, B. D. (1997). Teachers in transition: The impact of anti-racist professional development on classroom practice. *Teachers College Record, 99*(1), 162–178.

Lee, E. (1995). Taking multicultural, anti-racist education seriously. In D. Levine, R. Lowe, R. Peterson, & R. Tenorio (Eds.), *Rethinking schools: An agenda for change* (pp. 140–149). New Press.

Leonardo, Z. (2004). The color of supremacy: Beyond the discourse of "white privilege." *Educational Philosophy and Theory, 36*(2), 137–152.

Leonardo, Z. (2009). *Race, whiteness, and education.* New York: Routledge.

Leonardo, Z. (2013*). Race frameworks: A multidimensional theory of racism and education.* Teachers College Press.

Liptak, K. (2020). *Trump says Department of Education will investigate use of 1619 Project in schools.* CNN. https://www.cnn.com/2020/09/06/politics/trump-education-department-1619-project/index.html

Love, B. L. (2019). *We want to do more than survive: Abolitionist teaching and the pursuit of educational freedom.* Beacon Press.

MacMullan, T. (2005). Beyond the pale: A pragmatist approach to whiteness studies. *Philosophy & Social Criticism, 31*(3), 267–292.

Martin, D. B. (2019). Equity, inclusion, and antiblackness in mathematics education. *Race Ethnicity & Education, 22*(4), 459–478.

Matias, C. E., & Mackey, J. (2016). Breakin' down whiteness in antiracist teaching: Introducing critical whiteness pedagogy. *Urban Review, 48*(1), 32–50.

Matias, C. E., Mitchell Viesca, K., Garrison-Wade, D. F., Tandon, M., & Galindo, R. (2014). "What is critical whiteness doing in our nice field like critical race theory?" Applying CRT and CWS to understand the white imaginations of white teacher candidates. *Equity & Excellence in Education, 47*(3), 289–304.

May, S., & Sleeter, C. E. (Eds.) (2010). *Critical multiculturalism: Theory & praxis.* Routledge.

McIntosh, P. (1992). White privilege and male privilege: A personal account of coming to see correspondences through work in women's studies. In M. Andersen & P. H. Collins (Eds.), *Race, class, and gender: An anthology* (pp. 76–87). Wadsworth Publishing.

McLaren, P. (1997). Decentering whiteness. *Multicultural Education,* 4–11.

Michael, A., & Conger, M. C. (2009). Becoming an anti-racist white ally: How a white affinity group can help. *Perspectives on Urban Education,* 56–60.

Milner, H. R. (2003). Reflection, racial competence, and critical pedagogy: How do we prepare pre-service teachers to pose tough questions? *Race Ethnicity and Education, 6*(2), 193–208.

Milner, H. R. (2012). Beyond a test score: Explaining opportunity gaps in educational practice. *Journal of Black Studies 43*(6), 693–718.

Mosely, M. (2010). "That really hit me hard": Moving beyond passive anti-racism to engage with critical race literacy pedagogy. *Race Ethnicity & Education, 13*(4), 449–471.

National Council of Teachers of English. (2018). *Statement on anti-racism to support teaching and learning*. http://www2.ncte.org/statement/antiracisminteaching/

National Museum of African American History and Culture. (2021). *Power and privilege definitions*. https://nmaahc.si.edu/learn/talking-about-race/resources

Peller, G. (1990). Race consciousness. *Duke Law Journal*, 758–847.

Pewewardy, C. (2005). Shared journaling: A methodology for engaging white preservice students into multicultural education discourse. *Teacher Education Quarterly*, 41–60.

Picower, B. (2009). The unexamined whiteness of teaching: How white teachers maintain and enact dominant racial ideologies. *Race Ethnicity and Education, 12*(2), 197–215.

Pollock, M. (Ed.). (2008). *Everyday anti-racism*. The New Press.

Pollock, M. (2017). *Schooltalk: Rethinking what we say about—and to—students every day*. The New Press.

Richert, A., Donahue, D., & LaBoskey, V. (2008). Preparing white teachers to teach in a racist nation: What do they need to know and be able to do? In W. Ayers, T. Quinn, & D. Stovall (Eds.), *Handbook of social justice in education* (pp. 640–653). Routledge.

Sabzalian, L. (2019). The tensions between Indigenous sovereignty and multicultural citizenship education: Toward an anticolonial approach to civic education. *Theory & Research in Social Education, 47*(3), 311–346.

Samuel, A. (2009). Turning the focus from "Other" to science education: Exploring the invisibility of whiteness. *Cultural Studies of Science Education, 4*, 649–656.

Singh, A. A. (2019). *The racial healing handbook: Practical activities to help you challenge privilege, confront systemic racism, and engage in collective healing*. New Harbinger.

Singleton, G. E., & Linton, C. (2006). *Courageous conversations about race: A field guide to achieving equity in schools*. Corwin Press.

Sleeter, C. E. (1996). *Multicultural education as social activism*. State University of New York Press.

Sleeter, C. E. (2012). Confronting the marginalization of culturally responsive pedagogy. *Urban Education, 47*(3), 562–584.

Sleeter, C. E., & Grant, C. A. (1987). An analysis of multicultural education in the United States. *Harvard Educational Review, 57*, 421–444.

Smith, W. A. (2004). Black faculty coping with racial battle fatigue: The campus racial climate in a post-civil rights era. In D. Cleveland (Ed.), *A long way to go: Conversations about race by African American faculty and graduate students* (pp. 171–190). Peter Lang.

Tatum, B. D. (1997). *"Why are all the black kids sitting together in the cafeteria?" And other conversations about race*. Basic Books.

Thompson, A. (1997). For: Anti-racist education. *Curriculum Inquiry, 27*(1), 7–44.

Tochluk, S. (2010). *Witnessing whiteness: The need to talk about race and how to do it* (2nd ed.). Rowman & Littlefield.

UNC Charlotte. (2020). *Graduate certificate in anti-racism in urban education*. https://distanceed.uncc.edu/programs/gc-anti-racism-urban-education.

Vakil, S., & Ayers, R. (2019). The racial politics of STEM education in the USA: Interrogations and explorations. *Race Ethnicity and Education, 22*(4), 449–458. https://doi: 10.1080/13613324.2019.1592831

Vickery, A. E. (2017). "You excluded us for so long and now you want us to be patriotic?" African American women teachers contemplating the quandary of citizenship. *Theory and Research in Social Education, 45*(3), 318–348.

Watson, D., Hagopian, J., & Au, W. (Eds.). (2018). *Teaching for Black lives*. Rethinking Schools.

Wheaton College. (2020). *Becoming an anti-racist educator.* https://wheatoncollege.edu
/academics/special-projects-initiatives/center-for-collaborative-teaching-and
-learning/anti-racist-educator/

## CHAPTER 12

# Learning to Teach History for Justice

## Racial Literacies and Teacher Education

*Christopher C. Martell and Kaylene M. Stevens*

### INTRODUCTION

Racism is interwoven into our histories. In the United States and globally, race has long been used to create systems of advantage and has helped white people maintain their social power. In recent decades, this has been made more complex by the rise of populist nationalism, negative reactions of nations to global migration, and counterreactions to movements that seek justice for oppressed groups. Yet this is not surprising, as social systems have been designed to make whiteness and white supremacy almost invisible to many, despite the fact that it governs much of how the world and nation works. There are numerous recent historical events in the United States and the globe that highlight this. In response, numerous justice movements have organized, many led by people of color, including the Black Lives Matter and Women's March movements. With these ideas in mind, understanding how the concept of race was created, how it functions in the past and present, and how movements of people have organized to create a more equitable society must be a main purpose of history education.

The recent movement in history education toward inquiry-based learning has been important, but inadequate, for helping students address the larger issues of racial inequity in our society (Martell & Stevens, 2021; Salinas & Blevins, 2014). Over the past two decades, scholars have argued that the history classroom, and by extension history teacher education, should center on inquiry as it relates to historical thinking (Martin & Monte-Sano, 2008; VanSledright, 2011; Wineburg, 2001) and democratic citizenship skills (Barton & Levstik, 2004; Grant et al., 2017; Lévesque, 2008). While these ideas present key first steps, as Salinas and Blevins (2014) have argued, these views of historical inquiry do not deliberately challenge students to critically examine the past or look at the role that racial identity, power, and privilege have played in history. Without intentionally focusing the study of history on racial justice, students are unable to understand how our racialized society came to be. They are unable to develop racial literacies, where race serves as a tool of diagnosis, feedback, and assessment of conditions within society and people's lived experiences (King, 2016; Skerrett, 2011). To fill this gap, Martell and Stevens (2021) proposed using social inquiries in the history classroom, where students begin to "understand, disrupt and challenge the official curriculum and explore new and diverse perspectives that recognize and honor the unique experiences of linguistically and culturally diverse communities" (p. 38). Numerous other scholars have made similar arguments for a history education that centers the experience of people of color and positions racial justice as a key concept (Busey, 2014; Busey & Cruz, 2015; Chandler, 2015; Chandler & McKnight, 2009; Epstein, 2009; Epstein & Gist, 2015; Epstein et al., 2011; King, 2016; King & Brown, 2014; Rodríguez, 2018; Santiago, 2017, 2019; Santiago & Castro, 2019; Woodson, 2015, 2017). We hope this chapter adds to that important work by challenging the field of social studies teacher education to also center racial literacies and racial justice.

## A CONCEPTUAL FRAMEWORK: HISTORY FOR JUSTICE

We work from a stance that the study of history should be a tool to help citizens make the world better. We must understand our past to ensure that we make informed decisions in the present and future. Most of the problems our world will face over the next century will be caused or exacerbated by racial inequity. While fostering historical thinking and democratic citizenship are incredibly important, they should be a focus in history education only if they serve a larger purpose to make the nation and world more just. To accomplish this larger goal of history education to make the world better, we advocate that teachers take a *history for justice* stance in their practice (Martell & Stevens, 2021) and that seeking racial equity must be at the core of any justice work (Brown & Brown, 2011). To accomplish this, we propose a pedagogical framework that helps students learn how to "think like activists," which includes three main components. First, history students should investigate the past using social inquiries. Second, history teachers should design the curriculum to be both critical and multicultural. Third, history learning communities should be built around fostering transformative democratic citizenship.

### Thinking Like an Activist

Throughout history, most social change has been the result of activists organized in movements for justice. Yet, our history curriculum has long been organized around important individuals. Even when an important individual may be the spokesperson for a justice movement (i.e., Gandhi, Martin Luther King Jr., Malcolm X, Nelson Mandela), they were only able to have success because their work was usually built on decades of organizing by activists and community members. We need a radical reenvisioning of how we teach history in our schools. If students (and citizens) see history as only shaped by well-known (or powerful) individuals, then they may continue to believe that individuals are the only ones who can make change and put their faith in one elected leader to change society (this may explain why we have seen a rise in numerous leaders, especially in democratic or formerly democratic nations, espousing autocratic rule). Moreover, citizens may develop a view that they cannot contribute to social change and, as a result, are less likely to participate in social movements. This type of history education, which focuses on important individuals, may be a barrier to the popular support of movements, and especially movements for racial justice.

Rooted in the movement-building frameworks created by activists Moyer et al. (2001) and Lakey (2004), we argue that thinking like an activist comprises three main components: (1) cultural preparation, (2) critical analysis, and (3) collective action, which we describe below:

- Cultural preparation involves creating a new vision of what society can be instead of the status quo; it involves unlearning oppressive structures and building solidarity. Did a group of people at the time want to change society, and did they have a vision for how it might look different? If so, what was that vision and how was it different?
- Critical analysis, or developing sociopolitical consciousness, is the ability to recognize how oppression is constructed and how power structures are replicated. Did a group of people at the time outline and help educate the public about a particular type of oppression and ways that they could work against it? Did they make the case to the public that alternatives to the status quo would benefit all?
- Collective action is the work of activists; it is how movements enact change. Did a group of people at the time engage in collective action (Was there a "trigger event" that gained public attention? What methods were used to raise public awareness?)? Did the movement gain public support? Did the groups' collective actions lead to a resolution and change in society? (Martell & Stevens, 2021, pp. 9–10)

When students learn how to analyze history through these processes, they are more likely to understand how social change occurs and, we speculate, have a better understanding of how to enact social change in the present.

To support teachers in creating history classrooms that focus on activist thinking and the work of movements, we outline a pedagogical framework that includes three core components: social inquiry, critical multiculturalism, and transformative democratic citizenship (Martell & Stevens, 2021). We argue that most historical inquiries should be social in nature, since the core purpose of history should be to ask questions and gather and evaluate evidence through the lens of power relationships in the past, which has led to the present and influences our future. Social inquiries focus on understanding the welfare of human beings in a society over time and how equity has (or has not) been present in those societies, with a specific focus on how race and racism operate. Traditionally, the history curriculum has served as a tool of racism and other forms of oppression (Banks, 2004; Ladson-Billings, 2003). We contend that curriculum must be multicultural *and* critical. The curriculum must not only include many multicultural perspectives, but also specifically center on racism and other forms of oppression and how they have influenced the past (and present). Finally, history education has long been used to justify the status quo and uphold current racial and power arrangements (Banks, 2004; Ladson-Billings, 2003). Rooted in the work of Banks (2017), history education must serve as a place to foster transformative democratic citizenship. It must help students develop a sociopolitical consciousness and cultural competence, which are essential citizenship skills in any multicultural state and globally (Ladson-Billings, 1995, 2006, 2014). It should model democratic ideas and practices, but be an actual place for students, and especially students from nondominant groups, to engage in active and authentic citizenship.

## HISTORY FOR JUSTICE AND TEACHER EDUCATION

We argue that teaching history for justice should be at the center of social studies teacher education programs, including preservice teacher preparation and inservice professional development. Situated within the current research on teacher education, we make three contentions about designing teacher education and professional development programs for teachers and district leaders that are focused on history for justice.

There is strong evidence that teacher education programs that build on teachers' preexisting beliefs are most likely to influence teachers' practices (Martell, 2018; Wideen et al., 1998). Conversely, teachers with ingrained beliefs are unlikely to change their beliefs as the result of teacher education programs (Wideen et al., 1998). As such, teacher education programs must seek candidates who have preexisting beliefs that support social justice or who are open to new ideas related to the teaching of history. Whether they are preservice or inservice programs, their goal should be to seek candidates who show a commitment to teaching for diversity, inquiry, and democracy. To accomplish this, social studies teacher education programs should make clear their missions to prospective teachers to prepare teachers to approach their work in ways that aim to make the world more just. Based on decades of research, we argue that social studies teacher educators must: (1) anchor their justice-oriented programs within the discipline of history (and the subject of social studies more broadly), (2) include both conceptual and practical tools for teaching history for justice, and (3) support teachers as they grapple with sometimes difficult reflections on their own experiences.

## Teacher Education Must Be Rooted in Content

Research on teacher education highlights the need for programs to focus on content preparation, but only if it serves larger goals, such as helping teachers understand student learning as it relates to that specific content (Adler, 2008; Kennedy, 2016; Martell, 2018; van Hover, 2008). Traditionally, history teachers' content preparation through history coursework has been heavily lecture- and discussion-based. Any of us who have taken college-level history courses can attest that, much like middle or high school courses, they often involve passively listening to a professor describing narratives that other people (namely, historians) have created. Instead, social studies teacher education programs focused on history for justice should teach content in ways that ask future and current teachers to engage in social inquiries. The teachers should have ample opportunities to practice researching, writing, and rewriting their own narratives of the past with an intentional focus on equity, and specifically racial equity. This will allow them to experience learning content in a way that models a type of inquiry and justice-oriented pedagogy that they may not have experienced as students.

For example, in a social studies methods course, a teacher educator may ask students to search for documents from the incarceration of Japanese Americans during World War II and answer the question, "How could the government have incarcerated 120,000 civilians who had committed no violations of the law?" (or perhaps draft their own justice-oriented inquiry questions). There have been many different types of historical investigations around the topic of Japanese American incarceration (some may even ask the inappropriate question about whether it was justifiable). A social inquiry would instead position questions around injustice and ask students to examine the roots of it. Students may come to a number of conclusions, including that white farmers wanted to remove economic competition from Japanese Americans, white citizens had inaccurate views that Japanese American people were not loyal to the United States, or that it was a result of racism—since very few German and Italian Americans were incarcerated during this time.

These same practices should be used in professional development courses. Experienced history teachers could be asked to engage in a simulation of the California Gold Rush, where they are assigned to various racial groups and have to abide by the racial caste system of the time (cf. Martell et al., 2017). This would show the reality that Chinese American miners were not allowed citizenship or land ownership, Mexican American miners were targeted by the media and law enforcement as banditos, and Indigenous and African American miners were enslaved or segregated. These examples show how historical content is the medium that roots teaching for justice in the history classroom.

## Conceptual and Practical Tools

In their preparation programs, teachers need opportunities to develop both conceptual and practical tools for teaching (Grossman et al., 1999; Grossman et al., 2000; Martell, 2013, 2014, 2020; Valencia et al., 2009). Rooted in the work of Vygotsky (1978), Grossman et al. (1999) defined conceptual tools as the applicable ideas and theories teachers have about teaching, learning, and disciplinary acquisition that guide their instructional practices, while practical tools include the instructional practices and curriculum resources used in their classrooms. Conceptual tools offer teachers frameworks for thinking about their practice (i.e., critical race theory, constructivist learning theory), while practical tools have a more local and immediate utility (i.e., lesson plans, curricular resources). Keeping this in mind, teacher educators should organize teachers' development of conceptual and practical tools around the three components of history for justice: social inquiries, critical multiculturalism, and transformative democratic citizenship (described earlier in this chapter). For instance, teacher educators should expose beginning teachers to the three components of history for justice by asking them to interrogate curricular materials, analyze videos of teachers, and craft lesson plans. They could also ask to share the materials they create with colleagues, so they can build their pedagogical repertoires around history for justice. By focusing on both conceptual and practice tools, teachers will have not only opportunities to develop frameworks for thinking about history for justice, but also tangible resources for implementing it in their classrooms.

## Support Teachers in the Reflection Process

Learning to teach for justice through racial literacies lenses must involve teachers' examinations of their own racial and other social identities and the role that they play in privilege and oppression (Sibbett & Au, 2018). This can be difficult work for teachers and teacher educators and may involve feeling discomfort and fear (Woodson & Duncan, 2018). Teacher educators must acknowledge these emotions and build on them to help beginning and experienced teachers with their practice around justice. This includes having students consider their own family histories, as well as their learning and teaching experiences inside and outside school. Teacher educators might consider engaging preservice or inservice teachers in forms of reflection on their own lived experiences. For instance, Sleeter (2008, 2015, 2016) has used the technique of critical family histories with teachers, a process where they examine their own family histories around issues of inequity and injustice. This allows teachers, especially white teachers, to examine the role that race has played in their family's experiences. Specifically, Sleeter (2015) proposed using a process of the four Ps developed by Kumashiro and Lee (2013) when examining families' stories, which added "punishing" and "privileging" to the more traditional "pushing" and "pulling" factors that influence immigration.[1]

This allows people engaging in critical family histories to deeply consider the role that race, privilege, and oppression had in their family's past. This is an example of the type of reflective process that is necessary for preservice and inservice teachers.

## HISTORY TEACHER EDUCATION FOR JUSTICE

The education of history teachers starts before they enter a teacher preparation program and continues throughout their career in the classroom. We argue that it is instrumental that justice be a major theme through teacher development, including preservice teacher preparation and inservice professional development. To describe what a history teacher education for justice would look like, we imagine two different programs, one for preservice teachers and another for inservice teachers. In their descriptions, we hope to create a road map for what it would take to prepare teachers to teach for racial justice through social inquiry, critical multiculturalism, and transformative democratic citizenship. We envision these potential programs as spaces that would foster teachers' own racial literacies, as well as their abilities to support their students' racial literacy development.

### Teacher Preparation

To create a climate in education programs where teaching history for justice can thrive, teacher preparation programs need to be rooted in social inquiry, critical multiculturalism, and transformative democratic citizenship. For example, in both history content and methods courses, students would participate in social inquiries that include the voices of people of color and other unrepresented groups. They would learn by doing inquiries that ask questions about fairness and racial justice, for example, asking preservice teachers if policies have historically helped maintain power for dominant groups and how they may scaffold this concept to secondary and elementary students by looking at particular social injustices, such as redlining in federal housing policy or employment discrimination. Asking students to practice thinking about social inquiry themselves and how they may teach in the classroom fosters an environment where this type of teaching is routinely used. We hope that intentional lesson planning where students must create and design lessons around inquiry questions related to social identity and inequity becomes the foundation of teacher preparation programs.

Additionally, to drive home the concept of critical multiculturalism, history courses should require that a majority of content be related to underrepresented voices, and specifically the experiences of people of color, and how racial inequity (and other forms of inequity) have functioned over time. Preservice teachers would be taught not only about individual acts of discrimination; they would be taught to see the structures behind racism, including overlapping oppression or intersectionality. There are many texts that can help professors and teacher educators assist with understanding structural racism. For example, Ibram X. Kendi's (2017) book, *Stamped From the Beginning: The Definitive History of Racist Ideas in America,* which examines the power structures that fuel racism, could be used in history courses to provide preservice teachers with a justice-oriented perspective on American history. In this text, Kendi traces the intellectual history of racism from the first European settlers in the Americas to the present. Additionally, asking students to read texts such as Erika Lee's (2019) *America for Americans: A History of Xenophobia in the United States*, which traces the United States' long history of demonizing and stoking fear of immigrants back to the colonial era, can help them understand how immigration and racism have long been intertwined. These texts both center the experiences of nondominant groups and portray racism as a structural problem. To extend this into classroom practice, preservice teachers would use these justice-oriented historical texts, and others, to design curriculum units around topics of racism and other forms of oppression as structural problems.

Finally, in order to fully create a teacher program that embodies teaching history for justice, preservice teachers must be committed to transformative democratic citizenship. Teacher preparation programs should selectively screen applicants, searching for those who believe, or have the potential to believe, that the history classroom is a place to foster more active citizens who are working for a more just world. Teachers' commitment to justice should be included in the criteria for admissions in teacher education programs, specifically looking for students who are aware of their own cultural and racial biases and a willingness to challenge their own thinking. Once students are admitted to the program, they should spend time observing and reflecting on the practices of teachers who are teaching history for justice. Teacher education programs should create purposeful experiences for students to teach in multicultural spaces with experienced critical educator mentors, while also requiring preservice teachers to learn about and root their work within their students' communities. We imagine teacher preparation programs that are intentionally situated within specific racial or ethnic communities, and that prepare teachers to teach for justice based on local cultures and histories. Student teachers should be placed in classrooms where mentor teachers can model history teaching for justice. They should also attend community, political, and social events as well as volunteer in the community where they student-teach. For instance, for over two decades, the Teach Next Year Program at the University of Massachusetts Boston has specifically placed student teachers within the Boston Public Schools, creating a pipeline program with the specific intention that teachers will be hired in the district. During this program, social studies student teachers spend a year working and living in the neighborhoods of Boston. They work with experienced teachers who have lived and work in the community for decades (or perhaps their entire lives). Many of the students in the program are students of color who grew up and currently live in Boston. The program includes courses on the past and present Boston community, and focuses on the role of race (as well as class, gender, and other social identities) within the neighborhoods of Boston. Future social studies teachers must learn significant content related to Boston history and take education courses rooted in the local community. This type of teacher preparation offers a very different approach from a typical program, where future teachers are not necessarily prepared for specific communities.

## Teacher Professional Development

Inservice teachers will also need resources and support to start or continue the work of teaching for justice in the history classroom. Professional development around social inquiry, critical multiculturalism, and transformative democratic citizens would be similar to what is received in teacher preparation courses, only condensed. We envision this work also being done at the local level, in districts, with lead teachers supporting their colleagues to better teach for justice and designing model lessons that focus on social inquiry and critical multicultural content. For instance, a small team of teachers at Framingham High School in Massachusetts, which is a racially and economically diverse school located within the immigrant community just west of Boston, have been involved in a years-long process of revising the school's United States history curriculum to center racial justice in all of their units. They have attempted to center the voices of Indigenous, Black, Latinx, and Asian Americans with the curriculum. They intentionally began their curriculum with the experiences of Native people before European colonization and ended with the students writing their own communities' histories in the present. In addition, they have created a series of model lessons for each unit, which would help students understand the role that racial inequity has played in the past, as well as lessons on present-day connections to show students the outcomes of these historical events.

We also imagine schools and districts leading justice-oriented workshops on topics such as anti-racist teaching or working with students from specific cultural groups, which would focus on equity and systematic oppression, and encourage teachers to ask their students to challenge the status quo and build school communities where all students feel they belong. These workshops could use videos of classroom teachers, excerpts from key books, and lesson plan examples that look at power structures and challenge systems that continue to promote dominant groups. Our hope would be that these workshops would create spaces for teachers to share units focusing on topics of racism and other injustices. Returning to the example of Framingham High School, for the past two decades, the district has had teachers running professional development courses on creating anti-racist and culturally relevant classrooms, which has ultimately influenced much of the work being done by the teachers in the district today.

Finally, this type of professional development would also promote trans-formative democratic citizenship by providing examples of how teachers have promoted community action with their students, and providing practical examples and avenues that current teachers can use to become both more involved in the community they work in and more knowledgeable about their students' backgrounds. For example, a professional development workshop may begin by asking the teachers to describe what they know about their students' backgrounds and when was the last time they attended a community event. Teachers can then share stories of how they have invested in the communities where they work. This could serve as a starting place to help teachers take stock of what they know, including what false assumptions they may have, and what they need to know. They could also use this as an opportunity to share sample projects that help promote transformative democratic citizenship, such as creating "know your rights" seminars for immigrant students or students from overpoliced communities. Teachers could then engage in action research projects about the history and current political conditions of the communities they teach in.

## School Districts and Leaders

For history teaching for justice to occur in school districts, the leaders in those districts must commit to this mission. Like teacher preparation programs, they must recruit and hire justice-oriented faculty and create leadership positions centered on providing equity, with an intentional focus on hiring people from unrepresented racial groups. They should encourage their staff to challenge the status quo within schools and use social inquiry to challenge their own practices and policies within the school, evaluating the power structures and relationships in their schools around race and other social identities.

One of the objectives of critical multiculturalism is to analyze unequal power relationships in structures, such as schools, and search for solutions to make the playing field fairer. From this work, districts should create programs for racial equity, such as providing opportunities for students of color to take advanced history classes (and teach those courses in ways that align with a history for justice perspective) or provide feedback and guidance to teachers on the revision of history curricula. Districts and schools should also create mentoring programs and affinity groups for students of color to support them beyond the classroom walls.

Finally, schools, and their leaders, who want to make a commitment to transformative democratic citizenship must take every opportunity to involve their community, and especially parents and community members of color, in the school. In order to promote justice within the school, leaders need to provide as many opportunities as possible to receive feedback from faculty, specifically faculty and students of color, as well as other historically disadvantaged groups, to counteract the traditional assimilationist approaches to the culture and structure of schools. This also involves challenging experienced teachers and staff to examine their own biases and creating a space for reflective practice around issues of race and racism.

# REFERENCES

Adler, S. (2008). The education of social studies teachers. In L. S. Levstik & C. A. Tyson (Eds.), *Handbook of research in social studies education* (pp. 329–351). Routledge.

Banks, J. A. (2004). Teaching for social justice, diversity, and citizenship in a global world. *The Educational Forum, 68*, 296–305. https://doi.org/10.1080/00131 720408984645

Banks, J. A. (2017). Failed citizenship and transformative civic education. *Educational Researcher, 46*(7), 366–377. https://doi.org/10.3102/0013189X17726741

Barton, K. C., & Levstik, L. S. (2004). *Teaching history for the common good*. Lawrence Erlbaum Associates.

Brown, K. D., & Brown, A. L. (2011). Teaching K-8 students about race: African Americans, racism, and the struggle for social justice in the U.S. *Multicultural Education, 19*(1), 9–13. https://doi.org/10.1080/10665681003719590

Busey, C. L. (2014). Examining race from within: Black intraracial discrimination in social studies curriculum. *Social Studies Research and Practice, 9*(2), 120–131.

Busey, C. L., & Cruz, B. C. (2015). A shared heritage: Afro-Latin@s and Black history. *The Social Studies, 106*(6), 293–300. https://doi.org/10.1080/00377996 .2015.1085824

Chandler, P. T. (2015). What does it mean to "do race" in social studies? In P. T. Chandler (Ed.), *Doing race in social studies: Critical perspectives* (pp. 1–10). Information Age Publishing.

Chandler, P. T., & McKnight, D. (2009). The failure of social education in the United States: A critique of teaching the national story from "white" colourblind eyes. *Journal for Critical Education Policy Studies, 7*(2), 217–248.

Epstein, T. (2009). *Interpreting national history: Race, identity, and pedagogy in classrooms and communities*. Routledge.

Epstein, T., & Gist, C. (2015). Teaching racial literacy in secondary humanities classrooms: Challenging adolescents' of color concepts of race and racism. *Race Ethnicity and Education, 18*(1), 40–60. https://doi.org/10.1080/13613324.2013.792800

Epstein, T., Mayorga, E., & Nelson, J. (2011). Teaching about race in an urban history class: The effects of culturally responsive teaching. *The Journal of Social Studies Research, 35*(1), 2–21.

Grant, S. G., Swan, K., & Lee, J. (2017). *Inquiry-based practice in social studies education: Understanding the inquiry design model*. Routledge.

Grossman, P. L., Smagorinsky, P., & Valencia, S. W. (1999). Appropriating tools for teaching English: A theoretical framework for research on learning to teach. *American Journal of Education, 108*(1), 1–29. https://doi.org/10.1086/444230

Grossman, P. L., Valencia, S. W., Evans, K., Thompson, C., Martin, S. D., & Place, N. A. (2000). Transitions into teaching: Learning to teach writing in teacher education and beyond. *Journal of Literacy Research, 32*(4), 631–662. https://doi.org /10.1080/10862960009548098

Kendi, I. X. (2017). *Stamped from the beginning: The definitive history of racist ideas in America*. Nation Books.

Kennedy, M. M. (2016). How does professional development improve teaching? *Review of Educational Research, 86*(4), 945–980. https://doi.org/10.3102/003465 4315626800

King, L. J. (2016). Teaching Black history as a racial literacy project. *Race Ethnicity and Education, 19*(6), 1303–1318. https://doi.org/10.1080/13613324.2016.1150822

King, L. J., & Brown, K. (2014). Once a year to be Black: Fighting against typical Black History Month pedagogies. *Negro Educational Review, 65*(1–4), 23–43.

Kumashiro, K., & Lee, J. (2013). *The hidden four Ps and immigration.* https://www .christinesleeter.org/hidden-four-ps

Ladson-Billings, G. (1995). Toward a theory of culturally relevant pedagogy. *American Educational Research Journal, 32*(3), 465–491. https://doi.org/10.3102/00 028312032003465

Ladson-Billings, G. (2003). Lies my teacher still tells: Developing a critical race perspective toward the social studies. In G. Ladson-Billings (Ed.), *Critical race theory perspectives on the social studies: The profession, policies, and curriculum* (pp. 1–11). Information Age Publishing.

Ladson-Billings, G. (2006). "Yes, but how do we do it?": Practicing culturally relevant pedagogy. In J. Landsman & C. W. Lewis (Eds.), *White teachers, diverse classrooms: Creating inclusive schools, building on students' diversity, and providing true educational equity* (pp. 29–41). Stylus Publishing.

Ladson-Billings, G. (2014). Culturally relevant pedagogy 2.0: aka the remix. *Harvard Educational Review, 84*(1), 74–84. https://doi.org/10.17763/haer.84.1.p2rj131 485484751

Lakey, G. (2004). Strategizing for a living revolution. In D. Solnit (Ed.), *Globalize liberation: How to uproot the system and build a better world* (pp. 135–160). City Lights Books.

Lee, E. (2019). *America for Americans: A history of xenophobia in the United States.* Basic Books.

Lévesque, S. (2008). *Thinking historically: Educating students for the twenty-first century.* University of Toronto Press.

Martell, C. C. (2013). Learning to teach history as interpretation: A longitudinal study of beginning teachers. *The Journal of Social Studies Research, 37*(1), 17–31. https:// doi.org/10.1016/j.jssr.2012.12.001

Martell, C. C. (2014). Building a constructivist practice: A longitudinal study of beginning history teachers. *The Teacher Educator, 49*(2), 97–115. https://doi.org/10 .1080/08878730.2014.888252

Martell, C. C. (2018). Social studies teacher education: Problems and possibilities. In C. C. Martell (Ed.), *Social studies teacher education: Critical issues and current perspectives* (pp. 1–15). Information Age Publishing.

Martell, C. C. (2020). Barriers to inquiry-based instruction: A longitudinal study of history teachers. *Journal of Teacher Education, 71*(3), 279–291. https://doi.org /10.1177/0022487119841880

Martell, C. C., Bryson, J. R., & Chapman-Hale, W. C. (2017). Teaching racial inequity through the California Gold Rush. In P. T. Chandler & T. S. Hawley (Eds.), *Using inquiry to teach about race in social studies* (pp. 61–74). Information Age Publishing.

Martell, C. C., & Stevens, K. M. (2021). *Teaching history for justice: Centering activism in students' study of the past.* Teachers College Press.

Martin, D., & Monte-Sano, C. (2008). Inquiry, controversy, and ambiguous texts: Learning to teach for historical thinking. In W. Warren & D. A. Cantu (Eds.), *History 101: The past, present, and future of teacher preparation* (pp. 167–186). Information Age Publishing.

Moyer, B., MacAllister, J., Finley, M. L., & Soifer, S. (2001). *Doing democracy: The MAP model for organizing social movements*. New Society Publishers.

Rodríguez, N. N. (2018). From margins to center: Developing cultural citizenship education through the teaching of Asian American history. *Theory & Research in Social Education, 46*(4), 528–573. https://doi.org/10.1080/00933104.2018.1432432

Salinas, C. S., & Blevins, B. (2014). Critical historical inquiry: How might pre-service teachers confront master historical narratives? *Social Studies Research and Practice, 9*(3), 35–50.

Santiago, M. (2017). Erasing differences for the sake of inclusion: How Mexican/Mexican American students construct historical narratives. *Theory & Research in Social Education, 45*(1), 43–74. https://doi.org/10.1080/00933104.2016.1211971

Santiago, M. (2019). Historical inquiry to challenge the narrative of racial progress. *Cognition and Instruction, 37*(1), 93–117. https://doi.org/10.1080/07370008.2018.1539734

Santiago, M., & Castro, E. (2019). Teaching anti-essentialist historical inquiry. *The Social Studies, 110*(4), 170–179. https://doi.org/10.1080/00377996.2019.1600463

Sibbett, L., & Au, W. (2018). Critical social studies knowledge and practice: Preparing social justice oriented social studies teachers in the Trump era. In C. C. Martell (Ed.), *Social studies teacher education: Critical issues and current perspectives* (pp. 17–45). Information Age Publishing.

Skerrett, A. (2011). English teachers' racial literacy knowledge and practice. *Race Ethnicity and Education, 14*(3), 313–330. https://doi.org/10.1080/13613324.2010.543391

Sleeter, C. E. (2008). Critical family history, identity, and historical memory. *Educational Studies, 43*(2), 114–124. https://doi.org/10.1080/00131940801944587

Sleeter, C. E. (2015). Multicultural curriculum and critical family history. *Multicultural Education Review, 7*(1–2), 1–11. https://doi.org/10.1080/2005615X.2015.1048607

Sleeter, C. E. (2016). Critical family history: Situating family within contexts of power relationships. *Journal of Multidisciplinary Research, 8*(1), 11–24.

Valencia, S. W., Martin, S. D., Place, N. A., & Grossman, P. L. (2009). Complex interactions in student teaching: Lost opportunities for learning. *Journal of Teacher Education, 60*(3), 304–322. https://doi.org/10.1177/0022487109336543

van Hover, S. D. (2008). The professional development of social studies teachers. In L. S. Levstik & C. A. Tyson (Eds.), *Handbook of research in social studies education* (pp. 352–372). Routledge.

VanSledright, B. A. (2011). *The challenge of rethinking history education: On practices, theories, and policy*. Taylor & Francis.

Vygotsky, L. S. (1978). *Mind in society: Development of higher psychological processes*. Harvard University Press.

Wideen, M. F., Mayer-Smith, J. A., & Moon, B. (1998). A critical analysis of the research on learning to teach: Making the case for an ecological perspective on inquiry. *Review of Educational Research, 68*(2), 130–178. https://doi.org/10.3102/00346543068002130

Wineburg, S. S. (2001). *Historical thinking and other unnatural acts: Charting the future of teaching the past*. Temple University Press.

Woodson, A. N. (2015). "What you supposed to know": Urban Black students' perspectives on history textbooks. *Journal of Urban Learning Teaching and Research*, *11*(1), 57–65.

Woodson, A. N. (2017). "There ain't no white people here": Master narratives of the Civil Rights Movement in the stories of urban youth. *Urban Education*, *52*(3), 316–342. https://doi.org/10.1177/0042085915602543

Woodson, A. N., & Duncan, K. E. (2018). When keeping it real goes wrong: Race talk, racial blunders, and redemption. In C. C. Martell (Ed.), *Social studies teacher education: Critical issues and current perspectives* (pp. 101–112). Information Age Publishing.

## CHAPTER 13

# Knowing Is Not Enough, Action Is Required

## Toward Racial Literacy and Activism in Teacher Development

*Tiffany Mitchell Patterson*

We have no intention of stopping this fight until we have eradicated every single remnant of racism in this country.

—Angela Davis

## INTRODUCTION

In 2020, the brutal murders of Ahmaud Arbery, Breonna Taylor, Tony McDade, and George Floyd, among countless Black deaths, many of whom never garnered national attention, sparked a global uprising against police brutality and racism. This recent groundswell of activism is rooted in a long historical struggle for racial justice (Alexander, 2020; Blain & Zoellner, 2020) in this country. Kendi (2016) defines racism as "a marriage of racist policies and racist ideas that produces and normalizes racial inequities" (p. 18). Blatant visual acts of racism often serve as a catalyst for public reckoning and a reminder of the normalization of racism. The 2020 rebellion exposed longstanding racial inequities that permeate every sector of American society (Bell, 1992; Bonilla-Silva, 2013; Kendi, 2016; Yosso, 2005). Angela Davis reminds us that we must resist notions that racism cannot be overcome and continually work to dismantle it in every institution, brick by brick.

Racism in education is not an anomaly; it's the norm. From a critical race theory (CRT) perspective, education is largely rooted in narratives that are white, middle-class, male, cisgender, and heterosexual (Dixson & Rousseau Anderson, 2018; Ladson-Billings & Tate, 1995; Stovall, 2009; Tate, 1997). Racism in education is also evidenced in the school-to prison-pipeline, discipline policies, and overpolicing that disproportionately suspend students of color, and whitewashed dominant narratives curriculum. Acknowledging racism in education is an important first step, but hardly enough—concrete actions are required, too. Educators are "ethically bound to know better, see better and do better for the sake of children's learning" (Stevenson, 2014, p. 185). If we are truly invested in the learning of *all* students, racist educational structures, policies, and practices must be confronted and dismantled.

Reading, understanding, and disrupting racism in education is difficult, complex, and personal. Brown (2011) asserts that there is a fundamental lack of sociocultural knowledge about the norms of race and racism in society: "It's often those structural elements that aren't taken into consideration when there is a discussion about ending or challenging racism" (Davis, 2016, p. 34). In schools, the analyses of race and racism are often hindered for a myriad of reasons, including fear, discomfort, unwillingness, performative empathy, and downright apathy. Educational institutions often adopt a "color-blind" approach to avoid discussing race (King et al., 2018), thereby absolving them of the racism that occurs in that space. No longer can educational institutions intentionally and/or performatively avoid confronting racism.

Rooted in CRT, Guinier (2004) positions racial literacy as a way to contextualize, understand, and counter American racism through an interactive process that situates "race as a tool of diagnosis, feedback and assessment" (p. 115) and interrogates the relationship between "race, power, gender, class, geography and other explanatory variables" (p. 115). Racial literacy is an ongoing journey rooted in individual reflection and an examination of historical, contemporary, and institutionalized factors that uphold racism. Guinier (2004) reminds us that "racial literacy is about learning rather than knowing" (p. 115). Racial literacy means understanding the complexities and impact of institutional racism in education on school communities, classrooms, and students' lives.

Embedded in racial literacy is a call to action. Sealey-Ruiz (2011) contends that racial literacy asks teachers to take action against injustice in their school settings once they recognize it. Racial justice is the embodiment of racial literacy. Racial justice calls for the systematic fair treatment of people of all races and includes the "proactive reinforcement of policies, practices, attitudes and actions that produce equitable power, access, opportunities, treatment, impacts and outcomes for all" (Race Reporting Guide, 2015). Activism is central in the struggle for racial justice. Teacher activism requires that teachers have a political analysis of oppression (Picower, 2012a) and the will to fight against it. Ideally, as educators become racially literate, they are compelled to act. Racial justice activism is arduous. Activist and co-founder of Black Lives Matter Toronto Janaya Khan reminds us, "activism is not glamorous work: it's heart work" (Khan, 2017). Racially literate analysis resists quick fixes or discussions that only focus on solutions. Instead, racial literacy privileges informed action rooted in continuous learning and reflection (Smith & Crowley, 2018). Racial literacy teacher development could serve as an avenue to support and sustain educators in racial justice work.

This chapter does not presume to offer a magical formula, but, rather, puts forth a stance that the alignment of racial literacy and informed action can move more teachers toward racial justice in education. Building on the scholarship of CRT, racial literacy, and teacher activism, this chapter explores the challenges and opportunities of supporting activism through racial literacy teacher development. This chapter has two objectives: offer suggestions to support activism in teacher preparation programs, and advocate for continued learning opportunities for inservice teachers to sustain activism. By focusing on practical strategies, this chapter seeks to offer an entry point in an effort to build capacity and solidarity across the teaching–learning continuum, thereby increasing the likelihood of transformative change for both preservice and inservice teachers.

## RACIAL LITERACY AND ACTIVISM IN TEACHER PREPARATION PROGRAMS

Through racial literacy, preservice teachers can develop the ability to understand what race is, why racism exists, and how it is used to oppress and reproduce inequities in a historical and contemporary context (Brown, 2017; Horsford, 2011, p. 95). Students of color (25%) in teacher preparation programs are significantly underrepresented (U.S. Department of Education, 2016) as public school student populations are increasingly diverse. Similar to the current teaching force, students enrolled in teacher preparation programs are predominantly white. The "demographic divide" (Gay & Howard, 2000) across race, cultural, linguistic, and socioeconomic contexts between teachers (predominantly white and middle-class) and K–12 students (increasingly from racial/ethnic groups of color and low-income) continues to widen in both schools and teacher preparation programs. Teachers from different racial and cultural backgrounds than their students "often take cues from society on how to treat them" (Sealey-Ruiz, 2011).

Schools are more racially segregated today than over 60 years ago, with white students being the most racially isolated in public schools (National Center for Education Statistics, 2019). For many white students and parents, the racial demographics and the cultural, historical, and institutional factors that sustain them do not present a problem (Winans, 2010). This may lead some white preservice teachers to feel there is no need to teach or discuss race or racism, as if it doesn't apply in their teaching context. It is necessary to prepare white preservice teachers to teach students of color to prevent bias (Bazemore-Bertrand & Porcher, 2020). This is critically beneficial for all students. Developing racial literacy is imperative no matter the context, as "teacher candidates need to see that race and racism are relevant and real even if they are White" (Flynn et al., 2018). For teachers of color, there may be more of an inclination to have race-related discussions or be racially literate primarily due to their lived experiences of racism and discrimination. To be clear, though, even some teachers of color are uncomfortable discussing race (Howard, 2017). That discomfort may stem from a different place, resistance they might experience, and for a myriad of other reasons.

Across educational contexts and demographics, racial literacy becomes an urgent necessity in teacher preparation programs. Much like K–12 schools, racial literacy has struggled to make its way consistently and concretely into teacher preparation programs. Winans (2010) calls our attention to the struggle students will have when learning about race and racism, as they will have to "grapple with growing awareness of racial inequalities and their relationship to them" (p. 478). White preservice teachers must read and engage work that explores how racism feels, and understand their whiteness and that their momentary discomfort about discussing race are never synonymous with the lived experiences of a person of color (Matias & Liou, 2014). Given the demographics of teacher preparation programs, preservice teachers of color could also be dealing with racial battle fatigue (Smith et al., 2006) and the emotional toll of coping with racism on campus and in programs where they might be underrepresented. It can be challenging for a teacher educator to navigate the varied emotions that arise during discussions of race and racism. A teacher education program that fosters racial literacy must provide spaces for teachers to talk about their fears and uncertainties (Sealey-Ruiz, 2011).

Teacher education programs need to be restructured (with support from accreditation agencies) to ensure that teachers in teacher education programs are required to deeply study race beyond cursory discussions (Milner & Laughter, 2015). Many teacher education programs confine diversity preparation to a course, workshop, or module that students are mandated to complete for certification requirements (Bennett, 2013). For teacher preparation programs, racial literacy must extend beyond one multicultural education course to other education and content methods courses to allow for continual learning opportunities and deeper examination of race and racism in education. For racial literacy development to be central in teacher education programs, teacher educators must be racially literate. A primary component to developing students' racial literacy articulated in the research was their teachers' ability to understand and discuss racism (Kohli et al., 2017). The lack of racially literate faculty or those resistant to discussing race could lead to fewer opportunities to engage in this within a teacher preparation program. As most universities and colleges have "diversity" or "social justice" in their mission statement, faculty could advocate that an investment must be made to develop racial literacy competencies for faculty, hire more faculty of color or racially literate faculty, increase grants for conferences, or coordinate learning opportunities with faculty in other colleges that specialize in race and the teaching of racism.

Despite the challenges, in order to approach race and its effects on schooling, "we must acquire a strong racial literacy" (Brown, 2017, p. 86). Critical readings, media, discussions, assignments, and research could be utilized to cultivate racial literacy. Making curricular choices to teach and discuss race and racism in the classroom to enrich a mandated curriculum is a skill set and activism. Teacher preparation programs can model and engage preservice teachers in the hands-on practice of integrating social issues with the mandated curriculum (Katsarou et al., 2010). Further, race-focused action research and informed action projects could allow preservice teachers to immerse themselves in the action of racial literacy. Preservice teachers can reflect on their practices and research racial inequities or racial justice initiatives at their clinical placements. The goal of this work is to equip preservice teachers with the tools to observe, reflect, and engage in racial justice in schools. With this support in a teacher preparation program, preservice teachers could develop the skills to read racism but also do something about it.

Imagine if a generation of educators going into the profession acquired the knowledge of race as a social construct with the understanding that racism is operationalized in real systemic and intersectional ways in society. This knowledge could inspire preservice teachers toward activism by realizing that they can challenge and address racism within and outside of their classroom. With one or two courses with students, teacher preparation programs are often just scratching the surface. Though not an exhaustive list, here are a few ideas to use racial literacy in teacher preparation programs to inspire activism:

- Teach race and racism explicitly in preservice coursework and in more than one course to develop racial literacy.
- Employ critical readings, media, and assignments that center people of color and examine whiteness should be integral components of teacher preparation coursework.
- Provide opportunities for preservice teachers to practice and apply racial literacy principles in lesson plans and design curricular experiences on race and racism that enrich the academic curriculum.
- Recognize that students may vary in their knowledge of race and racism. Do not make assumptions. Support and development of racial literacy should be varied.
- Hire more faculty of color and racially literate faculty to engage preservice teachers in a deeper analysis of racial literacy.
- Create space and long-term assignments for preservice teachers to develop skills of activism centered on racism in schools during the program through action research or informed action projects.

## RACIAL LITERACY AND ACTIVISM IN PROFESSIONAL TEACHER DEVELOPMENT

Much of the literature on racial literacy teacher development focuses on teacher preparation programs. It is a natural space for teacher candidates to interrogate themselves by grappling with the complexities of race and racism through critical reflection, readings, activities, and discussions. In these spaces, courses that incorporate racial literacy competencies are most likely communal, inclusive, and blanketed in trust. In the profession, that cushion must be sought out, as conversations about race often exist in silos with educators who feel competent and compelled to engage in race dialogue with students. This work should not stop after teacher preparation programs, as race and racism is not static (King, 2016). Educators should have access to ongoing professional learning opportunities. In the life span of a child in K–12 schools, opportunities to discuss and analyze race might be few and far between. Given the context of schools, cultivating organizational capacity to talk about race with precision and specificity is a critical skill for leaders who are committed to improving the educational experience and outcomes of all students, particularly children and youth of color (Irby & Clark, 2018).

Developing racial literacy is a continual learning process about the ways "race, in conjunction with class and geography invariably shapes educational, economic and political opportunities for all of us" (Guinier, 2004, p. 117). Professional development could serve as a continual learning space for inservice teachers. Through professional development activities that engage educators in a critical examination of their beliefs and identities with the goal of increasing self-understanding, they are encouraged not only to be aware of their assumptions and potential biases but also to make explicit their visions, goals, and practical theories that guide their actions and interactions with all students (Cooper et al., 2011). One size does not fit all. Just as we seek the most successful ways to differentiate instruction for K–12 learners, teachers come to us with unique and specific needs (Wiseman & Fox, 2010). Teachers are at various stages of racial literacy, so there should be ongoing tiered learning opportunities to support their development. There is a need for collaborative professional development in schools where teachers seek to develop a unified discourse and shared practices of racial literacy instruction (Skerrett, 2011). If the capacity for advanced training on racial literacy does not exist within a school system, then financial support should be provided for teachers to purchase books, attend conferences, continue education, or utilize university partnerships to develop varied professional development sessions focused on racial literacy.

Many school districts have adopted a professional learning community (PLC) model that fosters ongoing collaboration with educators, usually inquiry-based and data-driven, with the goal of improving student outcomes. Nelson et al. (2010) argue that learning potential emerges as collaborative teams shift from sharing opinions to engaging in deep consequential conversations. These conversations are marked by transparency and a willingness to explore critical questions that examine teacher practice. What if critical questions included a racialized examination of teacher practices? What might be the impact on student outcomes? Challenging existing school structures of support such as PLCs builds capacity. It is essential to recognize the vital role of professional learning communities in providing teachers with opportunities for collaborative inquiry into, and learning about, more effective, context-specific practice (Skerrett, 2011). There should be more capacity for professional learning opportunities that explicitly address race, racism, and teacher practices. By doing so, solidarity can be cultivated. Engaging in social change within a school requires solidarity with like-minded educators and like-minded communities of support to sustain and deepen their efforts (Katsarou et al., 2010). In order to act and improve practice, teachers need support to engage in critical reflection in the profession. Beyond the classroom, teachers are organizing for social justice and finding solidarity in teacher activist groups. While it might be easier to find such groups in larger metropolitan cities, teacher activism is prevalent virtually everywhere. In the era of social media, one can connect easily with like-minded educators, joining and starting groups with the specific focus of racial justice in education. No one can sustain this fight alone; teachers must seek solidarity and support to avoid burnout.

From standardized curriculum to high-stakes testing, many schools have virtually every minute dedicated to a particular mandated program, particularly in low-income communities of color (Katsarou et al., 2010). Building capacity for thorough continual learning experiences is essential for growth in teacher practice on race and racism. This work cannot be sustained alone; therefore, professional development and learning communities can support continued development of racial literacy. Below are a few ideas for school leadership and educators:

- Increase access to ongoing and tiered professional development on race and racism in education.
- Bolster financial investments for curricular and pedagogical resources, books, and conference travel for educators to continually develop their understanding of racial literacy and pedagogy.
- Provide opportunities for professional learning communities to have dedicated time to focus explicitly on racial literacy and anti-racist teacher practices.
- Build capacity for racial literacy development by strengthening university and community partnerships to support this work in schools.
- Seek and build solidarity with like-minded educators within your school/district and through teacher activist groups in your area (e.g., New York Collective of Radical Educators, Teachers for Social Justice [Chicago], D.C. Area Educators for Social Justice, or Association of Radical Teachers in LA). Utilize social media to find groups and organizations in your area. If one doesn't exist, consider starting one. National organizations such as Rethinking Schools, Education for Liberation Network, Teaching for Change, and Learning for Justice also provide a wealth of support and resources.

## TOWARD RACIAL JUSTICE IN TEACHER DEVELOPMENT

Racial literacy and teacher activism are not mutually exclusive in the fight for racial justice in schools. Supporting racial literacy in teacher development provides a foundation for racial justice activism in schools. Racial literacy involves the ability to "read, recast, and resolve" racially stressful situations (Stevenson, 2014). Teachers need to learn how to see a racial moment, do something about it, and leave with a greater understanding of its complexity (King et al., 2018). In doing something, "activists develop commitment and deepen their motivations over time, in part through their experiences taking action against racism" (Warren, 2010, p. 213). Racial literacy development and activism are an evolving nonlinear process. Picower (2012b) outlines three key stages for fully realized teacher activists: (1) teachers must recognize inequality, fill gaps in historical knowledge, and develop empathy; and (2) as emerging social justice educators, engage in this work in their classrooms; then (3) join the fight to address oppressive institutional forces that impact schools. By centering race as a subject of academic pursuit, racial literacy provides a useful heuristic for guiding one's thinking about how racial moments fit within larger historical, economic, and sociopolitical movements (Smith, 2014). This journey will include mistakes, starts, and stops, but the more we can shift to a culture of racial literacy and activism in schools, the closer we are to achieving racial justice and anti-racism.

As a pedagogical framework, racial literacy gives teachers and students the means to engage in deeper racial understanding and problem solving (Smith, 2014). To truly teach in solidarity with schools and communities requires teachers to have both specific mindsets and skill sets (Katsarou et al., 2010) that can be cultivated in teacher preparation programs and sustained through continued learning opportunities. This pedagogical shift transforms the classroom to one that centers the voices and experiences of people of color and others that have been marginalized in the curriculum, and engages in race literacy work with students. When considering forms of oppression, such as racism, substituting readings about school segregation may be a successful critical social justice education teaching strategy, but it will not impact institutional racism (Picower, 2012a).

Teachers need meaningful professional learning opportunities to build upon their classroom experiences and increase their knowledge and skills, with the goal of increasing their capacity for advocacy, change agency, and efficacy concerning their work with diverse student populations (Wiseman & Fox, 2010). We must create opportunities and support networks now. Teachers should also work to engage in activism beyond the classroom. Examples of this activism include advocating for school policy and curriculum change reform, advocating for resources to support racial justice work, and engaging in collective social movements with the purpose of dismantling institutional racism. Supporting racial literacy and activism in teacher development can be fraught with challenges, but through capacity-building and solidarity, institutional changes can be made.

As Brown (2017) passionately states, the time has come when we can no longer wait until the "just right" time to address race and racism. As we transform teacher preparation programs, so must we also consider how to support continued learning for teachers in the classroom. Racial literacy includes understanding race and racism and ongoing activism. In what Love (2020) refers to as abolitionist teaching:

> Abolitionist teaching is not a teaching approach: It is a way of life, a way of seeing the world, and a way of taking action against injustice. It seeks to resist, agitate, tear down the educational survival complex through teachers who work in solidarity with their schools' community to achieve incremental changes in their classrooms and schools for students in the present day, while simultaneously freedom dreaming and vigorously creating a vision for what students will be when the educational survival complex is destroyed. (p. 89)

The ongoing global pandemic and systemic racism has provided a unique opportunity to engage in the reimagining and visioning work Love describes in education. To achieve this racial justice in education, we must advance racial literacy and activism in teacher development across the continuum of learning from teacher preparation to professional development. We must equip and sustain teachers with tools in the ongoing fight to eradicate systemic racism in all its forms. In the words of Audre Lorde (1984), "revolution is not a one-time event, it is becoming always vigilant for the smallest opportunity to make a genuine change in established, outgrown responses" (p. 134). The fight for racial justice in education needs more racially literate teacher activists. Knowing about racism is a start, but not enough—action is required.

## REFERENCES

Alexander, M. (2020, June 8). America, this is your chance. *The New York Times*. https://www.nytimes.com/2020/06/08/opinion/george-floyd-protests-race.html

Bazemore-Bertrand, S., & Porcher, K. (2020). Teacher preparation programs to prepare White preservice teachers. *Journal of Culture and Values in Education, 3*(1), 72–88. https://doi.org/10.46303/jcve.03.01.5

Bell, D. (1992). *Faces at the bottom of the well: The permanence of racism*. Basic Books.

Bennett, S. V. (2013). Effective facets of a field experience that contributed to eight preservice teachers' developing understandings about culturally responsive teaching. *Urban Education, 48*(3), 380–419. https://doi.org/10.1177/0042085912452155

Blain, K., & Zoellner, T. (2020, June 10). "Riots", "mobs", "chaos": The establishment always frames change as dangerous. *The Guardian*. http://www.theguardian.com/commentisfree/2020/jun/10/protest-black-lives-matter-police-activism

Bonilla-Silva, E. (2013). *Racism without racists: Color-blind racism and the persistence of racial inequality in America* (4th ed.). Rowman & Littlefield.

Brown, K. D. (2011). Breaking the cycle of Sisyphus: Social education and the acquisition of critical sociocultural knowledge about race and racism in the United States. *The Social Studies, 102*(6), 249–255. https://doi.org/10.1080/00377996.2011.563726

Brown, K. D. (2017). Why we can't wait: Advancing racial literacy and a critical sociocultural knowledge of race for teaching and curriculum. *Race, Gender & Class, 24*(1/2), 81–96.

Cooper, J., He, Y., & Levin, B. (2011). *Developing critical cultural competence: A guide for 21st century educators*. Corwin.

Davis, A. Y. (2016). *Freedom is a constant struggle: Ferguson, Palestine, and the foundations of a movement*. Haymarket Books.

Dixson, A. D., & Rousseau Anderson, C. (2018). Where are we? Critical Race Theory in education 20 years later. *Peabody Journal of Education, 93*(1), 121–131. https://doi.org/10.1080/0161956X.2017.1403194

Flynn, J. E., Worden, L. J., & Rolón-Dow, R. (2018). The responsibilities of White teacher candidates and teacher educators in developing racial literacy. *Multicultural Perspectives, 20*(4), 240–246. https://doi.org/10.1080/15210960.2018.1527156

Gay, G., & Howard, T. C. (2000). Multicultural teacher education for the 21st century. *Teacher Educator, 36*(1), 1–16. http://doi.org/10.1080/08878730009555246

Guinier, L. (2004). From racial liberalism to racial literacy: *Brown v. Board of Education* and the interest-divergence dilemma. *Journal of American History, 91*(1), 92. https://doi.org/10.2307/3659616

Horsford, S. D. (2011). *Learning in a burning house: Educational inequality, ideology, and (dis) integration*. Teachers College Press.

Howard, T. C. (2017, August 18). When we talk about race, let's be honest. *Education Week*. https://www.edweek.org/ew/articles/2017/08/18/when-we-talk-about-race-lets-be.html

Irby, D. J., & P. Clark, S. (2018). Talk it (racism) out: Race talk and organizational learning. *Journal of Educational Administration, 56*(5), 504–518. https://doi.org/10.1108/JEA-01-2018-0015

Khan, J. (2017). *Janaya Khan of Black Lives Matter on building a more inclusive Pride*. https://www.flare.com/tv-movies/ janaya-khan-pride-is-evolving/

Katsarou, E., Picower, B., & Stovall, D. (2010). Acts of solidarity: Developing urban social justice educators in the struggle for quality public education. *Teacher Education Quarterly, 37*(3), 137–153.

Kendi, I. X. (2016). *Stamped from the beginning: The definitive history of racist ideas in America* (Reprint edition). Nation Books.

King, L. J. (2016). Teaching Black history as a racial literacy project. *Race, Ethnicity and Education, 19*(6), 1303–1318.

King, L. J., Vickery, A. E., & Caffrey, G. (2018). A pathway to racial literacy: Using the LETS ACT framework to teach controversial topics. *Social Education, 82*(6), 316–322.

Kohli, R., Pizarro, M., & Nevárez, A. (2017). The "new racism" of K–12 schools: Centering critical research on racism. *Review of Research in Education, 41*(1), 182–202. https://doi.org/10.3102/0091732X16686949

Ladson-Billings, G., & Tate, W. (1995). Toward a critical race theory of education. *Teachers College Record, 97*(1), 47–68.

Lorde, A. (1984). *Sister outsider: Essays and speeches*. Crossing Press.

Love, B. (2020). *We want to do more than survive: Abolitionist teaching and the pursuit of educational freedom* (Reprint edition). Beacon Press.

Matias, C. E., & Liou, D. D. (2014). Tending to the heart of communities of color: Towards critical race teacher activism. *Urban Education, 50*(5), 601–625. https://doi.org/10.1177/0042085913519338

Milner, H. R., & Laughter, J. C. (2015). But good intentions are not enough: Preparing teachers to center race and poverty. *The Urban Review, 47*(2), 341–363. https://doi.org/10.1007/s11256-014- 0295-4

National Center for Education Statistics. (2019, February). *Indicator 7: Racial/ethnic concentration in public schools*. https://nces.ed.gov/programs/raceindicators/indicator_RBE.asp

Nelson, T. H., Deuel, A., Slavit, D., & Kennedy, A. (2010). Leading deep conversations in collaborative inquiry groups. *The Clearing House, 83*(5), 175–179.

Picower, B. (2012a). Teacher activism: Enacting a vision for social justice. *Equity & Excellence in Education, 45*(4), 561–574. https://doi.org/10.1080/10665684.2012.717848

Picower, B. (2012b). *Practice what you teach: Social justice education in the classroom and the streets*. Routledge.

Race Reporting Guide. (2015, June 20). *Race forward*. https://www.raceforward.org/reporting-guide

Sealey-Ruiz, Y. (2011). Dismantling the school-to-prison pipeline through racial literacy development in teacher education. *Journal of Curriculum & Pedagogy, 8*(2), 116–120. https://doi.org/10.1080/15505170.2011.624892

Skerrett, A. (2011). English teachers' racial literacy knowledge and practice. *Race Ethnicity and Education, 14*(3), 313–330. https://doi.org/10.1080/13613324.2010.543391

Smith, W. A., Yosso, T. J., & Solorzáno, D. G. (2006). Challenging racial battle fatigue on historically white campuses: A critical race examination of race-related stress. In C. A. Stanley (Ed.), *Faculty of color teaching in predominantly white colleges and universities* (pp. 299–327). Anker.

Smith, W. L. (2014). Not Stopping at First: Racial Literacy and the Teaching of Barack Obama. *Multicultural Perspectives, 16*(2), 65–71. https://doi.org/10.1080/15210960.2014.889567

Smith, W. L., & Crowley, R. M. (2018). Barack Obama, racial literacy, and lessons from "A More Perfect Union." *History Teacher, 51*(3), 445–476.

Stevenson, H. C. (2014). *Promoting racial literacy in schools: Differences that make a difference*. Teachers College Press.

Stovall, D. O. (2009). Race(ing), class(ing) and gender(ing) our work: Critical race theory, critical race feminism, epistemology and new directions in education policy research. In D. N. Plank, B. Schneider, & G. Sykes (Eds.), *Handbook on education policy research* (pp. 333–347). American Educational Research Association.

Tate, W. F. (1997). Critical race theory and education: History, theory, and implications. *Review of Research in Education, 22*, 195–247. http://doi.org/10.2307/1167376

U.S. Department of Education. (2016, July). *The state of racial diversity in the educator workforce*. https://www2.ed.gov/rschstat/eval/highered/racial-diversity/state-racial-diversity- workforce.pdf

Warren, M. R. (2010). *Fire in the heart: How white activists embrace racial justice*. Oxford University Press.

Winans, A. E. (2010). Cultivating racial literacy in white, segregated settings: Emotions as site of ethical engagement and inquiry. *Curriculum Inquiry*, *40*(3), 475–491. https://doi.org/10.1111/j.1467-873X.2010.00494.x

Wiseman, A., & Fox, R. K. (2010). Supporting teachers' development of cultural competence through teacher research. *Action in Teacher Education*, *32*(4), 26–37. https://doi.org/10.1080/01626620.2010.549708

Yosso, T. (2005). Whose culture has capital? A critical race theory discussion of community cultural wealth. *Race Ethnicity and Education*, *8*(1), 69–91. http://doi.org/10.1080/1361332052000341006

# I Stay Mad

## A Black Woman Social Studies Educator's Fight to Be Seen, Heard, and Heeded

*ArCasia D. James-Gallaway*

### INTRODUCTION

This chapter explores how my racial literacy, which shapes my praxis as a social studies (teacher) educator, has contributed to the enduring rage I feel and the resistance I have faced in working to enact an anti-oppression pedagogy. My purpose is to examine through a racial literacy framework, which is premised on the tenets of seeing, hearing, and heeding underserved Black children and communities, two circumstances of racial trauma as they pertain to my development as a social studies (teacher) educator. To do so, I draw from scholarly conceptualizations of Black women's anger (Austin, 1989; Lorde, 1981) and their models of critical self-reflection (Angelou, 1971; Davis, 1974; hooks, 1996; Lorde, 1982). In essence, this analysis represents a critical race theory counterstory (Cook & Dixson, 2013; Delgado, 1989) that rejects the presumption that Black women's anger is unjustified and that social studies' "innate" alignment with social justice principles invites little resistance.

### CONCEPTUAL INFLUENCES

Racial literacy's origins lie in critical race theory (CRT), which began in the 1970s as "a movement of left scholars, most of them scholars of color, situated in law schools, whose work challenges the ways in which race and racial power are constructed and represented in American legal culture and, more generally, in American society as a whole" (Crenshaw et al., 1995, p. xiii). By the mid-1990s, education scholars had introduced CRT to the field to enhance theorizations of race (Ladson-Billings & Tate, 1995). In recent years, this body of work has grown, and it focuses on clarifying how and why educational institutions perpetuate racial inequity.

Within this tradition, racial literacy helps to situate racism as a structural phenomenon that manifests social and racial inequity in systems and institutions such as education broadly and social studies specifically, also serving to advance discussions about redress. On this point, critical race theorist Lani Guinier (2004) submitted that "properly deployed, racial literacy . . . [represents] the ability to read race in conjunction with institutional and democratic structures" (p. 120), which seek to maintain and reinforce the status quo of white[1] supremacy and anti-Blackness. Guinier and her colleague Torres (2002) conceptualized racial literacy as apt for "identify[ing] patterns of injustice that link race to class, to gender, and to other forms of power" (p. 29). Such a focus on the salience of interlocking systems of oppression aligns this perspective with Black feminist theory (e.g., Combahee River Collective, 1979) and CRT's metaphor of intersectionality (Crenshaw, 1989). Moreover, "racial literacy teaches us that racism is not simply a function of individual psychology, prejudice, or bigotry. Indeed, well-meaning individuals can acquiesce in societal racism and most do" (Guinier & Torres, 2002, p. 370).

In working to operationalize racial literacy, I am developing a framework that may help one identify and assess it in practice, particularly within in-person interactions. This working model consists of three sequential propositions: seeing, hearing, and heeding. Seeing refers to the act of acknowledging the full humanity of another in terms of their racial heritage, contextualizing that history in concert with other categories of social difference such as gender, religion, class status, sexuality, or citizenship status. Hearing follows seeing, and it characterizes the result of recognizing one's full humanity and, thus, listening to and fully comprehending one's needs for and deservingness of racial and social justice. This principle may involve the literal act of listening, but it is not limited to such exclusively, as people who cannot hear (or see) are well able to engage this framework should they so choose. Last is heeding, which entails using one's (the seer's and hearer's) voice, power, and/or resources to advocate on behalf of those systematically underserved or to redistribute said resources to groups in need of them. Heeding means humanizing, for example, Black families who reject negative framing of their school involvement and articulate reasons for their so-called "low engagement"; then listening intently to and believing this marginalized group; and finally, implementing their feedback to amend practices and procedures, perhaps in collaboration with these families, to rectify ongoing issues. Ultimately, when enacted in concert, seeing, hearing, and heeding lead one to (re)conceptualize as inaccurate prevailing, denigrating ideologies that uphold white supremacy and subjugate underserved communities of color.

Alongside racial literacy, Black feminist and critical race theorizations about Black women's rage underpin this essay. These ideas offer clear and generative frames from which I can attempt to explain my sustained indignation regarding my relationship with social studies vis-á-vis white supremacy and anti-Blackness. Black feminists have helped establish that the stereotypical construction of the angry Black woman is reductive and denies our humanity because it works to preclude us from the full range and complexity of human emotions (Collins, 1990; Griffin, 2012). They have identified that we face persecution for expressing a common human sentiment, one that might be even more reasonable for us given the regularity with which we must confront society's misogynoir—its contempt for Black women (Bailey & Trudy, 2018). To communicate Black women's full humanity, many have penned personal, reflective, or autobiographical accounts of their lives that illustrate how they navigated a world that despises them (e.g., Angelou, 1971; Davis, 1974; hooks, 1996; Lorde, 1982). Using the written word to explore and document their agency and personhood in this way has served to fortify others like myself who come after them searching for legitimation and direction.

In 1981, Black feminist scholar Audre Lorde addressed the National Women's Studies Association as their keynote speaker, admonishing the white supremacy that had long stained the (white) feminist movement; she confessed "My response to racism is anger" (p. 7), and went on to validate this emotion, underlining that "anger is an appropriate reaction to racist attitudes" (p. 9). Legal scholar Regina Austin (1989) identified one potential source of this anger, highlighting society's limited capacity to recognize the simultaneity of oppression that distinguishes Black women and their lived experiences from that of other groups, who may not hold multiple subordinated identities; then Austin asked a series of questions, followed by clarifying comments, that exposed a manipulative technique intended to encourage feelings of psychological instability (i.e., gaslighting).

> When was the last time someone told you that your way of approaching problems, be they legal or institutional, was all wrong? You are too angry, too emotional, too subjective, too pessimistic, too political, too anecdotal, and too instinctual. I never know how to respond to such accusations. How can I "legitimate" my way of thinking? I know that I am not just flying off the handle, seeing imaginary insults and problems where there are none. (1989, p. 540)

These remarks speak to my experiences as a Black woman social studies preservice teacher and as a teacher educator in my quest to strengthen my racial literacy and Black feminist pedagogy (Henry, 2005; James-Gallaway & Turner, 2020; Joseph, 1995). Anger has consistently punctuated these experiences, and Lorde (1981) described how this outrage "has meant pain to me but it has also meant survival" (p. 9). This survival, Austin (1989) stressed, remains necessary despite much of society constantly wondering how a "tough, domineering, emasculating, strident, and shrill" Black woman "can possibly stand herself. All she does is complain. Why doesn't that woman shut up?" (pp. 539–540). This wish for Black women to stop "finding" issues to critique and to keep quiet represents society's unwillingness to confront its maleficence in forcing us to grow up within a symphony of anguish at being silenced, at being unchosen, at knowing that when we survive, it is in spite of a whole world out there that takes for granted our lack of humanness, that hates our very existence, outside of its service. (Lorde, 1981, p. 9)

Such misogynoir represents a regularity throughout U.S. history (Berry & Gross, 2020), one that angry Black women might face while acknowledging that their "anger is a source of empowerment" (Lorde, 1981, p. 9). Heeding Lorde's advice compels one to lean into this anger and consider that

the time has come for [Black women] to . . . declare that we are serious about ourselves, and to capture some of the intellectual power and resources that are necessary to combat the systematic denigration of minority women [or women of color]. It is time for [us] to testify on [our] own behalf, *in writing*. (Austin, 1989, p. 542, emphasis in original)

As frustrating as Black women's treatment has been and continues to be, Lorde (1981) reminded us that "if we accept our powerlessness, then of course any anger can destroy us" (p. 9); therefore, we must remember that "anger expressed and translated into action in the service of our vision and our future is a liberating and strengthening act of clarification" (p. 8).

Consequently, I draw on Austin's (1989) revelation that in testifying about my complicated relationship to social studies, I might contribute to the "document[ation of] the material [educational] ex[periences] of minority women" (p. 542). In doing so, I seek to articulate Black women's "concrete problems and needs, many of which are invisible even to minority [educators] because of gender and class differences" (p. 542). This act is essential, as Black women "have paid our dues, done more than our share of the doing and the dying, and are entitled to prosper with everyone else" (Austin, 1989, p. 543). In seeking such prosperity, next, I turn to defining moments in my social studies experiences, illustrating the influence of racial literacy on my anger as it relates to white supremacy and anti-Blackness.

## FIGHTING TO BE SEEN, HEARD, AND HEEDED

I am a social studies educator because I am mad, and I have been mad for a long while. My anger is rooted in my regular experiences with white supremacist ideologies that impede one's view of (1) me as fully human and (2) my history, Black history, as integral to American history and worthy of dedicated study. This lack of sight, as I understand it, is representative of Black people, experiences, and histories broadly, particularly those of Black women, because society does not typically afford us the luxury of individuality (Quashie, 2018). Thus, I know that this general unwillingness to fully see me and the legacies of struggle I represent are reflective of the commonality of this practice across many, if not most, interactions with other Black people or content centered on Black experiences or histories.

Like many, I came to social studies due to the distorted and anti-Black nature of my K–12 social studies education. Before beginning my undergraduate studies, I had been fortunate enough to take Advanced Placement courses and my prerequisite history, government, and political science classes at my local community college. Despite this early, "high-level" exposure, I still found myself astonished by the African American history education I received as a first-year university student. My experiences in this regard track closely with those of Audre Lorde (1982), contemplating how she had not learned of Crispus Attucks during her

> four years at Hunter High School, supposedly the best public high school in New York City . . . I had been taught by some of the most highly considered historians in the country. Yet, I never once heard the name mentioned of the first man to fall in the american revolution, nor ever been told that he was a Negro. What did that mean about the history I had learned? (p. 133)

Analogous to Lorde, my unpleasant surprise can be understood as a sense of betrayal at my K–12 social studies education that has since motivated me to work so that other Black students are not amazed by such information like I was (James-Gallaway & Turner, 2020). Working to employ racial literacy in tandem with Black feminist pedagogy, I strive to emphasize in my praxis, for instance, Black people's notable accomplishments in the past—achievements like building and ruling kingdoms such as Mali, Songhai, and Ghana; rebelling against enslavement like Toussaint Louverture and Nat Turner; leading raids as spies for the Union Army like Harriet Tubman; or constructing their own schools and teaching themselves to read and write like former bondspeople. My amazement-turned-betrayal quickly lit a fire under me to do what I could to ensure that other Black students were not denied a veracious, well-rounded social studies education.

## Preservice Teacher Education Program

Looking back, I can confidently say that my teacher education program was a source of racial trauma for me, especially because I was the only Black student—and thus, the only Black woman—in my secondary social studies cohort. This kind of racial isolation was not new to me, however, because I was early-on labeled "gifted and talented." This designation meant that I enrolled in advanced classes, which were predominated by the few white students who had not yet left for local private or suburban schools, and their families tended to wield great power over our public school district's urban, low-income, predominantly Black and Brown schools. However, by my senior year of undergraduate studies, I had started my journey toward critical consciousness, which had spurred my development of racial literacy. These new understandings helped incite some of my initial encounters with an anger that has yet to cease.

Throughout my teacher education program, I had been repeatedly terrorized by a certain group of white students in my cohort. On separate occasions, these individuals perpetuated race-evasive ideologies by dismissing illustrations of racism's prevalence in school and society. Their disavowals infuriated me, especially because I knew they were student-teaching in schools with scores of Black and Brown students. My journey into critical consciousness had only made their ignorance more evident and dangerous.

During my final semester of college, my cohort and I were student-teaching full time. We were, however, expected to attend weekly class on campus. One of these meetings occurred following our spring break in March 2012 shortly after George Zimmerman murdered Trayvon Martin, a Black 17-year-old who was walking home unarmed in Florida. I arrived at class distressed, given that another champion of anti-Blackness had claimed another Black child's life. Per usual, class discussion that day centered on race and racism. Engaging Beverly Tatum's (1997) metaphor about moving walkways, or conveyor belts, and racism, our professor asked us to provide examples of racism that might align with this metaphor. Given racism's regularity in everyday American life (Bell, 1992a, 1992b; Crenshaw et al., 1995; Ladson-Billings & Tate, 1995), I shared how what I perceived as an entitled white man had just earlier that day stepped in front of my friend, also a Black woman, and me in line as we waited to seek help in an airport. The airline professional who assisted him replicated his blatant disregard for our presence, as this individual, who had made eye contact with us as we waited in line, hurried to assist the white man in a suit while we continued to wait for help despite any indication that his needs demanded greater assistance than ours. I explained how this seemingly trivial act symbolized ongoing cycles of systemic racial oppression whereby Black people are continuously overlooked—unseen and, therefore, unheard—while white persons forge ahead. I noted how this situation literally relegated my needs, making me feel as if they mattered far less than those of white people.

Explaining this circumstance to class, I was met with swift, hostile pushback from an especially vocal white woman classmate. She adamantly refuted my experiences, estimating that despite my alleged confusion, my friend and I had *actually* been relegated not because of gendered racism, but because of either our age or our gender. Refusing to accept racism's permanence and impact on my life, my peer—a fellow social studies preservice teacher—willfully delegitimized my lived experience of racism.

I remember feeling my heart begin to race and my entire body temperature rise quickly, heating especially my abdomen and chest. I recall having to talk myself out of responding with a petty quip, one that would render her remarks equally as dehumanizing as hers had sought to make mine. But I declined. Instead, I let this burning anger slowly dissipate. I told myself that if she was unable to understand racism's brutality in the midst of national attention on Trayvon's untimely and undue murder, then there was nothing more I could say that might convince her otherwise. I understood that her actions were especially revealing and perilous, particularly in a social studies context, where identity and histories of racial oppression (should) feature integrally. I felt she had shown herself to be an avowed racist, so, as Maya Angelou urged (OWN, 2014), I chose to believe her.

Looking back, I understand this situation as shaped significantly by my unrelenting commitment to my community and inextricably linked to my racial literacy. This understanding helped me see that I, and therefore Black people broadly, were not being seen, heard, or heeded by most of my white social studies peers, particularly the white woman who vehemently repudiated my lived experience of racism. Because she refused to view me as a racialized person (not to mention as a person who experiences gendered racism), she renounced my racial reality, and thus that of her students, as well, something markedly pernicious for her students of color. Given that she could not see me, she could not hear as real or true my personal accounts with racism. These failings culminated in her inability to heed my testimony—and therefore, the testimonies and experiences of her students and colleagues of color. Racial literacy taught me to view her acts as indicative of issues in social studies and teacher education more generally. It is with these understandings of white supremacist, anti-Black ideologies that I started a subsequent chapter of my social studies professional career.

### Teaching Social Studies Methods

During graduate school, I served as the instructor of record for a social studies methods course. Returning to such a space some years later helped me realize that I had unresolved trauma with regard to teacher education broadly and social studies teacher education specifically—likely given its documented promotion of whiteness (Sleeter, 2017). In this class, there were 24 total students. Three of them were Korean American, and all the others were white; two students identified as male and all others as female. Based on their responses to questions at the beginning of the term about their socioeconomic status, upwards of 90% identified as having come from a middle-class or higher background. As with all courses I teach, my central pedagogical objective, informed expressly by racial literacy and Black feminist pedagogy (Griffin & James, 2018; James-Gallaway & Turner, 2020), emphasized social and racial justice as it pertained to social studies. Because I knew an educator's integration of equity perspectives stood likely to determine the extent to which their students of color felt seen, heard, and humanized under their care, I stressed to my students that this outlook was to extend to their site placements as well.

For me, this course was deeply difficult to teach, as most of the students' regular verbal commitments to anti-Black ideologies marked each class meeting and each assignment they submitted. These acts signified trauma for me in that before teaching each class, I constantly felt as if I needed to brace myself for impact and load my arsenal with ample defenses against the "polite" expressions of racism that I found to be characteristic of the Midwest, especially in comparison to my experiences on the East Coast or in the South. Unlike my encounters in other regions, common were student displays of race-evasive perspectives that ignored the reality and significance of race and, thus, racism. Often to no avail, I would respond with contemporary cases that challenged these presumptions, such as the overrepresentation of Black children in special education programs and juvenile detention facilities.

One instance revealed how appealing and rational anti-Blackness, an ideology shown not to be exclusive to white people, seemed to this cohort. A Korean American student's public comment rationalized her aunt, a business owner, closely following around her store all patrons who visited. With some probing, my student disclosed that her aunt's shop was located in a Black neighborhood and that virtually all of her customers were Black. The circumstance my student described and her complicity regarding it angered me, but I worked to manage my increased body temperature and elevated heart rate. After collecting myself and my thoughts, I highlighted the case of Latasha Harlins (Stevenson, 2013), an innocent Black girl whom a Korean American store owner shot in 1991 in Los Angeles. I pointed out that like my student's aunt, Soon Da Ju had assumed Black patrons to be thieves, and the end result for 15-year-old Latasha Harlins was her premature and undue death. Nonetheless, I saw no evidence that these challenges to their worldviews helped to shift their perspectives or teaching praxis.

Another case illustrates a similar point. Reviewing my student evaluations at the close of the semester confirmed my suspicions about my students' feelings toward me, ones that squared with misogynoir (Bailey & Trudy, 2018). Numerous comments, which are optional on evaluation forms, included the terms describing me as "scary" and "intimidating." Stereotypes that have long followed Black women regarding their being perpetually frightening and angry mark these remarks as far from original (Austin, 1989; Collins, 1990). One more lengthy evaluation lamented my asking students on the first day of class to publicly name their racial or ethnic identity, gender identity, and class status background; this student seemed to have held onto their resentment throughout the semester, as they detailed the ire and embarrassment they felt in having to admit that they came from a privileged, upper-middle-class family. It did not appear to matter that I also shared these aspects of my identity and explained that these parts of who we are largely inform the lens through which we view the world. This student's dismay at me and the exercise, however, is predictable, as scholarship has shown the regularity with which students with privileged social identities poorly evaluate Black women instructors (Chávez & Mitchell, 2020; Smith & Johnson-Bailey, 2011), especially in contexts where these women center their courses on social justice (Bailey & Miller, 2015).

Grading the final class assignment, a paper reflecting on takeaways from class, I encountered an assessment that well represents many students' thinking at the close of class. Commenting on how she might navigate behavior management as a classroom teacher, this student submitted that there would be some cases beyond her control. She noted a conversation with her cooperating teacher about one of their students, a 5-year-old Black boy; they resolved that his incarceration was the only plausible strategy for effectively improving his behavior. That is, her final essay underlined that "locking him up" characterized the only meaningful resolution for his "persistently outrageous" classroom conduct. As it had so many times before, my anger bubbled to the surface of my skin, warming my body and accelerating my heart rate. But class had ended, and it was likely that I would never again see this student; it was also likely that she may never read my feedback on this assignment. I was upset that she had spent 15 weeks in my class and, with confidence, promoted the incarceration of a Black child for his presumed behavior issues. She raised no questions about the strategies she and her mentor teacher were using to reach him, the deficit framing of his conduct, the context in which he might be living, whether his caregivers had access to essential resources such as safe housing or nutritious food, or if they had reliable transportation or adequate, dignified employment. To this student, none of these factors mattered, but my anger continues to make them matter to me.

Throughout this semester, my outrage remained palpable. I did not, however, stop trying to promote social and racial justice or stop seeking to enhance my students' racial literacy. Never missing one class or shirking my promise to assess their work in a timely, critical fashion, I did all in my power to translate my anger into my anti-oppression, Black feminist pedagogy. I cannot say I left class feeling as if most of my students saw me as fully human; instead, I walked away feeling as if most still viewed me as a caricature who fixated on issues that were either not present or were far less significant than I made them seem. As a result, I rarely felt heard; there are few to no moments to which I can point that indicated my students were able to clearly hear, and thus understand, why race matters for them as social studies teachers. Their impeded sight and listening rendered them largely unable to heed my warnings about race-evasive pedagogy or my concerns about dehumanizing their students (Bartolome, 1994). Nevertheless, struggles for social and racial justice necessitate that I continue to try so that my anger does not destroy me and render me powerless (Lorde, 1981).

## WHINE FOR WHAT?

Austin (1989) contended that bearing witness via testimony is tantamount to our survival and empowerment, which Lorde (1981) asserted can come from anger. Because I was able to analyze why my former classmates and former students resisted acknowledging the outsize role of white supremacy in U.S. society, I am able to contribute to what Austin (1989) described as the documentation of oppression. I recognize that this alone cannot and will not upend the anti-Blackness that is so central to life in the United States (Bell, 1992b). Nonetheless, it is crucial that women of color, Black women especially, leave behind a record that conveys our concrete experiences, which Austin (1989) noted may remain invisible to those who do not navigate the world as we must, given our social positions and positionings. Consequently, I offer such a testimony, which may serve to affirm our experiential knowledge. As critical race theorist Derrick Bell (1992b) asserted, "for some of us who bear the burdens of racial subordination, any truth—no matter how dire—is uplifting" (ix).

Critical race theory's counterstorytelling tenet furnishes an instructive frame through which one might make meaning from my accounts of anger in social studies. As an area that is often believed to be well-situated for exploring social justice issues, social studies still continues to see the denigration of Black people and their history, as just one example (King & Woodson, 2017; Shuster, 2018). In the schooling contexts I have discussed in this chapter, it should be evident that the social studies label did little to ameliorate the obstinate resistance to social and racial justice. Therefore, I have illustrated how an assumption about social studies—that it is ripe terrain for imparting in students dispositions of social justice—reflects an inaccurate perception about the stronghold of white supremacy and anti-Blackness in U.S. education. This shortsightedness underscores one way this essay may be understood as drawing on counterstory principles (Cook & Dixson, 2013; Delgado, 1989) that challenge such understandings of social studies. Furthermore, understanding the role of anger throughout these processes as something that has significantly animated my relationship to social studies provides greater context for disrupting stock stories or master narratives regarding Black women's experiences, especially our allegedly unjustified anger about systemic racism.

In many ways, I resolve that staying mad has enabled me to continue working to help create the social studies classrooms I wish I had as a young student. This anger has worked in tandem with my ever-developing racial literacy to enhance my pedagogy and continue my fight for a better educational future, one that is unfortunately often thwarted in social studies contexts (Crowley & Smith, 2015; King & Chandler, 2016; Martell, 2017). In the classrooms of which I dream, students would learn U.S. history through the perspectives of the Black, Indigenous, Latinx, and Asian peoples who were excluded from many aspects of the so-called American Dream. These courses would employ the concrete experiences of women of such heritages as lenses to examine the mainstay that is gendered racism, and they would also analyze the influence of such groups' economic status on their participation in society, providing context for the possibilities of cross-racial coalition-building in the ongoing struggle for social justice. Employing a social oppression analytic may open numerous possibilities for cultivating co-conspirators who work to mitigate white supremacy and anti-Blackness in education.

## COMING FULL CIRCLE

In bringing together my lived experiences, Black women's anger, and racial literacy to comment on my relationship to social studies, I have outlined occasions when my white peers and students refused to see me and Black people writ large as fully human. I characterized how this view-related limitation largely accounted for their difficulty to hear Black people's pleas for humanization—a process necessitating their racial literacy development. This call derived from our awareness that cultivating such a perspective would foster their recognition of the sociohistorical significance of race and ethnic identity—categories that have long determined access to vital resources, both symbolic and material (Crenshaw et al., 1995). These failures rendered them incapable of heeding our cries for humanizing consideration and dignity.

My navigation of these experiences has taught me that the fight for social and racial justice is a long one that will endure after my lifetime. In this struggle, however, I must believe that change is possible. A recent message from the white woman who negated my experience with racism, as I mentioned earlier in this chapter, in my teacher education program offers an illustration of possibility. In the wake of white police officer Derek Chauvin's brutal murder in Minnesota of George Floyd, a 46-year-old unarmed Black man, I received a message from this white woman expressing regret for her behavior in our social studies teacher education program. Having not communicated with her since, my unresolved rage returned, but after some time, I replied, letting her know how traumatizing her conduct had been. I even rehashed the very episode I recounted above in this chapter. Despite her saying that she had no memory of that specific exchange, she was apologetic and seemed to have realized the error of her ways. She wrote that she was working to focus on critically examining her privilege and seeking ways to invest in Black causes and Black-owned businesses.

Hence, we see how public attention on the all-too-common police-executed deaths of Black people may provoke white people's heightened racial consciousness. Such a trade, however, is unconscionable. The murder of Black people ought not to be required to enhance one's racial literacy. In that situation, the best I might have done was to hope that her "guilt [was] not a response to [my] anger, [but] . . . a response to [her] own actions or lack of action. If [her guilt] leads to change then it can be useful, since it becomes no longer guilt but the beginning of knowledge" (Lorde, 1981, p. 9). This point reflects my wish that anger, guilt, or any other potentially stifling emotion be mobilized toward a greater good. In this endeavor, I hope other members of society will help Black women, "de mules uh de world," according to Zora

Neale Hurston (1937/1978, p. 29), carry the load in doing such work—labor that indeed includes racial literacy.

## REFERENCES

Angelou, M. (1971). *I know why the caged bird sings*. Bantam.

Austin, R. (1989). "Sapphire bound!", *Wisconsin Law Review, 3*, 539–578.

Bailey, M., & Miller, S. J. (2015). When margins become centered: Black queer women in front and outside of the classroom. *Feminist Formations, 27*(3), 168–188.

Bailey, M., & Trudy. (2018). On misogynoir: Citation, erasure, and plagiarism. *Feminist Media Studies, 18*(4), 762–768.

Bartolome, L. (1994). Beyond the methods fetish: Toward a humanizing pedagogy. *Harvard Educational Review*, *64*(2), 173–195.

Bell, D. (1992a). *Faces at the bottom of the well*. Basic Books.

Bell, D. (1992b). Racial realism. *Connecticut Law Review, 24*(2), 363–379.

Berry, D. R., & Gross, K. N. (2020). *A Black women's history of the United States*. Beacon Press.

Chávez, K., & Mitchell, K. M. (2020). Exploring bias in student evaluations: Gender, race, and ethnicity. *PS: Political Science & Politics, 53*(2), 270–274.

Collins, P. (1990). *Black feminist thought: Knowledge, consciousness and pedagogy*. Unwin Hyman.

Combahee River Collective. (1979). The Combahee River Collective statement. In Z. R. Eisenstein (Ed.), *Capitalist patriarchy and the case for socialist feminism* (pp. 362–371). Monthly Review Press.

Cook, D. A., & Dixson, A. D. (2013). Writing critical race theory and method: A composite counterstory on the experiences of Black teachers in New Orleans post-Katrina. *International Journal of Qualitative Studies in Education*, *26*(10), 1238–1258.

Crenshaw, K. (1989). Demarginalizing the intersection of race and sex: A Black feminist critique of antidiscrimination doctrine, feminist theory and antiracist politics. *University of Chicago Legal Forum* 138–167.

Crenshaw, K., Gotanda, N., Peller, G., & Thomas, K. (Eds.). (1995). *Critical race theory: The key writings that formed the movement*. The New Press.

Crowley, R. M., & Smith, W. (2015). Whiteness and social studies teacher education: Tensions in the pedagogical task. *Teaching Education, 26*(2), 160–178.

Davis, A. (1974). *Angela Davis: An autobiography*. Random House.

Delgado, R. (1989). Storytelling for oppositionists and others: A plea for narrative. *Michigan Law Review, 87*(8), 2411–2441.

Griffin, R. (2012). I am an angry Black woman: Black feminist autoethnography, voice, and resistance. *Women's Studies in Communication, 35*(2), 138–157.

Griffin, A., & James, A. (2018). Humanities curriculum as White property: Toward a reclamation of Black creative thought in social studies and literacy curriculum, *Multicultural Education, 25*(3&4), 10–17.

Guinier, L. (2004). From racial liberalism to racial literacy: *Brown v. Board of Education* and the interest-divergence dilemma. *Journal of American History, 91*(1), 92–118.

Guinier, L., & Torres, G. (2002). *The miner's canary: Enlisting race, resisting power, transforming democracy*. Harvard University Press.

Henry, A. (2005). Black feminist pedagogy: Critiques and contributions. In W. Watkins (Ed.), *Black protest thought and education* (pp. 89–105). Peter Lang.

hooks, b. (1996). *Bone Black: Memories of girlhood*. Henry Holt & Company.

Hurston, Z. N. (1978). *Their eyes were watching God*. University of Illinois Press. Original work published in 1937.

James-Gallaway, A. D., & Turner, F. F. L. (2020). Mobilizing betrayal: Black feminist pedagogy and Black women graduate student educators. *Gender, Work, & Organization, 28*(S1), 24–38.

Joseph, G. (1995). Black feminist pedagogy in capitalist America. In B. Guy Sheftall (Ed.), *Words of fire: An anthology of African-American feminist thought* (pp. 482–471). New Press.

King, L. J., & Chandler, P. T. (2016). From non-racism to anti-racism in social studies teacher education: Social studies and racial pedagogical content knowledge. In A. R. Crowe & A. Cuenca (Eds.), *Rethinking social studies teacher education in the twenty-first century* (pp. 3–21). Springer.

King, L. J., & Woodson, A. N. (2017). Baskets of cotton and birthday cakes: Teaching slavery in social studies classrooms. *Social Studies Education Review, 6*(1), 1–18.

Ladson-Billings, G., & Tate. W. (1995). Toward a critical race theory of education. *Teachers College Record, 97*(1), 47–68.

Lorde, A. (1981). The uses of anger. *Women's Studies Quarterly, 9*(3), 7–10.

Lorde, A. (1982). *Zami: A new spelling of my name*. Crossing Press.

Martell, C. C. (2017). Approaches to teaching race in elementary social studies: A case study of preservice teachers. *The Journal of Social Studies Research, 41*(1), 75–87.

OWN. (2014, May 19). *One of the most important lessons Dr. Maya Angelou ever taught Oprah* [Video]. YouTube. https://www.youtube.com/watch?v=nJgmaHkcFP8

Quashie, K. (2018). To be (a) one: Notes on coupling and Black female audacity. *Differences, 29*(2), 68–95.

Shuster, K. (2018). *Teaching hard history: American slavery*. Southern Poverty Law Center.

Sleeter, C. E. (2017). Critical race theory and the Whiteness of teacher education. *Urban Education, 52*(2), 155–169.

Smith, B. P., & Johnson-Bailey. J. (2011). Student ratings of teaching effectiveness: Implications for non-White women in the academy. *Negro Educational Review, 62/63*(1–4), 115–140.

Stevenson, B. (2013). *The contested murder of Latasha Harlins: Justice, gender and the origins of the L.A. Riots*. Oxford University Press.

Tatum, B. D. (1997). *Why are all the Black kids sitting together in the cafeteria?: And other conversations about race*. Basic Books.

# Notes

### Chapter 2

1. Many thanks to Dr. Gerardo Aponte-Safe for his help in designing the survey involved in this study, to Dr. Hana Kang for her assistance with the quantitative data analysis, and to Dr. Jenni Conrad for her editing support.

2. Latinx is a gender-neutral alternative to Latina/o. We use this term to be inclusive of fluid gender identities.

3. All numbers rounded to two decimal places.

### Chapter 3

1. A pseudonym.

2. When referring to Indigenous peoples, it is preferable for teachers, scholars, and advocates to use terms specific communities and peoples choose to identify themselves (e.g., Piikani). However, there are challenges associated with such specificity (e.g., confidentiality might be compromised given the small sizes of communities, individuals within the same community may prefer different terms, and/or individuals may identify with multiple Indigenous communities). Throughout this chapter, I use various terms deemed appropriate for various situations as determined by Indigenous students, scholars, and community members. For example, "Indigenous" can be used to encourage solidarity across Nations, specific tribal affiliations can support sovereignty and unique identities when describing specific examples, and "Indian" or "American Indian" often aligns with educational policy language. However, "Indian" and "American Indian" remain problematic given their histories and related efforts to limit Indigenous educational self-determination.

3. To emphasize diversity within and among Indigenous groups, I opt to use plural forms of terms such as "histories," "peoples," "experiences," and "knowledges."

4. In addition to using quotation marks to identify direct quotes, I use them periodically to note language common within curricular resources but that is contested or inappropriate. For example, I use them around "Corps of Discovery" to emphasize that this term reinforces misconceptions (e.g., the idea that Lewis and Clark "discovered" a route to the Pacific) and settler colonial superiority (i.e., by naming and claiming an event using capitalization).

### Chapter 7

1. They are, in Gramsci's (1971) terms, organic intellectuals.

2. For Marx, this is the moment of consciousness for the proletariat to unite against the bourgeoisie, to realize that they do not need the owners of the means of produc-

tion, but they themselves can control the means of production through revolution and transformation of the very social hierarchy that has enslaved them.

## Chapter 11

1. In effort to decentralize whiteness within this text, I have decided not to capitalize white/whiteness within text, unless referenced in a citation (Matias et al. 2014).

## Chapter 12

1. Sleeter has posted her critical family history resources on her website here: http://christinesleeter.org/use-this-blog/

## Chapter 14

1. I lower-case the racial descriptor *white* while upper-casing ethnoracial terms referring to *people of* color to challenge the social, political, and cultural hierarchy that has historically privileged whiteness and subordinated peoples of color.

# Index

# About the Editor and the Contributors

**Sohyun An** is a professor of Social Studies Education at Kennesaw State University. Her research centers on curriculum and pedagogy of Asian American history, anti-racist social studies, and critical war studies. She was a former high school social studies teacher in South Korea.

**Karen Burgard** is an associate professor in the Department of Curriculum and Instruction at Texas A&M-San Antonio. In this position, she prepares future teachers for their diverse classrooms in central and south Texas. Her research investigates the intersection of race, heritage, and culture as it pertains to historical understanding. Her most recent work centers around the curriculum of public heritage sites and spaces, including historic museums, landmarks, and monuments.

**Eliana Castro** is an assistant professor of Secondary Education at The University of Vermont. Her research studies the role of race/ethnicity in K–12 settings, focusing on how scholars, teacher educators, practitioners, and other community members can both expose global racism through the social studies curriculum and disrupt it in schools. She is interested in understanding and contributing to the teaching and learning of race/ethnicity, racism, and related issues of power, identity, and institutions. Her work examines how history curricula can promote nuanced representations of intersectional racial/ethnic identities, such as Afro-Latinidad. Her most recent research combines teacher and student experiences to probe theories of teaching and learning, racial identity formation, and racial literacy. Castro's research has been published in the *American Educational Research Journal, Journal of Teacher Education, The Social Studies, Teaching and Teacher Education,* and the *Journal of Social Studies Research*. Castro's co-authored article in the *Journal of Research on Leadership Education*, "Twelve Years Unslaved: Lessons From Reconstruction and *Brown* for Contemporary School Leaders," was selected as the journal's Article of the Year in 2020.

**Tadashi Dozono** is an assistant professor of History/Social Science Education at California State University Channel Islands. Grounded in his teaching in New York City public schools, Tadashi centers the theorizing that LGBTQ and students of color engage daily because of their marginalization in order to critically reimagine social studies classrooms.

*Kristen E. Duncan* is an assistant professor of Social Studies Education at Clemson University. Her research interests include Black teachers' discussions of race and race in educational texts and at historic sites. She is a former middle school social studies teacher and elementary instructional coach and earned her Ph.D. at the University of Georgia.

*Tommy Ender* (he/him) is an assistant professor of Educational Studies in the Feinstein School of Education and Human Development, with a joint appointment in the Department of History, at Rhode Island College. A former middle school teacher and coach, Ender's research interests include Latino/a/x identities and cultures in education, critical theories and pedagogies in social studies, and music as history. He earned a Ph.D. from the University of North Carolina at Chapel Hill, with a focus on cultural studies and literacies. His work has appeared in *Curriculum Inquiry, Journal of Latinos and Education, International Journal of Multicultural Education, The History Teacher, Journal of Social Studies Research,* and numerous edited books.

*Andrea M. Hawkman* (she/her) is an associate professor of Social Studies Education in the College of Education at Rowan University. Her research focuses on the enactment of racialized pedagogies in the PK–20 classroom and the intersection of education policy and social studies education. She is the co-editor of *Marking the "Invisible": Articulating Whiteness in Social Studies Education*. Her scholarly work has also appeared in *Teaching Education, Theory and Research in Social Education, The Journal of Social Studies Research, The Urban Review,* and numerous edited books about social studies, teacher education, and race/ism. She is an avid soccer fan and enjoys traveling and spending time with her family.

*ArCasia D. James-Gallaway* is an interdisciplinary historian of education and a teacher educator at Texas A&M University, where she works as an assistant professor and ACES Fellow. Her scholarly aim is to bridge past and present perspectives on African American struggles for educational justice. Engaging critical perspectives and approaches such as critical race theory, Black feminist theory, oral history methodology, and Black Southern epistemology, her research agenda follows three overlapping strands of inquiry: the history of African American education, Black history education, and gendered anti-Blackness in education.

*Christopher C. Martell* is an assistant professor at the University of Massachusetts Boston. He teaches courses on elementary and secondary social studies methods. His scholarship and professional interests center on teacher development across the career span, including preservice teacher preparation, inservice professional development, and practitioner inquiry. He is particularly interested in how social studies teachers in urban and multicultural contexts use culturally relevant/sustaining pedagogy and historical inquiry, and teach for justice.

**Natasha Hakimali Merchant** is assistant professor of Multicultural and Social Studies Education at the University of Washington Bothell, where she teaches interdisciplinary courses exploring anti-colonial and liberatory education. Her research explores the curricular and pedagogical experiences of Islam in secondary social studies classrooms.

**LaGarrett King** is an associate professor of Social Studies Education at the University at Buffalo and the Founding Director for the Center for K–12 Black History and Racial Literacy Education. Dr. King's award-winning research includes Black history education, critical theories of race, the history of curriculum, and teacher education.

**Tiffany Mitchell Patterson** is a manager of social studies at District of Columbia Public Schools, with over a decade of experience as a social studies educator. Her research interests include racial and social justice in education, Black feminism, and teaching Black and historically excluded narratives in social studies education. Activism, intersectionality, and anti-racist/anti-oppressive education lie at the core of her teaching practice, research, and community work. Education is her revolution.

**Gabriel A. Reich** is an associate professor of secondary history education at VCU's School of Education in the Department of Teaching and Learning. Dr. Reich began his educational career as a high school history teacher in New York City. He earned a Ph.D. from New York University's Steinhardt School of Culture, Education, and Human Development in 2007. Dr. Reich's area of special interest within the discipline of social studies education is the developing field of historical consciousness, which includes historical thinking and understanding. He has published in a variety of scholarly publications, such as *The Journal of Curriculum Studies, Theory and Research in Social Education,* and *Historical Encounters.*

**Noreen Naseem Rodríguez** is an assistant professor of Teacher Learning, Research, and Practice in the School of Education and Affiliate Faculty in the Department of Ethnic Studies at the University of Colorado Boulder. Her research engages critical race frameworks to explore the pedagogical practices of teachers of color and the teaching of so-called difficult histories through children's literature and primary sources. She is co-author of *Social Studies for a Better World: An Anti-Oppressive Approach for Elementary Educators* with Katy Swalwell and co-edited the forthcoming *Critical Race Theory and Social Studies Futures: From the Nightmare of Racial Realism to Dreaming Out Loud* with Amanda Vickery. Before becoming a teacher educator, Noreen was a bilingual elementary teacher in Austin, Texas for nine years.

**Maribel Santiago** is an assistant professor of Justice and Teacher Education at the University of Washington and a 2019 National Academy of Education/

Spencer Postdoctoral Fellow. She specializes in the teaching and learning of race/ethnicity in K–12 history. Her work centers on the production and consumption of Latinx social studies: *what* students, policy makers, and educators learn about Latinx communities, and *how* they conceptualize Latinx experiences. Dr. Santiago is part of an emerging collective of social studies education scholars complicating notions of Latinidad that often omit Indigenous and Black Latinx histories. As part of this effort, Dr. Santiago leads the History TALLER (pronounced tah-yĕr) research group, dedicated to exploring the Teaching and Learning of Language, Ethnicity, and Race (TALLER). Her work has been published in *Cognition and Instruction*, *Teachers College Record*, and *Theory & Research in Social Education*.

**Christine Rogers Stanton** is an associate professor of Social Studies Education at Montana State University in Bozeman, Montana. Prior to focusing her career on teacher education and research, she worked as a teacher and instructional coach in schools on and bordering the Wind River Indian Reservation in Wyoming. Dr. Stanton's work focuses on repositioning youth and community members as scholars, educators, and leaders to advance social justice, anti-colonial education, trauma-reducing praxis, and community- and place-conscious teaching and learning. The common thread connecting these areas of scholarship centers recognition of sovereignty, self-determination, and treaty responsibilities within and beyond education. Her scholarship has appeared in *Educational Researcher, The American Journal of Education, Curriculum Inquiry, Qualitative Inquiry, Social Education, Theory & Research in Social Education, The Journal of Social Studies Research, The Journal of American Indian Education*, and others. Dr. Stanton is the descendant of white settlers who occupied lands of the Piikani (Blackfeet), Pawnee, Očhéthi Šakówiŋ (Lakota), and many other Nations. She has lived and worked on lands belonging to the Northern Arapaho, Eastern Shoshone, and Apsáalooke (Crow), among others. Dr. Stanton thanks Indigenous partners and mentors who have supported her learning, especially Brad Hall, Dodie White Eagle, Amanda LeClair-Diaz, Dani Morrison, Jordan Dresser, Sweeney Windchief, Nicholas Rink, Marsha Small, Sergio Maldonado, and Marty Conrad.

**Kaylene M. Stevens** is a lecturer at Boston University Wheelock College of Education & Human Development. She teaches courses on historical literacy, research methods, and elementary and secondary social studies methods. Her research and professional interests focus on gender equity in the social studies classroom, race-conscious teaching for social studies, and culturally relevant pedagogy and curriculum.